THE ETHICS AND PRACTICE OF REFUGEE REPATRIATION

THE ETHICS AND PRACTICE OF REFUGEE REPATRIATION

Mollie Gerver

EDINBURGH
University Press

Edinburgh University Press is one of the leading university presses in the UK. We publish academic books and journals in our selected subject areas across the humanities and social sciences, combining cutting-edge scholarship with high editorial and production values to produce academic works of lasting importance. For more information visit our website: edinburghuniversitypress.com

Edinburgh University Press Ltd
The Tun – Holyrood Road
12(2f) Jackson's Entry
Edinburgh EH8 8PJ

First published in hardback by Edinburgh University Press 2018

Typeset in 11/13 Palatino LT Std by
IDSUK (DataConnection) Ltd

A CIP record for this book is available from the British Library

ISBN 978 1 4744 3747 9 (hardback)
ISBN 978 1 4744 3748 6 (paperback)
ISBN 978 1 4744 3749 3 (webready PDF)
ISBN 978 1 4744 3750 9 (epub)

CONTENTS

ACKNOWLEDGEMENTS

A special thanks to the subjects who invited me into their homes, patiently told me their life stories, and answered difficult questions about repatriation.

I would like to thank Kai Spiekermann for his support throughout the research process. He encouraged me to continue utilizing empirical data for philosophy, and provided extensive feedback for every chapter and stage of the research process. I would also like to thank Chandran Kukathas for his comments and encouragement, and especially his early recommendation that I focus on cases involving difficult puzzles. This proved especially fruitful, helping me structure the book and each chapter. A special thanks to Eiko Theilemann for his comments, and for reminding me of the relevance of my work for public policy.

Thanks to Luc Bovens and Kieran Oberman for providing me extraordinarily in-depth comments, and a thought-provoking discussion on my work.

Various individuals provided me helpful advice and feedback on numerous chapters. Thanks to Laura Valentini for her comments on my methodology; to Martin Williams for his comments on the introduction; to David Vestergaard Axelson for his comments on Chapter 5; to Anne Phillips, Sarah Goff, Tom Parr, and Sarah Fine for their comments on Chapter 7; and to Derek Bell, Peter Jones, Beth Kahn, and Andrew Walton for their comments on Chapter 8.

A special thanks to Maud Gauthier-Chung, Jacob Huber, Nimrod Kavner, Johan Olsthoom, Kaveh Pourvand, Paola Romero, Anahi Wiedenbrug, and Marta Wojciechowska for their thoughtful discussions and questions.

I thank the London School of Economics for providing me the funding to conduct this research, and for providing much-needed insurance during fieldwork. Thanks to Newcastle University's school of Geography, Politics, and Sociology, my academic home during final stages of my research on repatriation. Thanks to the participants of the weekly seminar series at Essex University's Department of Government for their helpful comments on Chapters 2 and 4. Thanks to Catherine Lu for her thought-provoking discussions on reparations, and for providing me the opportunity to more carefully study this topic at the Yan P. Lin Centre at McGill University.

My research in South Sudan was only possible because of the assistance, knowledge, and network of various aid workers, volunteers, and former refugees I met in East Africa and Israel. There are more names than I can write here, but thanks to Dobuol Chuol Nyaang, Rami Gudovitch, Sharon Livne, Moran Mekamel, Bol Duop, and Michael Mann-Goldman for introducing me to former refugees after they repatriated or were deported to South Sudan. Bol and Michael not only assisted me in research, but provided me company, coffee, and security updates during challenging days in Juba.

A special thanks to Rebecca Akoun, Liat Chouai, and Aaron Johnson for ten years of stimulating conversations and fresh perspectives. Thanks to my friend and partner Benedict Elliott Smith for providing me critical comments, questions, and writing advice, including the penning of this sentence. Finally, I thank my parents for instilling in me a sense of curiosity and respect for the refugees in our community.

Chapter 1

INTRODUCTION

At 7:12 pm on March 13, 2012, a man began screaming on Kenya Airlines flight 101. Two British Border Control officers shoved him forcefully into his seat, handcuffing him. "Mugabe will kill me!" he cried out.

The woman sitting to my left looked concerned. "Don't worry," an officer told her, "they always stop screaming when the flight lifts off." The man in handcuffs heard this, and said, "I will continue screaming until you get me off this flight." The border officer shook his head. "Trust me," he told the woman next to me, "they always stop screaming."

The man threatened self-harm, but nobody responded. He instead threatened to scream the entire flight, but he was ignored. Finally, as a last resort, he threatened to defecate in his seat. Officials quickly unlocked his handcuffs, and escorted him off the flight.

Everyone relaxed.

Though this event had transfixed the passengers, a similar incident unfolded moments later and passed without notice. A second man, wearing no handcuffs, started making a low moaning noise. He was ignored by the border agents, who were some distance away, and was sitting between two unarmed civilians, one holding a clipboard, the other saying, "It will be fine." He did not believe her, and continued to make the moaning noise, his voice increasing in volume, his eyes staring at the seatback pocket, and his body shaking in discomfort. He was eventually escorted by the civilians off the flight.

While the screaming man on my flight was being deported, given that he was subject to considerable force, the second man was likely repatriating, accompanied by staff members of an organization or the United Nations (UN).[1]

Around the world, refugees often repatriate with the help of an organization or the UN, with millions repatriating to Côte d'Ivoire, Iraq,

Afghanistan, and dozens of other countries between 2010 and 2018. Some return because they cannot access residency status, work visas, or social services. Others return because, if they remain, they will be forced into enclosed refugee camps, or detention centers where they are told when to eat, drink, sit, and stand. Some return because, though they can live outside camps or detention, they struggle to access sufficient nutrition or medical care. In returning home, they are not officially deported – nobody physically forces them onto a flight – but they do find their lives too difficult to stay, and so seek help from organizations who pay for transport, arrange travel documentation, and at times accompany them on the journey home.[2]

Such organizations struggle to determine whether they ought to help refugees return home. They feel they face a dilemma: On the one hand, helping with return is ethical because otherwise refugees will remain in detention, camps, or poverty. On the other hand, helping with return may be wrong, precisely because refugees are returning involuntarily, given that those who remain will be forced into detention, camps, or a life of poverty. It may be wrong to help with involuntary repatriation, especially if the risks of return are substantial.

In an attempt to better understand this dilemma, I spent a year in East Africa, the Middle East, and South-east Asia, interviewing 172 refugees and migrants who had repatriated, or were considering repatriation, from Israel. I chose to focus on their cases partly because non-governmental organizations (NGOs) in Israel claimed to be especially ethical when helping with return, taking steps that differ from those of organizations in other countries. I wished to find out if they had truly succeeded in ensuring an ethical return. Initially, there were reasons to believe they had. Unlike organizations in other countries, NGOs in Israel spent a significant amount of time interviewing each refugee to ensure they were not coerced into returning. NGOs also had resources to travel regularly to countries of origin, finding out about the conditions refugees faced after returning, and relaying this information to refugees still in Israel. Importantly, they took no government funds, relying on private donors alone to avoid acting as an arm to the government's immigration goals. Some were also active in lobbying for a more just refugee policy, and so refused to assist with returns that were the result of this unjust policy, such as helping refugees return from detention.

I quickly learned, while in South Sudan in 2012, that many refugees had returned to avoid detention. But even if this is true, the NGOs' actions may have been ethical. It may have been better to help them return than force refugees to remain in detention. A dilemma remained despite the NGOs' best of intentions and resources. As such, the case illustrates the depth of the dilemma, and the need for a philosophical analysis.

This book provides this analysis, drawing upon original fieldwork to understand the context of dilemmas arising in repatriation, and solving these dilemmas using the tools of analytic philosophy. In doing so, the book provides the first rigorous set of ethical guidelines for organizations and governments helping with repatriation. In the following Section 1.1 I describe more precisely what repatriation is and why it matters. In Sections 1.2 and 1.3 I provide a brief history of repatriation since the Second World War (WWII), and the repatriation occurring in Israel since 2010. I then describe seven primary dilemmas arising in repatriation (Section 1.4), and the fieldwork I conducted to understand these dilemmas (Section 1.5).

1.1 WHAT IS REPATRIATION?

Repatriation refers to refugees moving to the countries from which they or their parents fled. Some refugees are returning to a place they call home, and which they have lived in recently. Others are returning to a place they do not call home, having fled as young children decades prior. Some are not returning at all, moving to a country they have never seen, their parents having fled before they were born. The book refers to all three types of repatriation, focusing particularly on those repatriating with the help of organizations using no coercion, merely providing free transport, and at times providing stipends, travel documentation, and accompaniment on journeys.

Such repatriation is often enthusiastically embraced by governments hoping to avoid deportation, while still decreasing the number of refugees within their borders.[3] Repatriation has a ring of legitimacy, especially if organized by separate humanitarian organizations, or a separate wing of the government uninvolved in deportations. Those who help with repatriation may not agree with the government's sentiment, but they argue that helping is better than doing nothing at all.

These agents have referred to their activities as "repatriation facilitation."[4] I adopt this term, referring to those helping with return as "repatriation facilitators." They are non-armed actors, and distinguish themselves from the border officials handcuffing individuals on flights, or the doctors injecting psychiatric drugs into those who resist.[5] I focus on those holding clipboards and pens rather than guns or needles.

Some of these facilitators are part of the government, such as one official in the Assisted Voluntary Return Unit in Israel's Ministry of Interior. He insisted on his neutral status. "I'm not involved in deportations at all," he explained, "I want them to leave Israel happy."[6] In Spain, a government civil servant similarly emphasized that she was uninvolved in deportation, and merely helping refugees access a smooth form of repatriation.[7] In addition to government officials, government-employed social workers may assist unaccompanied minors return to their countries of origin. Judges may have a role in determining if an adult can repatriate, if the adult has a mental illness and lacks the capacity to make decisions on their own behalf.[8] Sometimes private companies provide repatriation, as in the United States where hospitals pay private firms to facilitate the return of patients without the legal right to remain.[9]

There are also NGOs and intra-governmental organizations (IGOs) who help with repatriation, such as the International Organization for Migration (IOM) and the United Nations High Commissioner for Refugees (UNHCR).[10] These bodies, and many more, make repatriation either possible or easier, and have contributed to millions of refugees repatriating over the last decade alone.

These refugees repatriating raise questions overlooked in public dialogue on migration. One question is empirical: it is not clear what happens to refugees after they return home. Another question is philosophical: it is not clear what repatriation facilitators ought morally to do. While the government acts wrongly when detaining refugees,[11] perhaps repatriation facilitators do not. An assisted coerced return seems better than an unassisted deportation or a life in detention. Nor is it clear that helping with uncoerced return is always permissible. Even if a refugee is returning without any coercion, it might be wrong to help a person take a risk to their lives, however voluntary their choice may be. The criteria for when repatriation is wrong are different from the criteria for when deportation is wrong.

This book establishes such criteria. In doing so, I shall avoid committing myself to a particular theory of whom states should not deport. Instead, I aim to consider whether, in cases where nearly all agree that deportation is wrong, helping with repatriation is right.

Of course, there is much debate over when deportation is wrong and this may, by extension, impact when repatriation is wrong. I shall assume, for simplicity, that deportation is wrong when deportees' lives will be at immediate risk in their home countries, whether from violence, extreme poverty, or a natural disaster. This claim is supported by a range of philosophers who, though disagreeing on who states can deport, agree that deporting migrants to all life-threatening conditions is wrong.[12] States are similarly beginning to recognize that it is wrong to deport individuals to countries where they will likely die of hunger or general violence, even if they have not fled persecution.[13] For simplicity, I will call all individuals "refugees" if their life will be threatened if they return, regardless of why. I further elaborate on this theory, and defend it against recent objections, in Appendix A.[14]

Though I assume deportations to life-threatening conditions are wrong, this assumption is not central to the book. Those disagreeing with this assumption can still accept my general conclusions. For example, in Chapter 2 I conclude that assisting refugees repatriate from detention is wrong if this causes the government to increase its use of detention. If you think that only those fleeing persecution have a right to asylum, then this conclusion is only relevant for those fleeing persecution. If you think that only those fleeing violence have a right to asylum, then this conclusion is only relevant for those fleeing violence. My goal is not to consider who deserves asylum but whether, if someone deserves asylum, it is wrong to help them repatriate.

This question has been largely overlooked in today's debates on immigration. Debates tend to focus on who states should admit, rather than who states should help return.[15] The few academics addressing return assume return must always be voluntary.[16] It remains unclear whether voluntary returns are always ethical when the risks of return are substantial. And it remains unclear whether involuntary returns should be provided if voluntary return is not possible. To address these questions, we must ask not only what returns are just in the abstract, but what particular actors ought to do when governments are pressuring refugees to leave.

My focus on individual actors, though rare in discussions on immigration, is not entirely unheard of. There are debates over whether individual smugglers ought to transport refugees across borders. There are debates over whether individual citizens ought to resist unjust immigration laws, such as by hiring those without permits. There are debates over whether individual migrants ought to cross borders without authorization, and whether these migrants are permitted to use violence in the process.[17] Outside of immigration ethics, there are debates over when individual organizations should help populations in need, and whether working with corrupt governments is justified to help these populations.[18] There are debates over how individual civil servants ought to respond when faced with difficult dilemmas, and how much discretion such civil servants should have.[19] All of these debates shift our gaze from the state in the abstract onto concrete actors, asking what these actors ought to do. I take the same approach in exploring when repatriation assistance is ethical.

1.2 A BRIEF HISTORY OF REPATRIATION

This question has been especially relevant since WWII, when in 1943 the United Nations Relief and Rehabilitation Organization (UNRRO) assisted roughly seven million individuals return home as war raged on. It is not clear if UNRRO acted ethically, given that refugees' return may have been unsafe. Following the end of WWII 20 million refugees refused to repatriate, afraid to live in the Soviet-controlled Eastern Bloc, and UNRRO's successor organization helped only 73,000 individuals return home between 1946 and 1952.[20] When UNHCR was formally established soon after, rates of repatriation steadily rose, culminating in ten million individuals returning to the newly-created Bangladesh between 1971 and 1972. Throughout the late 1970s and 1980s UNHCR focused on repatriation within Africa, as African governments became increasingly unwilling to host refugee populations.[21] In 1983, for example, UNHCR helped an estimated 35,000 Ethiopian refugees repatriate from Djibouti, where they could no longer access aid or work permits.[22]

With the end of the Cold War UNHCR announced that the "decade of repatriation" had begun.[23] Throughout the 1990s rates of repatriation increased, with over twelve million refugees repatriating between 1991 and 1997.[24] One reason for the increase was refugees' greater ability to return home, as when one million refugees were able to return to Ethiopia and Eritrea with a change in government in 1991.[25] Many refugees, however, struggled to access basic necessities in their countries of asylum, giving them little choice but to return home.

UNHCR continued helping with repatriation into the 2000s, focusing particular attention on millions returning from Iran and Pakistan to

Afghanistan.[26] It helped far fewer refugees return from 2010 onwards, but will likely help more in the years to come. Not only are conditions for refugees deteriorating in Pakistan and Iran, compelling two million to return between 2015 and 2018, conditions are similarly deteriorating in other parts of the globe.[27] Over one million Somali refugees were told by the Kenyan government they will be required to repatriate, leading UNHCR to help tens of thousands to repatriate to Somalia in the last year alone.[28] UNHCR has more recently begun planning the repatriation of Syrian refugees, given that refugees are struggling to access asylum in wealthier countries, and are often forced to remain in enclosed camps in poorer countries.[29]

UNHCR assists not only refugees return home, but Internally Displaced Persons (IDPs). It helped IDPs returning from regions within Afghanistan to Kabul in 2002, IDPs returning from regions within the DR Congo to Ituri in 2007, and IDPs returning from regions within Sri Lanka to Ampara in 2009.[30] Indeed, UNHCR helps far more IDPs return annually than refugees, as the majority of those fleeing disasters remain within their home states. For example, it helped 2.9 million IDPs return home in 2010 and 3.2 million in 2011, while helping only 197,000 refugees return in 2010 and 532,000 in 2011.[31] When UNHCR helps IDPs repatriate, it faces similar ethical dilemmas to those arising with refugee repatriation, including the dilemma of whether to assist with return that is involuntary and unsafe.

In addition to UNHCR, IOM helps with large-scale repatriations, assisting an estimated 1.3 million individuals repatriate since 1979. Its rates of assistance are steadily increasing, with 31,270 individuals returning home via IOM in 2011, 43,786 in 2014, and 98,403 in 2016.[32] Of those it helps, at least some are returning to life-threatening conditions, as in 2002 when it assisted refugees repatriate from the island of Nauru to Afghanistan, and in 2003 when it helped refugees repatriate from Belgium to Iraq.[33] Importantly, IOM assists migrants repatriate to countries without sufficient nutrition or healthcare. Such migrants, I assume, are refugees with a moral right to remain in the host state, even if no legal right to remain. If this is true, then when IOM helps them repatriate they are engaging in morally problematic assistance.

Governments often provide their own repatriation, rather than relying on UNHCR and IOM. The Israeli government began providing repatriation from 2012 and the UK government began providing repatriation from 2015. The German government's repatriation is far older, dating back to the 1970s, and was especially active in the 1990s when it informed Bosnian refugees they were required to return home.[34] It will likely become increasingly active in the future, as Germany has announced that all Syrian refugees will be required to eventually repatriate.[35] If this repatriation is similar to that of Bosnian refugees, refugees will face a choice between deportation if they remain and a grant if they return.

In many cases, repatriation is not facilitated by a single organization or government agency. Instead, multiple organizations and agencies are involved in repatriation, each taking on a slightly different task. In Kenya wealthy donor states fund UNHCR, UNHCR interviews refugees to ensure their return is informed, and the Danish Refugee Council facilitates the return itself.[36] In Spain the government funds repatriation, and the Young Men's Christian Association (YMCA) has facilitated the return itself.[37] The European Union (EU) has a similar model, allocating approximately €1.7 billion to member states since 2008, and member states paying IOM to facilitate repatriation on their behalf.[38]

Sometimes a state provides funding, a charity provides repatriation, and a given government agency publicizes the repatriation. This occurred in the UK, where the government paid the charity Refugee Action to facilitate return,[39] and the Home Office used a controversial method publicizing this return: it placed billboards on vans around the UK, telling migrants to "Go home or face arrest."[40] Refugee Action condemned the billboards, they were eventually taken down,[41] but the Home Office ceased Refugee Action's funding shortly after, providing repatriation itself.[42]

1.3 REPATRIATION FROM ISRAEL

Though repatriation is common globally, it was uncommon in Israel until 2010, when a small number of refugees began returning home to South Sudan with the help of an NGO. Most who returned knew little about the region they were repatriating to, having fled as children during the Second Sudanese Civil War, fought mainly between the Sudanese government and southern Sudanese forces.[43] Throughout the 1980s and 1990s they had arrived in Egypt, where they faced xenophobic attacks at work and on the street, but also felt remaining was safer than returning. They continued living in Egypt into 2005, when southern and northern Sudanese forces signed the Comprehensive Peace Agreement

(CPA). The CPA allowed for a referendum for an independent South Sudan in 2011, but they were uncertain whether independence would bring security, or whether independence would be established at all.

The same year as the 2005 CPA, Egyptian police opened fire on protesters sitting in front of the UN offices, killing fifty-three refugees,[44] and encouraging eleven youths to pay smugglers to take them across the Sinai Desert and up to the border fence with Israel.[45] Once there, they crossed through a small opening in the fence, stepped into Israeli territory, and were eventually granted temporary residency permits. Others soon followed and, though an unknown number were immediately deported back to Egypt,[46] hundreds were allowed to stay when sympathetic border soldiers refused to deport them. The soldiers instead drove them to the Negev Desert in the south of Israel, dropped them off at a bus station, and told them to find organizations that assisted refugees.

Organizations sometimes met the refugees at the bus station, but so did kind strangers. Nyandeng, who arrived in Israel as a young girl in 2007, remembers her first day:

> At the station, an Ethiopian woman came and asked what we were doing there. . . . She bought me and my siblings and mother food and gave us money to take the bus to Jerusalem and said we should call her if we had no place to go and we would stay with her. We took a taxi and my mother told the driver to take us to a church – it didn't matter which one. He took us to a guesthouse and there was a man there, at reception. My mother told him we needed help. Without thinking he gave us a room for free with food.[47]

Soon after, Nyandeng and her younger sister and brother began attending school, and her mother found a job at one of the dozens of hotels employing East African refugees as cleaners. They rented an apartment in Naharia, a town in the north of Israel, but as the months passed they failed to gain any official residency status. There were 1,000 other asylum seekers in the country by 2007 and, like them, Nyandeng's mother could not legally work. They eventually received limited rights when, a year later, the High Court of Justice ordered that the government provide temporary residency status to all asylum seekers, and allow them to apply for refugee status. Nyandeng's family and others received three-month visas, and freedom from arrest. They still never received refugee status, as the government had yet to establish a Refugee Status Determination (RSD) procedure. Under such a procedure, common in developed countries, refugees undergo intensive interviews with government officials, providing evidence that they fled persecution due to their ethnic, political, religious, or social identity.

One reason that refugees like Nyandeng and her family could not access full residency rights was that they were not Jewish. Had they been Jewish, they would have qualified for citizenship under Israel's Law of Return. The Law, which dates back to Israel's creation in 1948, aims to ensure that every Jew has a state they can call home and which they can turn to in need. The logic behind this law is that, because Jews failed to access asylum during the Holocaust, a Jewish state is necessary to provide protection to Jews fleeing persecution, and ensure that Jews have access to a state that protects their interests. Were Israel to accept a significant number of non-Jewish refugees, then Israel would no longer have a Jewish majority, the Jewish character of the state would be undermined, and the Law of Return itself would no longer be accepted. Indeed, this general policy of maintaining a Jewish majority is a reason Israel refuses to allow the return of Palestinian refugees, those who had fled territory currently under Israeli control. For example, Palestinian refugees who once lived in Jerusalem and fled to Jordan in 1948 cannot return to Jerusalem and obtain residency permits in this city. When Sudanese refugees crossed into Israel, they were viewed in the same light as Palestinians: a threat to the Jewish majority, and so a threat to the Law of Return.[48]

This threat was dismissed by activists hoping to help refugees like Nyandeng. Such activists emphasized that, even if African asylum seekers were given refugee status, they needn't stay indefinitely, but only until it was safe to return home. Even if they did stay indefinitely, they would comprise a small percentage of the overall population, and so Jews would maintain a majority. Importantly, some activists claimed this would have no repercussions on Palestinian refugees who wished to return to their former homes currently under Israeli control. Palestinian refugees were one issue, they stated, and African refugees another.[49]

These activists failed to persuade policymakers to grant full residency status to Sudanese refugees, but refugees still faced superior conditions in Israel compared to Egypt. As a result, more refugees began arriving. By 2010 there were approximately 1,200 southern Sudanese in the country, and approximately 35,000 other asylum seekers from Eritrea and Sudan.

All had crossed over from Egypt since 2005, and their claims for asylum were never heard, their legal status remaining in limbo.[50] Given their precarious position, in 2010 some wished to return home.

They asked an NGO in Jerusalem for help returning. The NGO, called the International Christian Embassy (ICE), offered southern Sudanese refugees free flights to Juba, a stipend worth $1,500, and the necessary documents to enter Sudanese territory.[51] The organization worked with officials in UNHCR and the Hebrew Immigrant Aid Society (HIAS), a refugee rights organization.[52] Several dozen refugees returned, finding jobs soon after, and the project was deemed a success. Another NGO, Operation Blessing International (OBI), took over the project in 2011, still working with UNHCR and HIAS. When OBI took over, many Darfur refugees from northern Sudan also wished to repatriate. They, too, accepted OBI's free flight to Juba, paying for their own buses or flights to Darfur. By 2012, OBI and HIAS had helped 900 individuals repatriate.[53]

In 2011 South Sudan became an independent country. A year later the Israeli government announced that return to South Sudan was safe, as the country was no longer part of Sudan. OBI continued helping with return, and the Ministry of Interior also set up its own repatriation program, called Operation Returning Home (ORH).[54] It was supposedly voluntary, but the Ministry of Interior threatened to detain anyone who stayed. In response, South Sudanese activists organized protests, and raised a court petition, but it was rejected by the court and all were ordered into detention.[55]

"It was so strange," one aid worker recalls. "When refugees found out they would be detained, they just stopped protesting, all at once. They went out, bought the nicest clothes, and boarded the flight back."[56] After return, at least twenty-two individuals were killed or died of a disease within a year, representing at least 2 per cent of returnees.[57] When I traveled to South Sudan in December 2013, civil war broke out two days later, and I learned of an additional five who were killed, representing approximately 3.7 per cent of my sample of 136 returnees to South Sudan.[58] The exact mortality rate was likely higher, as I never reached the most insecure areas, and most returnees were never contacted by researchers or aid workers after returning.

Many of the NGO staff members helping with return were uncertain whether their actions were ethical. Based on the data I collected, they faced seven moral dilemmas, prevalent in repatriation globally.

1.4 SEVEN DILEMMAS

Below is an overview of these dilemmas, described in greater depth in the seven main chapters of this book.

1.4.1 Coercion

The first dilemma concerns coercion. Refugees often return to avoid detention, destitution, deportation, or life in an enclosed camp. If refugees are returning for these reasons, their returns are perhaps coerced.[59] We might suppose humanitarian organizations should not assist with coerced return.[60] Yet organizations defend their assistance by noting that, if refugees do not return, they will remain indefinitely in detention, destitution, or enclosed camps, and eventually be deported home.

This dilemma is especially acute in mass repatriation programs in developing countries, where the vast majority of repatriation takes place. Refugees in Pakistan and Iran often face detention, poverty, and police brutality, leading millions to repatriate with the help of UNHCR.[61] Somali refugees in Kenya are often forced into enclosed camps and threatened with deportation if they remain.[62] UNHCR has criticized enclosed camps and deportations, but has further expanded its repatriation program. It claims providing repatriation is better than providing no option at all.[63] It is not clear it is.

In Chapter 2 I describe the global prevalence of this dilemma and attempt to resolve it. I conclude that organizations can permissibly help with coerced repatriation if they try to end coercion, do not contribute to coercion, and inform refugees of the risks of returning.

1.4.2 Misinformation

In Chapter 3 I address a dilemma that arises when organizations and states do not inform refugees of the risks of returning, because they lack information about these risks. It is not clear who has a duty to inform refugees about risks, or whether refugees themselves are responsible for finding such information. I conclude that states and organizations have weighty duties to find information, even when the costs are high.

1.4.3 Regret

Chapter 4 addresses a dilemma relating to regret. Many refugees returning are informed about the risks, but regret their decision nonetheless, wishing they had remained in their country of asylum. This occurred in 2010 when thousands of refugees returning to Iraq regretted their decisions to return via UNHCR, wishing they had remained in Iran.[64] In such cases, perhaps the UN should stop facilitating return if future returnees will likely feel similar regret. But this claim is controversial: denying someone transport because they might feel regret seems wrongly paternalistic. When I book a flight to an unsafe country, the airline is not required to consider whether I will regret my decision. In Chapter 4 I argue that, though regret is not usually a reason to deny repatriation, sometimes it is.

1.4.4 Payments

In Chapter 5 I address dilemmas concerning payments. Government agencies often provide generous stipends to refugees agreeing to return home, at times using no coercion at all. We might suppose that such agencies are engaging in a justified form of immigration control, assuming refugees' choices are genuinely voluntary. Yet, perhaps such agencies act unethically because they are encouraging refugees to risk their lives in repatriating. A similar dilemma arises when UNHCR provides stipends to refugees returning home, as when it paid hundreds of dollars to each refugee returning to Afghanistan in the 2010s. I argue that government payments are justified when return is safe and voluntary. When returns are neither safe nor voluntary, because refugees are forced into enclosed camps if they remain, UNHCR payments are justified when they do not contribute to further coercion against refugees.

1.4.5 Children

In Chapter 6 I address cases involving children. In many cases children's rights will be at risk if they repatriate, but their parents seek repatriation nonetheless. In such cases it is not clear if parents have a right to return with their children. I argue that they often do not, and organizations and states should not provide repatriation assistance in such cases.

1.4.6 Discrimination

Chapter 7 concerns refugees whose lives will not be at risk if they repatriate. In a range of cases, refugees from unwanted ethnic groups are provided generous return assistance by governments who wish to fulfill the racist preferences of voters. In the case of Israel, those of African descent were given stipends to repatriate, while non-Africans were not. In such cases a dilemma arises: on the one hand such payments may seem morally acceptable, as the government is using no coercion, and many migrants hope to receive money to leave. On the other hand, such payments may be wrong, given the racist motives of governments and voters. I argue that such stipends are wrong, but may still be morally permissible if refugees consent to the stipends and the stipends do not harm others.

1.4.7 *Restitution*

Chapter 8 considers the rights of refugees who have already repatriated. In particular, I consider whether refugees have a right to valuable property restitution when others are in far greater need. It is not clear, for example, whether princes who fled Czechoslovakia had a right to the castles they left behind, or whether South Sudanese refugees who grew wealthy abroad had a right to the land confiscated during their displacement. I argue that such refugees do not have a right to the property they lost, but that states have good reason to return this property nonetheless.

1.5 FIELDWORK FOR PHILOSOPHY

In addressing these dilemmas, I will draw upon a range of cases around the globe. I shall also draw upon interviews I conducted in South Sudan, Ethiopia, Uganda, and other countries of origin, where individuals described to me why they arrived in Israel, their reasons for returning from Israel, and the conditions they faced after returning. Their stories serve a similar purpose to medical cases in bioethics, court judgments in jurisprudence, and thought experiments in moral philosophy. The cases serve as the dilemmas we start with which have yet to be addressed in philosophy and public policy.

Philosophers addressing ethical dilemmas typically draw upon cases found in existing empirical literature, rather than cases they learned about through their own fieldwork. I will also refer to existing literature, citing cases of return from around the world. However, there are very few in-depth studies of repatriation; the few that exist tend to describe the aggregate experience of repatriating populations, and often only before return. With some exceptions, studies rarely explore how individuals may have been subject to different injustices both before and after repatriation. I aim to capture this diverse range of cases with my own in-depth empirical research on repatriation from Israel.

A diverse range of cases is useful for normative theorizing. For example, in fictional trolley examples used in moral philosophy, a person must always decide if it is just to kill one person to save five, but the details of each example vary. In one case you see a runaway train about to run over five workmen on a track. You can save the five men by pushing a large bystander onto the track, stopping the train, killing him, but saving the five lives. In another case you also see a runaway train about to kill five workmen, but this time can only save them by pulling a switch, diverting the train onto another track, killing one man standing on the track but saving the five workmen. Many have the intuition that it is morally impermissible to push the large man onto the track in the first case, but perhaps permissible to pull the switch in the second.[65] The variation between cases highlights whether our intuitions change in response to new variables, helping us determine if these variables are normatively significant. I will employ a similar approach when formulating general ethical guidelines for repatriation.

To select cases that were sufficiently varied, I drew upon varied sources on repatriation globally, and conducted varied fieldwork on repatriation from Israel. For the latter, I conducted interviews with refugees who explained to me precisely why they came to Israel, what they experienced in Israel, why they decided to repatriate, who helped them repatriate, and what their conditions were after repatriating. To ensure I had a broad array of cases, I traveled to multiple towns within countries, and spoke to those living in urban and rural areas, in both safe and unsafe regions.

My first set of interviews took place between 2008 and 2010, when I spoke to NGO staff members in Israel who helped with return, and twelve refugees living in Israel, one of whom was interested in returning. I later traveled to Juba, Aweil, and Wau in South Sudan in March and April 2012, interviewing twenty-seven individuals after they returned from Israel to South Sudan. When I arrived in Juba the Israeli government announced that all were required to repatriate,[66] and almost all remaining South Sudanese in Israel returned by 2012. I traveled to East Africa again to interview these new returnees, first conducting fieldwork in Kampala and Entebbe in 2013, as many had migrated to these cities shortly after returning to South Sudan. While there, I interviewed thirty returnees, the majority children. In August 2013 I again traveled to Israel to interview a government official who was facilitating return,[67] and NGO staff assisting individuals' return as of 2013.

That year I traveled to South Sudan a second time, landing on December 13 to interview additional individuals who had returned. Two days later civil war broke out, and I stayed for six more weeks, interviewing sixty-one returnees who stayed in Juba. Roughly half the individuals I interviewed were Nuer citizens forced by Dinka militias to flee their homes to UN IDP camps. In June 2014 I traveled to Ethiopia, interviewing nine returnees from the Nuer tribe who had fled or migrated to Gambella, a town situated along the border with South Sudan. In February 2018 I traveled to Nairobi, Kenya, re-interviewing a subject I last saw in Israel in 2009, and a subject I last saw fleeing Juba in 2014. I also interviewed an additional subject who had fled South Sudan in 2013.

In total, I interviewed 128 returnees to South Sudan, including forty-eight minors. I also learned of the conditions of eight additional return-ees, and so could confirm the conditions of 136 individuals in total, representing approximately 11 per cent of the roughly 1,200 South Sudanese nationals who returned between 2010 and 2014.

To select these subjects, I arrived in each country and called two to five contacts provided to me by repatriation facilitators, volunteers, and friends in Israel. I then used a snowball methodology to interview their acquaintances, their acquaintances' acquaintances, and so forth, until all links were exhausted. After each interview, I coded responses for subjects' reasons for returning, including detention or threats to deportation in Israel. I also coded the interviews for properties related to post-return conditions, including whether they had access to food, income, medical care, education, and shelter, and whether they were again displaced. Finally, I recorded the number of subjects who died from illness, ethnic-based killings, or crossfire after returning.

I could not obtain a full list of phone numbers of those who returned and, even if I had, I would not have been able to interview a random sample of this list, as I could not access extremely remote areas. None-theless, I strived to interview a diverse range of subjects. I specifically strived to counteract survivorship bias, which arose because I was less able to learn about those who were killed or returned to insecure areas I could not reach. To counteract this bias, I traveled extensively within each town, and the surrounding rural areas, to meet with returnees who did not have access to secure healthcare, a cell phone, or a close tarmac road. During the war, I also conducted interviews in and around both UN IDP camps in Juba, including one in the Jebel neighborhood, where ethnic cleansing and fighting were especially widespread. And though I could not interview those who were killed, I attempted to establish a mortality rate. When I learned of a subject who was killed, and who I would have met had they survived, I included them in the sample of 136 subjects whose conditions I could confirm.[68]

In addition to interviewing South Sudanese subjects who returned, I interviewed a smaller sample of other refugees and migrants who repatriated via a distinct NGO called the Center for International Migration and Integration (CIMI). This NGO worked with IOM and a special Voluntary Return unit set up in the Ministry of Interior.[69] The sample included a family of four who had repatriated in 2012 to Sudan, and then fled to Ethiopia; two Eritrean refugees who had accepted money to resettle to Ethiopia; a father and his eight-year-old daughter who repatriated to Ethiopia; and three migrants who repatriated to Nigeria, two to Guinea, one to the Philippines, and fourteen to Thailand. I additionally interviewed a family of four intending to repatriate to Colombia who later changed their mind and remained in Israel. All of these cases are in many ways different than the cases of repatriation to South Sudan, but have certain important similarities – most notably the level of misinformation they received – and so provide useful comparisons.

One might suppose that we cannot rely on the responses of those who returned. They may have misrepresented how much they were coerced to return, how misinformed they were, and how difficult their conditions were after returning, especially if they were not satisfied with their choice. My method of sampling strived to mitigate this possibility. Because I interviewed individuals living in a diverse range of countries and regions, a significant portion were very satisfied with their return, but still recall being misinformed or coerced into returning, later fleeing their homes. If even these individuals recall similar challenges to those who regretted repatriating, this provides stronger evidence as to the accuracy of such testimonials. I also witnessed conditions described by respondents, such as overcrowding, unhygienic latrines, lack of food, and soldiers firing into IDP camps. As such, I could corroborate the responses of many interviewees regarding these conditions.

This original data on repatriation from Israel is central to this book. However, I situate it within the broader range of repatriation cases. The case of Israel is not unique because of the dilemmas repatriation facilitators faced. What was unique was the NGOs' greater financial investment to avoid these dilemmas. If such extraordinary measures failed to succeed, this highlights the depth of the problem and the need for an ethical analysis.

Such ethical analysis is central to this book, which is both philosophical and practical. It is philosophical because it addresses broader questions concerning consent, assistance, and discrimination, questions of interest for philosophers outside the field of immigration. It is practical because these broader questions are relevant for refugees around the world who, though living dramatically different lives, raise similar dilemmas for the agents helping them repatriate. The book describes refugees returning from Pakistan and Myanmar who, though experiencing different types of repatriation, raise similar dilemmas concerning how organizations should respond when coercion is rife. The book describes refugees returning from Norway and Iran who, though facing different types of misinformation, raise similar dilemmas concerning how organizations should respond when misinformation is rife. In focusing on these and other dilemmas, the book moves beyond asking how refugees have been wronged, and asks who is responsible for these wrongs. It moves beyond asking what principles governments should follow, and asks how these principles ought to be applied in practice. It asks not only what practices will protect refugees' safety, but what practices will respect refugees' rights when safety cannot be ensured. In doing so, the book provides a comprehensive set of guidelines for those helping refugees, helping create more ethical and informed repatriation.

NOTES

1. He was likely escorted by a representative of Refugee Action, a refugee-rights NGO facilitating all repatriation at the time. See International Organization for Migration (IOM), "Return and Reintegration," <http://unitedkingdom. iom.int/return-and-reintegration> (last accessed July 1, 2015).
2. UNHCR Global Trends 2010, <http://www.unhcr.org/en-us/statistics/ country/4dfa11499/unhcr-global-trends-2010.html> (last accessed July 30, 2017); UNHCR Global Trends 2011, <http://www.unhcr.org/en-us/ statistics/country/4fd6f87f9/unhcr-global-trends-2011.html> (last accessed July 30, 2017); UNHCR Global Trends 2012, <http://www.unhcr.org. uk/fileadmin/user_upload/pdf/UNHCR_Global_Trends_2012.pdf> (last

accessed July 30, 2017); UNHCR Global Trends 2013, <http://www.unhcr. org/en-us/statistics/country/5399a14f9/unhcr-global-trends-2013.html> (last accessed July 30, 2017); UNHCR Global Trends 2014, <http://www. unhcr.org/en-us/statistics/country/556725e69/unhcr-global-trends-2014. html> (last accessed July 30, 2017); UNHCR Global Trends 2015, <http:// www.unhcr.org/en-us/statistics/unhcrstats/576408cd7/unhcr-global-trends-2015.html> (last accessed July 30, 2017); UNHCR Global Trends 2016, <http://www.unhcr.org/5943e8a34.pdf> (last accessed July 30, 2017).

3. The reasons a government may not want to deport are varied. In Israel's case, various international aid packages and trade benefits are conditional on general human rights in the country. Deportations may be a point against Israel's human rights record, which can impact its trade status. See European Commission, "Implementation of the European Neigh-bourhood Policy in 2009: Progress Report Israel," Brussels, May 12, 2010, <http://ec.europa.eu/world/enp/pdf/progress2010/sec10_520_en.pdf> (last accessed July 5, 2011) and the "Justice, Freedom and Security" section in individual country progress reports, <http://ec.europa.eu/world/enp/ documents_en.htm#3> (last accessed July 5, 2011).

4. UNHCR, "Voluntary Repatriation: International Protection," 1996 at Chapter 3, Section 1.

5. Liz Fekete, "Europe's Shame: a report on 105 deaths linked to racism or government migration and asylum policies," European Race Bulletin, London: Institute of Race Relations, March 1, 2009; Leanne Weber and Sharon Pickering, "Exporting Risks, Deporting Non-Citizens," in (ed.) Francis Pakes, *Globalization and the Challenge to Criminology*, Abingdon, UK: Routledge 2013 at 110–28.

6. Interview with Assisted Voluntary Return (AVR) official, Tel Aviv, August 7, 2013.

7. Barak Kalir, "Between 'Voluntary' Return and Soft Deportation," in (eds) Zana Vathi and Russell King, *Return Migration and Psychosocial Wellbeing*, New York: Routledge 2017: 56–72 at 59.

8. For a contemporary discussion on social workers' roles in helping asylum seekers, see Ravi Kohli, "Social Work with Unaccompanied Asylum-Seek-ing Young People," *Forced Migration Review* 12(2002):31–3. See High Court of Justice 4845/12, Aid Organization for Refugees and Asylum Seekers (ASSAF), *The Hotline for Migrant Workers and the Association of Civil Rights in Israel v. The Ministry of Interior and the Ministry of Welfare*.

9. Philip Cantwell, "Relevant 'Material': Importing the Principles of Informed Consent and Unconscionability in Analysing Consensual Medical Repa-triations," *Harvard Law and Policy Review* 6(2012):249–62; Mark Kucze-wski, "Can Medical Repatriation be Ethical? Establishing Best Practices," *American Journal of Bioethics* 12(9)(2012):1–5; Lori A Nessel, "The Practice of Medical Repatriation: The Privatization of Immigrant Enforcement and Denial of Human Rights," *Wayne Law Review* 55(2009):1725–56.

10. Alex Betts, Gil Loescher, and James Milner, *UNHCR: The Politics and Practice of Refugee Protection, Second Edition*, Abingdon, UK: Routledge 2012.

11. Megan Bradley, *Refugee Repatriation: Justice, Responsibility, and Redress*, Cambridge: Cambridge University Press 2014; Lauren Fouda, "Compulsory Voluntary Repatriation: Why Temporary Protection for Sudanese Asylum-Seekers in Cairo Amounts to Refoulement," *Georgetown Journal on Poverty Law and Policy* 10(3)(2007):511–37 at 511; Katy Long, *The Point of No Return: Refugees, Rights, and Repatriation*, Oxford: Oxford University Press 2013.

12. Joseph Carens, "Aliens and Citizens: The Case for Open Borders," *The Review of Politics* 49(2)(1987):251–73; David Miller, "Immigration: The Case for Its Limits," in (eds) A. Cohen and C. Wellman, *Contemporary Debates in Applied Ethics*, Malden, MA: Blackwell Publishing 2005 at 202.

13. Alexander Betts, "Survival Migration: A New Protection Framework," *Global Governance* 16(2010):361–82; European Council on Refugees and Exile, "Complimentary Protection in Europe," July 2009, <http://www.refworld.org/pdfid/4a72c9a72.pdf> (last accessed July 1, 2012); Ruma Mandal, "Protection Mechanisms Outside of the 1951 Conventions ('Complimentary Protection')," Legal and Protection Policy Research Series, UNHCR 2005.

14. There are some exceptions to this rule, which I address in Appendix A.

15. Carens 1987 ibid.; Matthew Gibney, *The Ethics and Politics of Asylum: Liberal Democracy and the Response to Refugees*, Cambridge: Cambridge University Press 2004; Miller 2005 ibid. at 202.

16. Megan Bradley's work is perhaps the most impressive discussion on the philosophy of repatriation, and she addresses the role of UNHCR. However, her focus is mostly on what a just return would entail, rather than the actions that UNHCR should take when a just return is not possible. Katy Long similarly presents a nuanced and rigorous analysis of what an ethical return entails, but does not focus on what actions particular agents should take when a truly just return is not possible. See Bradley 2014 ibid. and Long 2013 ibid.

17. Javier Hidalgo, "The Duty to Disobey Immigration Law," *Moral Philosophy and Politics* 3(2)(2006):1–22; Javier Hidalgo, "The Ethics of People Smuggling," *Journal of Global Ethics* 12(3)(2016):311–26; Javier Hidalgo, "Resistance to Unjust Immigration Restrictions," *Journal of Political Philosophy* 23(4)(2015):450–70; Julian F. Müller, "The Ethics of Commercial Human Smuggling," *European Journal of Political Theory* (forthcoming).

18. Niheer Dasandi and Lior Erez, "The Donor's Dilemma: International Aid and Human Rights Violations," *British Journal of Political Science* (forthcoming); Jennifer Rubenstein, *Between Samaritans and States: The Political Ethics of Humanitarian INGOs*, Oxford: Oxford University Press 2015.

19. Bernardo Zacka, *When the State Meets the Street: Public Service and Moral Agency*, Cambridge: Harvard University Press 2017.

20. Katy Long, "When Refugees Stopped Being Migrants: Movement, Labor and Humanitarian Protection," *Migration Studies* 1(1)(2013):4–26.

21. Katy Long, *The Point of No Return*, Oxford: Oxford University Press 2013 at 80–1.

22. Jeff Crisp, "The Politics of Repatriation: Ethiopian Refugees in Djibouti, 1977–1983," *Review of African Political Economy* 33(30)(1984):73–82.

23. Sadako Ogato, "Statement by Mrs. Sadako Ogata, United Nations High Commissioner for Refugees, at the International Management Symposium, St. Gallen, Switzerland, 25 May 1992," <http://www.unhcr.org/uk/admin/hcspeeches/3ae68faec/statement-mrs-sadako-ogata-united-nations-high-commissioner-refugees-international.html> (last accessed January 8, 2018).

24. Jeff Crisp, "Mind the Gap! UNHCR, Humanitarian Assistance and the Development Process," New Issues in Refugee Research, Working Paper No. 43, May 2001 at 8.

25. James Milner and Gil Loescher, "Responding to Protracted Refugee Situations," Forced Migration Policy Briefing 6, January 2011 at 7, <https://yorkspace.library.yorku.ca/xmlui/bitstream/handle/10315/8011/Milner-Responding-Brief.pdf?sequence=1> (last accessed January 9, 2018).

26. UNHCR, "Voluntary Repatriation," February 2009, <http://www.unhcr.org/49ba2f5e2.pdf> (last accessed April 25, 2018).

27. Oxfam, "Returning to Fragility: Exploring the Link between Conflict and Returnees in Afghanistan," January 2018, <https://reliefweb.int/sites/reliefweb.int/files/resources/rr-returning-fragility-afghanistan-310118-en.pdf> (last accessed February 21, 2018).

28. Human Rights Watch, "Kenya: Involuntary Refugee Returns to Somalia," September 14, 2016, <https://www.hrw.org/news/2016/09/14/kenya-involuntary-refugee-returns-somalia> (last accessed January 7, 2018).

29. Jeff Crisp, "Why It's Far Too Early to Talk of Return for Syrian Refugees," News Deeply, August 11, 2017, <https://www.newsdeeply.com/refugees/community/2017/08/11/why-its-far-too-early-to-talk-of-return-for-syrian-refugees-2> (last accessed January 22, 2018).

30. Government of Sri Lanka, "UNHCR Helps First IDP Returns to Ampara," July 3, 2009, <http://www.priu.gov.lk/news_update/Current_Affairs/ca200907/20090703unhcr_support_govt.htm> (last accessed January 7, 2018); UNHCR, "Afghanistan: Refugee and IDP Returns," May 14, 2002, <http://www.unhcr.org/news/briefing/2002/5/3ce10537b/afghanistan-refugee-idp-returns.html> (last accessed February 9, 2018); UNHCR, "Displaced Congolese Return to Ituri with UNHCR Help," November 14, 2007, <https://reliefweb.int/report/democratic-republic-congo/displaced-congolese-return-ituri-unhcr-help> (last accessed January 7, 2018).

31. UNHCR, "UNHCR Global Trends 2010," <http://www.unhcr.org/uk/statistics/country/4dfa11499/unhcr-global-trends-2010.html> (last accessed January 7, 2018).

32. IOM, "Assisted Voluntary Return and Reintegration IOM Statistics Report," 2015, Geneva.

33. David Corlett, *Following them Home: The Fate of the Returned Asylum Seekers*, Melbourne: Black Inc. 2005 at 200–3; Human Rights Watch, "The International Organization for Migration (IOM) and Human Rights Protection in the Field: Current Concerns," <http://pantheon.hrw.org/legacy/backgrounder/migrants/iom-submission-1103.htm#_ftn14> (last accessed January 7, 2018); International Organization for Migration, "Displaced Families Quit Southern Mali, Cities, Return to North," May 2, 2014, <https://reliefweb.int/report/mali/displaced-families-quit-southern-mali-cities-return-north> (last accessed April 23, 2018); Catherine Ramos, "Unsafe Returns: Refoulement of Congolese Asylum Seekers," Justice First, at 10, http://justicefirst.org.uk/wp-content/uploads/UNSAFE-RETURN-DECEMBER-5TH-2011.pdf> (last accessed February 24, 2018).

34. Marina Martinovic, "Refugees Reloaded – Lessons from Germany's Approach to Bosnian War," DW, February 2, 2016, <http://www.dw.com/en/refugees-reloaded-lessons-from-germanys-approach-to-bosnian-war/a-19021249> (last accessed January 6, 2018).

35. German Federal Ministry of Interior, "Return Policy," <https://www.bmi.bund.de/EN/topics/migration/law-on-foreigners/return-policy/return-policy-node.html> (last accessed January 25, 2018); Andreas Rinke, "Germany's Merkel Says Refugees Must Return Home Once War is Over," Reuters, January 30, 2016, <https://uk.reuters.com/article/us-europe-migrants-germany-refugees/germanys-merkel-says-refugees-must-return-home-once-war-is-over-idUKKCN0V80IH> (last accessed January 6, 2018).

36. UNHCR, "Voluntary Return and Reintegration of Somali Refugees from Kenya: Pilot Phase Evaluation Report," 2015, at 2, <http://www.unhcr.org/560b962f9.pdf> (last accessed January 28, 2018).

37. Kalir 2017 ibid.

38. European Commission, "EU Trust Fund for Africa: New Programs Adopted to Reinforce Protection of Migrants and Fight against Smugglers and Traffickers," December 6, 2017, <http://europa.eu/rapid/press-release_IP-17-5144_en.htm> (last accessed January 19, 2018); European Commission, "Questions & Answers: Making Return and Readmission Procedures More Efficient," March 2, 2017, <http://europa.eu/rapid/press-release_MEMO-17-351_en.htm> (last accessed January 19, 2018).

39. Scott Blinder, "Deportations, Removals, and Voluntary Departures from the UK," October 4, 2017, <http://www.migrationobservatory.ox.ac.uk/wp-content/uploads/2016/04/Briefing-Deportations-2.pdf> (last accessed January 19, 2018).

40. Patrick Wintour, "'Go Home' Billboards Not a Success, Says Theresa May," *The Guardian*, October 22, 2013, <https://www.theguardian.com/politics/2013/oct/22/go-home-billboards-pulled> (last accessed February 28, 2018).

41. Many other organizations, members of the public, and politicians also con-demned the billboards, including the United Kingdom Independence Party (UKIP) leader Nigel Farage. See Matthew Taylor, "'Go Home' Campaign Creating a Climate of Fear, Say Rights Groups," *The Guardian*, August 8, 2013, <https://www.theguardian.com/uk-news/2013/aug/08/go-home-climate-of-fear-rights-groups> (last accessed February 28, 2018).

42. Blinder 2017 ibid.; Wintour 2013 ibid.

43. The Second Sudanese Civil War lasted from 1983 until 2005, leaving approx-imately two million dead from both the war itself and the consequences of the war, including famine and disease. For a more complete background on the history of South Sudan, see Anders Breidlid, Avelino Androga Said, and Astrid Kristine Breidlid, *A Concise History of South Sudan: New and Revised Edition*, Kampala, Uganda: Fountain Publishers 2014.

44. Michael Slackman, "After Cairo Police Attack, Sudanese Have Little but Rage," *The New York Times*, January 3, 2006, <http://www.nytimes.com/2006/01/03/world/africa/after-cairo-police-attack-sudanese-have-little-but-rage.html> (last accessed February 24, 2018).

45. Galia Sabar and Elizabeth Tsurkov, "Israel's Policies towards Asylum Seek-ers, 2002–2014," Istituto Affari Internazionali Working Paper, May 15, 2015.

46. Dana Weiler-Polak, "Israel's 'Hot Return' of Sudan Refugees Prompts UN Concern," *Haaretz*, December 30, 2009, <https://www.haaretz.com/1.5116374> (last accessed February 28, 2018).

47. Interview with Nyandeng, Entebbe, May 9, 2013. All names have been changed to protect anonymity.

48. Barak Kalir, "The Jewish State of Anxiety: Between Moral Obligation and Fearism in the Treatment of African Asylum Seekers in Israel," *Journal of Ethnic and Migration Studies* 41(4)(2015):580–98; Tally Kritzman-Amir, "'Otherness' as the Underlying Principle in Israel's Asylum Regime," *Israel Law Review* 42(3)(2009):603–27; Vered Slonim-Nevo and Maya Lavie-Ajayi, "Refugees and Asylum Seekers from Darfur: The Escape and Life in Israel," *International Social Work* 60(3)(2017):568–87; Hadas Yaron, Nurit Hashimshony-Yaffe, and John Campbell, "'Infiltrators' or Refugees? An Analysis of Israel's Policy towards African Asylum Seekers," *International Migration* 51(4)(2013):144–57.

49. I made this argument myself as a student activist.

50. Gilad Nathan, "The Policy towards the Population of Infiltrators, Asylum Seekers, and Refugees in Israel and European Countries," Israel Knesset Research and Information Center 2012 at 13 (Hebrew).

51. Because the NGO had connections to southern Sudanese officials, it ensured that all who wanted to repatriate accessed documentation to enter what was then Sudanese territory. At the time, this was an option that the Israeli government could not provide, as Sudan was an enemy state to Israel. Sudan remains an enemy state to Israel, though South Sudan – created in 2011 – is not.

52. Interview with HIAS director, Jerusalem, December 12, 2012.

53. Ibid.

54. Laurie Lijnders, "Deportation of South Sudanese from Israel," *Forced Migration Review* 2013(44)(2013):66–7.

55. Administrative Petition (Jerusalem) 53765-03-12: *ASSAF v. Ministry of Interior* (7.6.12); Lijnders 2013 ibid. at 66.

56. Interview with Sharon, ASSAF volunteer, Tel Aviv, December 16, 2013.

57. Yuval Goren (Hebrew), "Aid Organizations: Over 22 Refugees Expelled to South Sudan Die within the First Year," June 5, 2012, <http://www.nrg. co.il/online/1/ART2/477/197.html> (last accessed February 25, 2018).

58. Interview with Gatluak, Juba, January 4, 2014; interview with Matthew, Juba, January 4, 2014; interview with Simon in IDP camp, Juba, January 4, 2014.

59. If they are coerced into returning home, then their returns violate the international law principle of *non-refoulement*, which holds that states ought not to force refugees back to countries where their lives will be at risk. But even if their return does not violate any international law, because they are not refugees in the legal sense, their forced return may still be unethical. For an overview on the legal principle of *non-refoulement*, see Jean Allain, "The *Jus Cogens* Nature of *Non-Refoulement*," *International Journal of Refugee Law* 13(4)(2001):533–58.

60. This is a conclusion reached by a number of academics. See Jeff Crisp and Katy Long, "Safe and Voluntary Refugee Repatriation: From Principle to Practice," *Journal on Migration and Human Security* 4(3)(2016):141–7 at 146; Michael Barnett, "UNHCR and the Ethics of Repatriation," *Forced Migration Review* 10(2001):31–4.

61. Human Rights Watch, "Pakistan Coercion, UN Complicity: The Mass Forced Return of Afghan Refugees," February 13, 2017, <https://www.hrw. org/report/2017/02/13/pakistan-coercion-un-complicity/mass-forced-return-afghan-refugees> (last accessed February 26, 2018).

62. Human Rights Watch, "Kenya: End Abusive Round-Ups," May 12, 2014, <https://www.hrw.org/news/2014/05/12/kenya-end-abusive-round-ups> (last accessed January 22, 2018); Human Rights Watch, "Kenya: Involuntary Refugee Returns to Somalia," September 14, 2014, <https://www.hrw. org/news/2016/09/14/kenya-involuntary-refugee-returns-somalia> (last accessed January 22, 2018).

63. UNHCR, "Voluntary Return and Reintegration of Somali Refugees from Kenya: Pilot Phase Evaluation Report," 2015, <http://www.unhcr. org/560b962f9.pdf> (last accessed January 28, 2018).

64. UNHCR Briefing Note, "Iraqi Refugees Regret Returning to Iraq, Amid Insecurity," October 19, 2010, <http://www.unhcr.org/uk/news/ briefing/2010/10/4cbd6c9c9/unhcr-poll-iraqi-refugees-regret-returning-iraq-amid-insecurity.html> (last accessed February 26, 2018).

65. Judith Jarvis Thomson, "The Trolley Problem," *The Yale Law Journal* 94(6) (1985):1395–1415.

66. For the text of the letter sent to the South Sudanese, see PIBA, "A Call for the People of South Sudan," January 31, 2011, <http://www.piba.gov. il/SpokesmanshipMessagess/Documents/2012-2192.pdf> (last accessed July 3, 2012).

67. Interview with head of Voluntary Return Unit, Tel Aviv, July 28, 2013.

68. I did not include those I learned about only because they had died, as this would bias my sample in the opposite direction, over-representing those who had died.

69. Interview with CIMI director, Jerusalem, September 22, 2011.

Chapter 2

COERCION

George was followed home. As he reached for his keys to his apartment in Tel Aviv, he was startled by a voice from behind.

"Pack your belongings," a policeman ordered, informing him he had a week to return to South Sudan or be detained indefinitely in Israel.

George had originally fled South Sudan for Egypt during the Second Sudanese Civil War in the 1980s. He failed to find secure protection in Egypt and so crossed the Sinai Desert in 2008, entering Israeli territory with the help of smugglers. Like 60,000 other asylum seekers who had crossed over, George could not apply for refugee status or legally work as of 2012.[1]

As the policeman drove away, George called OBI. He asked for help returning to South Sudan, and was given a free flight home and travel documentation. By 2012, nearly all South Sudanese in Israel had repatriated via similar means.

It is against international law to indefinitely detain asylum seekers without first establishing if they are refugees.[2] What is less obvious is whether organizations like OBI should help individuals return to avoid such detention.

The UN claims it should.[3] Over the last three decades, it has assisted over ten million refugees repatriate, many from detention, and many more from enclosed camps.[4] It helps because, even if governments detain refugees or force them into enclosed camps,[5] the UN is using no coercion itself, and is helping refugees obtain freedom through repatriation.[6] It is analogous, one could claim, to civil servants clandestinely helping individuals flee persecuting regimes. During the Rwandan Genocide and the Holocaust, such civil servants were celebrated as helping individuals escape injustices.[7] Of course those who fled were coerced; that is why it was commendable to help them.

Yet, unlike fleeing from danger to safety, refugees who return home may be trading one injustice for another. In this case, "repatriation facilitators," including NGOs and UN agencies, cannot normally justify their actions by appealing to the outcomes of return. In this eventuality, NGOs have justified their assistance by reference to refugees' consent. But it is unclear if there is consent, given the presence of coercion.

In the following section I will describe one version of this dilemma, which I call the "Coercion Dilemma." Coercion Dilemmas occur when facilitators help with coerced returns without causally contributing to the coercion. In Section 2.2 I will then address "Causation Dilemmas," where facilitating return does causally contribute to coercion.

Before proceeding, it is necessary to precisely state the aims and clarify the assumptions of this chapter to avoid misunderstanding about the highly contentious questions addressed.

I shall consider whether facilitators are morally permitted to assist with return, rather than whether they are legally permitted to do so.[8] The refugees under consideration are primarily those who the UN claims should not be forcibly returned, but instead given asylum or the opportunity to apply for refugee status. These are individuals whose lives will likely be at risk from persecution if they return. Using the UN definition permits discussion of the UN's dilemmas according to the UN's own standards. In a similar vein, I use the definition of coercion provided by IOM, a major global repatriation facilitator. According to IOM, coercion occurs when one is repatriating to avoid detention, but also when one lacks basic necessities if they stay, such as food or shelter.[9] More specifically, I assume states unjustly coerce refugees to leave if they have the capacity to provide basic services to refugees within their territory, but refuse to provide such services.[10]

Though I mostly focus on refugees who fled persecution in their home countries, and are repatriating to such persecution, I will at times discuss individuals who fled general violence, food insecurity, and a lack of medical care. As noted in the introduction, I assume that coercing such "survival migrants"[11] to return home is morally impermissible. At the very least, it is impermissible if the state has the capacity to accept such individuals, and if accepting these migrants is the only way to ensure that they obtain basic human rights. This claim is supported not only by philosophers who believe in open borders, such as Joseph Carens,[12] but also by those who defend states' right to exclude immigrants, such as David Miller, Matthew Gibney, and even some states themselves.[13] As such, it serves as a "minimal ethical standard," determining who the state should not deport,[14] while leaving open the question of who repatriation facilitators should help return. I will therefore refer to individuals as "refugees" even if their return is unsafe for reasons related to general violence or food insecurity, rather than persecution.

Though I make the above assumptions throughout the chapter, one may accept my general conclusions, while still disagreeing on who deserves asylum. My goal is not to settle the debate about who states should protect, but to resolve the dilemma of who should be helped to return by the aforementioned organizations, if governments are coercing individuals to leave.

2.1 THE DILEMMA OF INVOLUNTARY RETURN

Coercion Dilemmas occur when humanitarian organizations are faced with a choice. They can either help with return, or watch refugees face confinement in camps and detention, or an inability to access basic necessities. I will first describe this dilemma, and then consider how it might be resolved.

2.1.1 Describing the Dilemma

In 1991 two million Kurdish refugees fled Iraq, most hoping to reach Turkey. They reached a mountainous area separating the two countries, but Turkish officials refused to grant them entrance. NGOs active in the area had a choice. They could do nothing, forcing refugees to stay in the mountains, or help them return to Iraq, and risk being killed.

Within four days, 1,500 died from exposure, the rest uncertain what would happen if they remained. As in Israel, no NGOs claimed that the Turkish government's response was morally permissible. But helping with return seemed preferable, because the Turkish government refused to change its policy regardless.[15]

This same dilemma arose ten years later, in 2001, when three and a half million Afghan refugees faced regular detention, deportation threats, and extortion in Pakistan and Iran.[16] These continue today, as one refugee in Pakistan testified in 2017:

> In early August . . . the police came to our house . . . [at] about 4:30 a.m. They entered our house without asking, pushed all the women to one side and took all of the men, including me, to the

police station . . . They held us there all day and did not give us water or let us go to the toilet. Our relatives came and paid to get us out. In early October, I saw in a newspaper that the police would do more search operations and that they were going to put Afghans in prison. So we knew we had to leave.[17]

To leave he turned to UNHCR, and the agency provided him transport to Afghanistan, joining hundreds of thousands of refugees similarly compelled to repatriate.[18] It is not clear whether such refugees ought to have been assisted with repatriation. Their choices were involuntary, but perhaps an involuntary choice is better than no choice at all.

A similar dilemma is found when states lack the capacity to accept refugees. In such cases, states may both deny refugees the right to work, and also lack the means to provide them aid to survive. This was the case between 1982 and 1984 when Djibouti denied refugees work visas and rations, and refugees felt compelled to return to Ethiopia with the help of UNHCR.[19] In 2014 the Tanzanian government gave refugees the choice between living in camps or returning to Burundi without access to basic necessities.[20] More recently, the Ugandan government has struggled to provide sufficient food for refugees, compelling some to repatriate home.[21] In such cases, we may feel that poor states are not blameworthy for failing to provide aid to refugees, but there is still a background injustice if wealthier countries could provide this aid to poorer states, and refuse to, compelling refugees to leave.[22] In such cases, it remains unclear whether NGOs and the UN should help with return.

This dilemma has been especially pronounced in Kenya, where refugees confined to enclosed camps often seek return to Somalia to regain their freedom, despite the risks involved. These refugees evoke the Somali proverb *laba kala daran mid dooro*, which means "choosing the best of two bad situations." As one refugee explained in the early 2000s: "The conflict we fled [in Somalia] at least we could get out, we could move around even if a bullet hits you. And now we miss that . . . now we cannot move around. You just sit around."[23]

This refugee sought assistance returning from UNHCR, but UNHCR had yet to set up a repatriation program. It finally did in 2013 when the Kenyan government announced that refugee camps would be closed, and stern action taken against refugees remaining.[24] UNHCR created "help desks," asking refugees whether and why they wished to return and, if their choice seemed voluntary, they were given transport back

to Somalia.[25] In reality, their choices were often involuntary, but perhaps UNHCR acted ethically if their lives in Kenya would be unlikely
to improve.

One might suppose that Coercion Dilemmas are not relevant when
claims for asylum are heard in wealthier countries, where genuine refugees are given residency rights and freedom. Yet, even when claims are
heard, strict evaluation criteria mean many refugees are denied refugee
status, especially those fleeing life-threatening poverty.[26] They are then
detained and wish to repatriate. Some do, with the help of organizations, and end up again displaced or killed after return.[27] Even if one
believes that states have acted legally according to a strict definition of
international law, it seems unlikely they are acting ethically, and so it
remains unclear whether organizations should assist with such returns.

Consider, for example, the case of Habibullah, a refugee from
Afghanistan who boarded a boat in an attempt to reach Australia in
2001. His boat was intercepted by an Australian naval ship and, according to Habibullah and a witness, a naval officer placed a gun to his head
and pulled the trigger, never telling him the gun was not loaded. He
was traumatized, taken to a detention center, and given a heavy dose of
sleeping pills rather than psychological care. His condition deteriorated,
his application for asylum was rejected, and he remained in the camp,
eventually accepting an IOM flight to his home village in Afghanistan.
Once home he was threatened by a villager who claimed he was a
Taliban spy, and fled to Pakistan shortly after.[28] Assuming Habibullah
was a refugee when attempting to reach Australia, and that he wanted
to return because of trauma and detention, it was not clear if IOM
ought to have helped him return. Perhaps IOM made the right decision,
given the deteriorating conditions he experienced in detention. Perhaps
it made the wrong decision, given the involuntary nature of his choice.

The Coercion Dilemma is not limited to cases of refugees returning
home. It is also relevant for IDPs returning from one region to another.
In 2014 over 2,000 individuals living in the Kiwanja IDP camp in DR
Congo were left homeless when government officials burned their
shelters to the ground, telling them they must return home. UNHCR
faced a choice: it could help these IDPs return to their home villages,
knowing their choices were involuntary and unsafe, or do nothing at all,
forcing them to live without shelter and security.[29] A similar dilemma
arose in South Africa in 2008 when forty-three refugees and migrants
were killed by anti-immigrant mobs, thousands more injured, and

20,000 displaced by the week's end. Those who were displaced struggled to access basic necessities. All were classified as IDPs by UNHCR, which was unable to provide them safe accommodation where they were, but could offer them assistance returning to the neighborhoods from which they fled. Those choosing to return often had little choice, as they needed to return to access life-sustaining businesses.[30] It is not clear if UNHCR ought to have helped them return, given that their choices were involuntary.

The above Coercion Dilemmas have been largely overlooked in discussions on immigration. Such discussions focus almost entirely on state injustices, rather than the dilemmas of organizations providing repatriation.[31] The few scholars discussing the ethics of UNHCR and IOM tend to assume that assisting with a coerced return is, by definition, impermissible.[32] Their position is that UNHCR and IOM have a "repatriation culture" and use a distorted definition of "voluntariness," where a refugee in detention or destitution is considered sufficiently free to consent to return.[33] This critique is incomplete. Though the definition of voluntariness is skewed and the culture of repatriation problematic, UNHCR and IOM may be helping with involuntary returns because doing nothing is worse.

When OBI began its repatriation program in 2010, the Israeli government had yet to detain a significant number of refugees, and had yet to prevent them from working, but OBI was still facing a Coercion Dilemma. At the time, refugees were denied legal residency, a small number were detained, and all were uncertain whether they would be deported in the near future.[34] They could not apply for refugee status and, even if they could, their claims would likely be denied, as Israel provides refugee status to only 0.25 per cent of applicants.[35]

Though conditions were difficult in Israel, most did not wish to return to South Sudan. The country was part of Sudan until 2011, and had only recently emerged from a war which began in 1983, fought mainly between southern Sudanese opposition forces, and the ruling northern Sudanese forces.[36] From 1991, the southern Sudanese forces had split into two opposing groups, one mainly from the Dinka ethnic group, and the other mainly from the Nuer ethnic group.[37] When South Sudan achieved independence from northern Sudan in 2011, a coalition government was formed in Juba comprising both Nuer and Dinka citizens, but the president stifled dissenting voices,[38] and inter-ethnic violence continued into 2012. That year alone thousands of civilians were killed.[39] As a result of the instability, the country lacked basic services, including food security and healthcare.[40]

Given conditions in South Sudan, and given that Israel let South Sudanese work in 2011, many refuges stayed in Israel. Vanessa, one such refugee, explained why she had initially left South Sudan, and why she did not accept OBI's help to return from Israel in 2011:

> I am from Unity State, and we fled the war to Khartoum when I was a young girl ... I married there, had four kids, and crossed into Israel via Egypt in 2007. [In Israel] I was in prison for half a year, but then released, so decided to stay. It was good. I worked, at first, in the Renaissance hotel in Tel Aviv. The kids went to school.[41]

But others wished to return, such as Joseph:

> My state is Lega State ... I was born in Khartoum in 1982, but came back to South Sudan from 1995 until 2000, so I was familiar with Juba. I went to Egypt in 2000, and in 8 August 2005 I went to Israel ... I went to prison for one year, and after one year they released us. I worked in a hotel, but could not get an ID, or legally start a business. So I saved $20,000. I was in touch with my family in Juba, and so asked for help returning.[42]

Joseph was one of the first refugees to return with the help of OBI. At the time, many human rights organizations opposed OBI's assistance, claiming Joseph and others had few rights, and so their return was involuntary.[43] In response, OBI hired a refugee rights organization, HIAS, to interview each refugee, asking them, "Why do you want to return?" If an individual said they were only returning to avoid detention, their return was viewed as involuntary and not supported.

In total, OBI helped roughly 900 individuals return between 2009 and 2012.[44] Once an asylum seeker left Israel they could not re-enter Israeli territory.[45] But OBI was convinced that this choice, though irreversible, was entirely voluntary.

OBI's intentions seemed genuinely humanitarian. It was a Christian humanitarian organization with a strong history of providing food, shelter, and medical assistance to all denominations in developing countries.[46] It had never, until 2010, been involved in repatriation. Nor had HIAS, a humanitarian organization founded in 1881 to assist Jews fleeing pogroms in Russia and Eastern Europe, and which later focused on helping 3,600 non-Jewish refugees resettle from Vietnam, Cambodia, and Laos into the United States.[47] HIAS said it opposed repatriation in other contexts, refusing to assist with repatriation from Kenya to Somalia due to risks involved.[48] In Israel it made an exception, as it could conduct individual interviews to ensure there was no coercion.

HIAS and OBI had succeeded to an extent. Of the 128 subjects I interviewed, sixty-nine returned because they thought life was better in South Sudan, rather than only to avoid difficult conditions in Israel. However, there was a marked distinction between those who returned prior to and after 2012.

That year, thousands of Israeli citizens marched through the streets of Tel Aviv, calling for the expulsion of African asylum seekers, described by the prime minister as "flooding the country"[49] and by one politician as a "cancer to the body."[50] Legislation was passed to detain asylum seekers,[51] and all South Sudanese were told they must return or face imprisonment.[52] Only those with severe medical problems were permitted to remain. Vanessa describes life during this period, and why she changed her mind about staying in Israel:

> Every day started with a mess. You go outside and they tell you, "Go back to your country! Why are you here? Your country has money! Go home!" In June they took my husband's visa and said, "We will not give you a new visa." We were left without work for two months. I said, "What? What will I do . . .?" So I thought, "I will say thank you to God that we are healthy and go back."

Vanessa called OBI, which eventually agreed to help her return.[53] Hundreds of others soon followed. Of those I interviewed, thirty-seven returned to avoid detention, and thirty-six returned partially or wholly because they could no longer work, fearing they would lack basic necessities if they stayed. Fourteen left because they feared deportation.

It is not immediately clear whether OBI's first policy of refusing to help with coerced return was better than its second policy of supporting such return. Neither was more principled than the other. It may seem principled to only help with voluntary returns, but this would force refugees to stay in detention. The case demonstrates that the dilemmas of repatriation cannot easily be avoided even when working independently from the government, and even with the best of intentions and resources.

2.1.2 Resolving the Dilemma

To resolve the Coercion Dilemma, we must address a pressing question: can refugees truly give their consent when faced with coercion? In many cases outside the sphere of repatriation, consent may very well be valid even if there are only injurious alternatives. A patient is perfectly capable of giving consent to life-saving surgery, even though the alternative to surgery is death. As such, some philosophers argue that cases of "third party coercion" are also cases of valid consent.[54] Imagine that Abbey threatens to shoot Babu if he does not buy Cathy's watch. Cathy sells Babu her watch because she does not want him shot by Abbey. Babu's consent seems valid for Cathy, even if not for Abbey. Of course, Cathy would have an obligation to later give back the money to Babu once the threat has subsided, but Cathy has not wronged Babu at the time of the transaction and, if she cannot later undo the transaction, then she has not wronged Babu even though his consent was under duress. One could similarly argue that refugees' consent is valid for repatriation facilitators, even if it is not valid for the government.

However, according to a number of theories, consent would be invalid for Cathy if she could easily persuade Abbey to put her gun down.[55] Cathy should do this, instead of selling her watch. In other words, Cathy's duty is to get Abbey to stop threatening Babu, and therefore Babu's consent is not valid for Cathy. This approach is consistent with the Good Samaritan principle, which holds that agents should help those in great need, if they easily can. If there is nothing that Cathy can do, then Babu's consent is perfectly valid for her, but not if she can easily stop Abbey's violent threat.

With repatriation to dangerous countries, we may ask if a facilitator can easily raise money for basic necessities and legal aid to avoid coercive conditions. If instead it raises money for repatriation, then it fails to honor the Good Samaritan principle. Of course, basic necessities may be an ongoing cost, while repatriation is a one-off. But if a refugee lacks necessities after they have returned, it is unclear if the repatriation facilitator can simply ignore their needs. If they owed them this aid before return, an action absolving them of this duty without alleviating the need seems unethical.

In addition to Good Samaritan duties, organizations may have cost-lier duties. Humanitarian organizations in particular were created to protect vulnerable populations, and so should be held to a higher standard in protecting these populations. They may be morally required to lobby for policy changes, provide legal aid, and raise money for necessities. Demanding costly duties from Cathy, by contrast, could infringe on her right to a personal life. While organizational staff also have a personal life, they have voluntarily agreed to allocate an insulated portion of their lives to the goals of the organization, so their personal lives are not infringed.

Some may claim that, though organizations like OBI and HIAS have weightier duties to help refugees, semi-governmental organizations do not. Such organizations are created to help refugees and governments. IOM, for example, states that it is "dedicated to promoting humane and orderly migration for the benefit of all," including governments hoping to decrease the number of refugees within their borders.[56] We might suppose IOM, when allocating its time and resources, should weigh the benefits for refugees against the benefits for governments. This might involve, for example, spending some resources and time lobbying for better conditions for refugees, but ensuring there are ample resources and time to facilitate returns, even if this comes at the expense of lobbying. UNHCR may have similar duties, given that it is funded by states and purports to represent states as a UN agency.

Though IOM and UNHCR were created partly to help states, they were created to only help in a certain manner. UNHCR was created to help states fulfill their duties towards refugees fleeing persecution because of their ethnicity, religion, social identity, or political opinion. It would be contrary to UNHCR's mandate if it physically coerced such refugees back to a country where they would face persecution, even if this advanced states' interests. By extension, it would be contrary to UNHCR's mandate to help these refugees with repatriation without also helping end coercion, even if this would advance states' interests. A similar claim is relevant for IOM, which claims to advance the interests of states in a manner consistent with the legal rights of migrants.[57] Some migrants are refugees according to international law, and so IOM's mandate requires it to try to end the coercive conditions these refugees face.

Many refugees, of course, are not fleeing persecution, but fleeing general violence, extreme poverty, or natural disasters. UNHCR's and IOM's official mandates do not require them to prevent their coerced return. Nonetheless, UNHCR and IOM may still have a special duty to help prevent their coerced return. This is because agents can have a duty to help individuals when they have significant power.[58] When an agent has power, it has a greater ability to help others, and so may have greater duties to help.[59] For example, a doctor on a flight may have a duty to save a life, because she can more easily do so, even if the doctor never recited the Hippocratic Oath, and never claimed to be undergoing medical training to help all those in need. If repatriation facilitators have a greater ability to lobby for the rights of all refugees – including those fleeing general violence and poverty – they should do so, even if this is not in their mandate. At the very least, they ought to work harder to protect the rights of refugees than an individual like Cathy, a private citizen with less power.

There are situations where repatriation facilitators – whether UNHCR, IOM, or NGOs – do work hard to end coercive conditions, but fail to create any change. In such cases, assisting with return may be legitimate. For example, when Kurdish refugees were trapped between Iraq and Turkey, NGOs tried and failed to persuade the Turkish government to provide them with asylum. More refugees were likely to die from exposure, and so NGOs acted ethically when helping with their return. Similarly, had OBI and HIAS worked hard to end detention, but failed, perhaps helping with return would have been legitimate, so long as South Sudanese nationals were aware of the risks.

This conclusion is predicated on the assumption that helping with repatriation does not itself cause governments to expand their use of coercion. If there is such a causative link, then further considerations become relevant, which I will now address.

2.2 THE CAUSATION DILEMMA

Causation Dilemmas occur when an organization helps refugees repatriate, and this contributes to government coercion. There are four types of such dilemmas and, in all four, return should generally not be facilitated, with some exceptions.

2.2.1 *Simple Counterfactual Causation*

In "Simple Counterfactual Causation" an agent causes an event if, had the agent not acted as she had, the event would not have occurred and, in acting as she did, the outcome did occur.[60] In other words,

A causes B if A's actions were necessary for B to occur, and B did in fact occur.

If the government is detaining refugees to encourage return, and an organization makes return possible, this can motivate the government to detain more refugees than it otherwise would. IOM is an example of an organization that may have such an impact. Globally, the organization visits survival migrants in detention, writes down their details, and tries to secure their passports so they can repatriate.[61] If governments are only detaining refugees so that they repatriate, and refugees are only repatriating because of IOM, then IOM is causally contributing to detention, in the sense that its actions are necessary for the detention to occur.

UNHCR may contribute to coercive policies in a similar manner. In 1994 and 1995 UNHCR began facilitating the repatriation of Rohingya refugees from Bangladesh back to Burma. Soon after, the Bangladeshi government increased its pressure on refugees to return precisely because return was now possible, as it was being funded by UNHCR.[62] Similarly, in 2012, one Israeli Knesset report stated that OBI had established that repatriation for South Sudanese was possible, and the government should endorse a more aggressive return policy for those who had not yet returned.[63]

The case of Israel raises an additional complication, overlooked in the examples above. OBI was not the only agent facilitating return. The government began its own repatriation program in 2012, eventually returning thousands of asylum seekers.[64] In other countries, UN agencies, multiple private charities, and refugees themselves pay for transport home. When there are multiple agents helping with repatriation, then one agent pulling out will not stop repatriation, nor stop the coercive conditions which lead to repatriation. If existing bodies have the capacity to repatriate all refugees, a single organization may very well not causally contribute to coercion. For were it to discontinue its repatriation services, refugees would still be able to repatriate at the same rate, via a different facilitator. Even in such cases, a given facilitator might still be necessary for coercion if other facilitators are incapable of facilitating all repatriation. OBI may have increased the number of refugees who could return from detention compared to a world where only the government provided repatriation. If the government was detaining refugees so more would return, and more could return because of OBI, OBI's actions may have been necessary for the government's rate of detention.

When humanitarian organizations are necessary for coercive policies – either because they make repatriation possible for all or more refugees – then coercion is not a mere background condition, but is dependent on repatriation. This leads to a simple argument for discontinuing repatriation services, related to the Good Samaritan principle. Refraining from helping with return is costless. If this costless act of omission helps refugees avoid detention, then, as organizations created to help others, they should exploit this omission to efficiently achieve their goals.

We might argue that, in some cases, causally contributing to coercion does not harm refugees. In my sample, some refugees did not particularly mind that the government threatened to detain them or revoke their visas, because they would have returned regardless, for reasons unrelated to coercion. Some missed their families, or wished to contribute to the development of their country.

Even for these cases, it may be wrong for humanitarian organizations to help with return, because it is wrong to causally contribute to coercive policies, even if those subject to coercion do not feel subjectively worse off. For example, imagine again that Abbey puts a gun to Babu's head, telling him to buy Cathy's watch, but Babu wanted to buy the watch regardless. When Cathy sells her watch, she may be making Babu's life better in some ways, but she is also causally contributing to Abbey's act of raising a gun to another person's head. In such cases, Cathy should refuse to sell Babu her watch if she knows that this refusal will make Abbey put her gun down. She should wait until Abbey does this, and only then sell Babu her watch.

In a similar way, humanitarian organizations should avoid encouraging governments to detain refugees, as the act of detention is especially unjust, even if many refugees would have returned regardless. Repatriation facilitators should wait until the government ends detention, and only then agree to help with return.

2.2.2 Causation as Influence

There are instances where an organization, in helping with return, is not necessary for coercion, and so does not cause coercion in the counterfactual sense. For example, in 1985 UNHCR was considering whether to help over 100,000 Tigrayan refugees repatriate from Sudan. At the time, the Relief Society of Tigray and the Sudanese Office of the Commissioner for Refugees were already helping all wishing to repatriate, and so had UNHCR provided repatriation this would have been unlikely to impact the rates of return, or the extent of coercive policies.[65] Similarly, by 2013 the Israeli government had the capacity to repatriate all South Sudanese refugees who wished to return home, and so had OBI continued with repatriation this would have been unlikely to impact the rate of return nor the government's coercive policies.

In such cases, facilitators may still be acting wrongly according to other criteria. Sometimes, a person acts wrongly by influencing an event, even if their actions were not necessary for the general event to occur.[66]

For an example of such a phenomenon, imagine there is an assassin, and she pulls her trigger, leading the bullet to shoot out of her barrel into the heart of a victim, unjustly killing him on the spot. She also has a thousand backup assassins, who are all working independently from her, and who would have killed the victim, had she not killed him first. As such, she was not necessary for his death, or even almost necessary for his death. She still causally contributed to his death if she influenced the particular way the death transpired.[67] This would be the case if, in a world without her, the bullet would have flown in a slightly different direction, piercing the victim's heart in a different place, while in a world without other assassins, her bullet would have still flown in the same direction as it really did, piercing the victim's heart in the same way. She causally contributed to the event by being necessary for the way the event transpired, even though she was not necessary for the general event to occur.

In such cases, even if the assassin causally contributed to the event by influencing it, we might still claim that she did not influence it in a way that harmed the victim; he would have been killed regardless. Nonetheless, as noted above, we have duties to avoid causally contributing to injustice, even if the victims are made no worse off from the causal contribution. If influence is a form of causation, then the assassin may be acting wrongly by influencing the injustice of killing another human being, regardless of whether the victim is worse off compared to a world where the assassin does not pull her trigger. In a similar sense, a single organization may be wrongly causing an unjust event by influencing it, even if the general injustice would still have occurred had it not provided repatriation.

In cases where we causally contribute to injustice by influencing the event, such causal influence may still be justified if the influence is significantly helpful for the victim. The assassin, for example, may know she can more accurately shoot the victim directly at the center mass of his body, leading to a quicker death compared to the backup assassins. If the assassin is in no way responsible for the presence of other assassins, and is shooting the victim only to reduce suffering, pulling the trigger may be morally justified. In a similar manner, an organization can justifiably help with repatriation in cases where, though the help causally contributes to unjust coercion, it can also ensure a much safer return than would otherwise take place. For example, an organization may be justified in helping Ethiopians repatriate from Saudi Arabia, given that Ethiopians attempting to repatriate on their own often rely on unsafe smugglers.[68] It remains the case that, unless an organization is quite certain that its actions significantly help refugees, it should avoid helping with repatriation, to avoid causally contributing to injustice.

2.2.3 Uncertainty

In some cases, a given organization has essentially no influence. It is neither necessary for coercion, nor does it influence coercion or the safety of return. This may be the case if there are multiple organizations, each one providing equally safe repatriation, such that if one pulled out, the coercion and safety of return would be the same. Similarly, there may be only one organization, but the government is detaining refugees both to encourage return, and also to placate anti-refugee protesters, or to deter new refugees from arriving in the country. We might suppose that an organization assisting with return here does not causally contribute to coercive policies. For had it not helped with repatriation, there would still be other decisive reasons for the government to detain refugees in the exact same manner. In such cases, an organization may still have a strong reason to avoid helping with return.

An agent has a reason to avoid an act if she subjectively suspects that her act may increase the probability of a harmful event occurring, even if she is not ultimately necessary for the outcome nor influencing the outcome. Imagine two assassins pull their triggers at the same time, both bullets flying out their barrels simultaneously, piercing the victim's heart in the same location at the same moment, such that neither assassin influenced his death.[69] One reason that each assassin acted wrongly is that, at the time she pulled her trigger, she could never be 100 per cent certain the other would pull her trigger too. In choosing to pull her own trigger, she increased the probability, in her mind, of the death occurring.

When there are multiple facilitators helping with return, then each can never be 100 per cent certain that the others will make return possible. In choosing to help with repatriation, they risk increasing the chances of repatriation occurring, and so the chances of coercion occurring. Similarly, when the government has multiple reasons for using coercive policies, an organization can never know for certain that the government will still detain refugees in the event that repatriation is no longer a possibility. As such, repatriation should be discontinued, so that organizations are certain they are not causally contributing to injustice.

Nonetheless, an exception may be made if the government has a large number of reasons for detaining refugees, such that detention would almost certainly continue even if repatriation ceased. Helping with such coerced returns is not ideal, but may be morally permissible, as the causal impact on coercion is unlikely, and the benefits significant if the return is safer than alternatives.

We have, as such, reached a general conclusion: Coerced repatriation should generally only be facilitated if it does not significantly contribute to coercive policies, and if all efforts have been made to first stop the coercive policies. Such repatriation is permissible on balance, assuming refugees are aware of the risks. When they are not aware of the risks, a distinct dilemma arises, to be addressed in the next chapter.

2.2.4 Causing Coercion of Others

There is a final version of the Causation Dilemma. In many cases organizations helping particular refugees repatriate do not contribute to the detention of these particular refugees, but contribute to the detention of other refugees. In 1994 when UNHCR helped Rohingya refugees repatriate from camps, the assistance encouraged the Bangladesh government to force other refugees into enclosed camps, but the assistance did not harm the actual refugees repatriating; they would likely still be in camps had they remained.[70] UNHCR therefore faced a dilemma: it could discontinue repatriation, forcing refugees currently in the country to remain in camps, or help these refugees repatriate, encouraging the Bangladesh government to force other refugees into camps. In the UK, IOM faced a similar dilemma when, in assisting with repatriation from detention, it may have legitimized the UK asylum policy, encouraging the detention of other refugees.[71]

Though it may have encouraged the detention of other refugees, refusing to help with repatriation would harm the refugees who were already detained.

OBI first faced this dilemma in 2012 when it helped the first refugee repatriate from detention. Once OBI helped him repatriate, the government likely detained a new refugee, filling the prison cells to maximum capacity. In this case, OBI faced a choice: it could do nothing, forcing refugees currently in detention to remain in detention, or help these refugees repatriate, freeing up detention cells, contributing to the detention of other refugees.

In Israel, human rights organizations argued that OBI ought to do nothing. Helping with repatriation set back the interests of refugees as a whole, even if particular refugees were better off in returning home. OBI responded that doing nothing would use refugees as pawns for the larger aims of refugee rights, and it was wrong to use individuals as pawns for these ends. They argued that a refugee who wished to repatriate had a right to do so, and to deny them this right would be inconsistent with the values of humanitarian assistance.[72] Humanitarian assistance ought not to simply calculate the aggregate benefit for refugees, but ought to treat each refugee as ends in themselves, even if doing so contributes to injustices towards others.

This same dilemma arises in the fictional case of Cathy. Imagine, as before, that Abbey puts a gun to Babu's head, telling him to buy Cathy's watch. If Cathy sells her watch, Abbey will then threaten hundreds of others in the same manner, many of whom will lack the funds to buy her watch, and potentially be shot themselves. It is not clear whether Cathy should protect Babu by selling her watch, or protect all future potential victims by refusing to sell him her watch.

While we cannot entirely resolve this variant of the Causation Dilemma, one guiding consideration is the role that various agents hold. Some agents hold the role of *general advocates*. General advocates strive to help all members of a group. If Cathy were a member of an organization aiming to help the victims of Abbey's gun-wielding tactics, then Cathy would be a general advocate, and ought to take actions which mitigate Abbey's coercion against all, rather than only Babu. If Cathy were certain that Abbey would threaten others if she sold Babu her watch, then Cathy would have one reason to refrain from selling Babu her watch.

In contrast to general advocates, some agents claim to be acting as *personal advocates*. A personal advocate helps particular individuals obtain rights. They are morally permitted to prioritize the rights of those they represent over others. A lawyer is a personal advocate, and permitted to prioritize her wrongfully accused client even if, in doing so, she frees her client and another individual is wrongfully accused instead. She is permitted to represent her client partly because the client is permitted to advocate for himself. Given that the client is unable to advocate for himself, having little knowledge of the law, he has outsourced this task to the lawyer, and the lawyer is acting permissibly in prioritizing his interests. If Cathy is a personal advocate for Babu, she is permitted to prioritize his interests over the interests of others. Just as we feel Babu has a right to protect himself from the fulfillment of Abbey's threat, he has a right to Cathy's assistance to avoid the fulfillment of Abbey's threat.

Though a personal advocate is permitted to prioritize the interests of those they represent, this prioritization is not absolute. If a lawyer will certainly contribute to wrongful accusations against dozens of others, she has a weighty reason to refrain from representing those wrongfully accused. If Cathy is certain that Abbey will continue her coercion against thousands of others, then Cathy ought to think twice about helping Babu.

Many repatriation facilitators are general advocates. UNHCR has an explicit mandate to help all forced to flee their homes due to persecution, and tends to extend assistance to those fleeing famine, natural disasters, and general violence.[73] General advocates like UNHCR ought to avoid assisting particular refugees at the expense of other equally vulnerable refugees. This is because, by its own standards, it claims to be instituting policies which can best protect all, rather than particular refugees. If UNHCR is a general advocate, it failed in its duties in 1994 when it helped some Rohingya refugees repatriate from detention, contributing to the detention of others. It ought not to have provided relief to some at the expense of others.

In contrast to UNHCR, OBI presented itself as a personal advocate serving the particular refugees seeking repatriation. If OBI was a personal advocate it was permitted to offer a given refugee repatriation even if another refugee would likely be detained as a result. This permission was nonetheless not absolute: were it to learn that a significant number of other refugees would be detained as a result of its assistance to some refugees, it would have a weighty reason to discontinue repatriation assistance.

IOM, to a lesser extent, also presents itself as a personal advocate, helping particular asylum seekers repatriate. IOM has defended its repatriation by appealing to the interests of individuals: it helps particular individuals repatriate because this is what these particular individuals desire. Indeed, historically IOM has been dismissed as a "travel agency."[74] Just as a travel agency arranges flights for one's customers, and does not claim to be improving mobility for all, IOM arranges return flights for refugees, rather than improving rights for all. If a travel agency has a right to sell tickets to individuals wishing to return home, even if this contributes to the detention of others, perhaps IOM has a right to give tickets to refugees wishing to return home, even if this contributes to the detention of others. As with OBI, however, IOM is not morally permitted to be a personal advocate regardless of its effects on others. If it learns that helping some individuals repatriate contributes to a major increase in the detention of others, it ought to reconsider its repatriation policies.

2.3 CONCLUSION

When a refugee is detained, her choices are far from voluntary. Given that this is the case, humanitarian organizations have two options, neither ideal. They can help with an unsafe return, and free refugees from detention, or refuse to help, forcing refugees to stay. In reality, this dilemma comes in two forms, requiring two distinct policies.

In some cases, the government will arrest refugees, force them into detention, or deny them visas regardless of whether they return. In these cases humanitarian organizations should lobby for an end to such policies, and appeal to donors to provide food security and shelter. If they fail, it may be ethical to facilitate return, so long as refugees are aware of the risks.

In other cases, repatriation causes coercion. Facilitators are not mere third parties, as their actions impact government policies, intentionally or not. The more refugees are able to repatriate, the more the government will try coercing them to repatriate. In such cases, organizations should not help with return, unless their assistance has only a small impact on coercion, and ensures a much safer return than would otherwise take place. When assistance contributes to the coercion of other refugees, rather than the refugees returning home, then organizations who claim to be general advocates should discontinue their assistance, while those working as personal advocates should ensure their impact on others is minimal.

In light of these conclusions, repatriation facilitators ought to change their current policies and practices. Today, facilitators spend little of their budget on lobbying for the end of coercive conditions, and more on flights, stipends, and coordinating return. This is partly because humanitarian organizations often rely on government grants, at times competing with other organizations to repatriate refugees at the lowest possible cost, at the fastest possible rate. But even organizations who raise their own funds, such as OBI, continue allocating their entire budget to repatriation, feeling pressure from refugees who want to return as quickly as possible to avoid detention. Though refugees have good reason to return quickly, repatriation facilitators have good reasons to slow down return, freeing up resources for lobbying, and dissuading governments from detaining refugees. Such a policy shift for organizations may mean fewer refugees can return, but fewer may want to, if conditions improve in the host country.

When George called OBI in 2012, it might have implemented a different policy in light of these conclusions. It might have attempted to persuade the government to provide George residency rights, or to provide greater residency rights for South Sudanese nationals in general. OBI could also have waited to facilitate his return, to see whether the government would eventually free him from detention, seeing that he had no way of going back.

For George, and millions of others, immigration control involves not just force, but assistance. How organizations provide assistance can impact how governments respond, and how refugees react. If we are to have a fuller picture of what an ethical refugee policy entails, we must shift our focus away from the policeman who followed George home, and onto NGOs who sit in small offices, answering calls from refugees who feel they need help returning, and quickly. While the urgency is clear, the best policy is not.

NOTES

1. Interview with George, Juba, January 2, 2014.
2. Michael Barnett, "UNHCR and the Ethics of Repatriation," *Forced Migration Review* 10(2001):31–4; B. S. Chimni, "From Repatriation to Involuntary Repatriation: Towards a Critical History of Durable Solutions to Refugee Problems," *Refugee Survey Quarterly* 23(3)(2004):55–73.
3. Michael Barnett and Martha Finnemore, *Rules for the World: International Organizations in Global Politics*, Cornell: Cornell University Press 2004 at

75; UNHCR, "Voluntary Repatriation: UNHCR Global Consultations Background Paper," Geneva: UNHCR, EC/GC/02/5, para 29, cited by Megan Bradley, "Back to Basics: The Conditions of Just Refugee Returns," *Journal of Refugee Studies* 21(3)(2008):285–303 at 292.

4. UNHCR Global Trends, <http://www.unhcr.org/statistics/STATISTICS/4852366f2.pdf> (last accessed July 31, 2017); Jeff Crisp, "Mind the Gap! UNHCR, Humanitarian Assistance and the Development Process," New Issues in Refugee Research, Working Paper No. 43, May 2001 at 8.

5. Matthew Gibney, "Is Deportation a Form of Forced Migration?" *Refugee Survey Quarterly* 32(2)(2013):116–29.

6. Repatriation assistance usually involves the paying for transport home when refugees lack the funds to do so, and the arranging of travel documentation. There is also, in some cases, the provision of food aid during the first year after return. See UNHCR, *Handbook – Voluntary Repatriation: International Protection*, Geneva: 1996.

7. Lee Ann Fujii, *Killing Neighbours: Webs of Violence in Rwanda*, Ithaca: Cornell University Press 2009; Bo Lidegaard, *Countrymen: How Denmark's Jews Escaped the Nazis*, London: Atlantic Books 2013.

8. UNHCR, *Handbook – Voluntary Repatriation: International Protection*, Geneva: 1996.

9. See Glossary on Migration, IOM, 2004, at 34. <http://publications.iom.int/bookstorelinebreak/free/IML_1_EN.pdf> (last accessed October 12, 2014).

10. When very poor states lack the resources to support refugees, then wealthier states may have a duty to provide these funds. If they do not, then they may be viewed as the agents coercing refugees to leave.

11. Alexander Betts, "Survival Migration: A New Protection Framework," *Global Governance* 16(2010):361–82.

12. Carens 1987 ibid.

13. Betts 2010 ibid; Matthew Gibney, *The Ethics and Politics of Asylum*, Cambridge: Cambridge University Press 2004; David Miller, "Immigration: The Case for Its Limits," in (eds) A. Cohen and C. Wellman, *Contemporary Debates in Applied Ethics*, Malden, MA: Blackwell Publishing 2005 at 202.

14. Javier Hidalgo, "Resistance to Unjust Immigration Restrictions," *Journal of Political Philosophy* 23(4)(2015):450–70.

15. Katy Long, *The Point of No Return: Refugees, Rights, and Repatriation*, Oxford: Oxford University Press 2013 at 107.

16. Human Rights Watch, "Closed Door Policy: Afghan Refugees in Pakistan and Iran," 14(2)(2002). <https://www.hrw.org/reports/2002/pakistan/pakistan0202.pdf> (last accessed February 25, 2018).

17. Human Rights Watch, "Pakistan Coercion, UN Complicity: The Mass Forced Return of Afghan Refugees," February 13, 2017, <https://www.

hrw.org/report/2017/02/13/pakistan-coercion-un-complicity/mass-forcedreturn-afghan-refugees> (last accessed February 26, 2018).

18. Susanne Schmeidl, "Repatriation to Afghanistan: Durable Solution or Responsibility Shifting?" *Forced Migration Review* 33(2009):20–2 at 20.

19. Jeff Crisp, "The Politics of Repatriation: Ethiopian Refugees in Djibouti, 1977–1983," *Review of African Political Economy* 30(1984):73–82.

20. US Department of State IDIQ Task Force, Order No. SAWMMA13F2592, "Field Evaluation of Local Integration of Former Refugees of Tanzania,"p. iii, April 15. 2014, <https://www.state.gov/documents/organization/235057.pdf> (last accessed February 25, 2018); IRIN,"Special Report on Repatriation of Burundian Refugees," April 15, 2015, <http://www.irinnews.org/report/49519/east-africa-special-report-on-repatriation-of-burundian-refugees> (last accessed February 25, 2018).

21. James Hathaway, *The Rights of Refugees under International Law*, Cambridge: Cambridge University Press 2005 at 380; Mugume Davis Rwakaringi, "Could This Country be Among the World's Best for Refugees?" January 27, 2017, <http://bhekisisa.org/article/2017-01-19-00-uganda-opens-its-arms-to-refugees-but-hardship-still-stalks-the-south-sudanese> (last accessed April 23, 2018).

22. Chimni 2004 ibid. at 65. Khalid Koser and Richard Black, "The End of the Refugee Cycle? Editorial Introduction," in (eds) Khalid Koser and Richard Black, *The End of the Refugee Cycle? Refugee Repatriation and Reconstruction*, New York and Oxford: Berghahn Books 1999 at 2–17.

23. Awa M. Abdi, "In Limbo: Dependency, Insecurity, and Identity Among Somali Refugees in Dadaab Camps," *Refuge* 22(2)(2005):6–14 at 10.

24. Human Rights Watch, "Kenya: End Abusive Round-Ups," May 12, 2014, <https://www.hrw.org/news/2014/05/12/kenya-end-abusive-round-ups> (last accessed January 22, 2018); Human Rights Watch, 'Kenya: Involuntary Refugee Returns to Somalia,' September 14, 2014, <https://www.hrw.org/news/2016/09/14/kenya-involuntary-refugee-returns-somalia> (last accessed January 22, 2018).

25. Melissa Fleming,"In Kenya, UN Refugee Chief Urges Support for Refugees and Host Communities," UNHCR, December 21, 2017, <http://www.unhcr.org/afr/news/latest/2017/12/5a3aaf074/kenya-un-refugee-chief-urges-support-somali-refugees-host-communities.html> (last accessed January 22, 2018).

26. Richard Black and Saskia Gent, "Sustainable Return in Post-Conflict Contexts," *International Migration* 44(3)(2006):15–38; Brad K Blitz, Rosemary Sales, and Lisa Marzano, "Non-Voluntary Returns? The Politics of Return to Afghanistan," *Political Studies* 53(2005):182–200.

27. Black and Gent 2006 ibid. at 19.
28. David Corlett, *Following Them Home: The Fate of the Returned Asylum Seekers*, Melbourne: Black Inc. 2005 at 105–11 and 200–3.
29. UNHCR, "Return of Displaced People in Eastern DR Congo Should be Voluntary," December 5, 2014, <https://reliefweb.int/report/democratic-republic-congo/unhcr-return-displaced-people-eastern-dr-congo-should-be-voluntary> (last accessed January 6, 2018).
30. Christopher Munnion, "South Africa Riots: Violence against Immigrants Spreads to Cape Town," *The Telegraph*, May 23, 2008, <http://www.telegraph.co.uk/news/2014045/South-Africa-riots-Violence-against-immigrants-spreads-to-Cape-Town.html> (last accessed January 5, 2018); Jonny Steinberg, *A Man of Good Hope: One Man's Extraordinary Journey from Mogadishu to Tin Can Town*, London: Jonathan Cape 2015 at 285–6.
31. Bradley 2008 ibid.; Megan Bradley, *Refugee Repatriation: Justice, Responsibility and Redress*, Cambridge: Cambridge University Press 2014; Long 2013 ibid.
32. Barnett 2001 ibid.
33. Barnett and Finnemore 2004 ibid. at 75; Barbara Harold-Bond, "Repatriation: Under What Conditions Is It a Durable Solution for Refugees?" *African Studies Review* 32(1)(1989):41–69; Corlett 2005 ibid.at 201.
34. Christian Mumras (Hebrew), "The activities of Israel to Promote the Return of South Sudanese Asylum Seekers," in (ed.) Tally Kritzman-Amir, *Where Levinsky Meets Asmara: Social and Legal Aspects of Israeli Asylum Policy*, Jerusalem: Van Leer Institute 2015.
35. Mumras 2015 ibid.; Ruvi Ziegler, "No Asylum 'For Infiltrators': The Legal Predicament of Eritrean and Sudanese Nationals in Israel," *Immigration, Asylum, and Nationality Law* 29(2)(2015):172–91 at 181.
36. See note 43 in Chapter 1.
37. International Crisis Group, "South Sudan: Jonglei – 'We Have Always Been at War,'" Africa Report 221, December 22, 2014.
38. Douglas Johnson, "Briefing: The Crisis in South Sudan," *African Affairs* 113(451)(2014):300–9.
39. Judith McCallum and Alfred Okech, "Drivers of Conflict in Jonglei State," *Humanitarian Exchange Magazine* 57 (May 2013).
40. Médecins Sans Frontières (MSF) "South Sudan: Violence against Healthcare," July 1, 2014, <http://www.msf.fr/actualite/publications/south-sudan-conflict-violence-against-healthcare> (last accessed February 26, 2018).
41. Interview with Vanessa, Juba, December 25, 2013.
42. Interview with Joseph, Juba, April 10, 2012.
43. Interview with HIAS director, Jerusalem, December 12, 2012; Mumras 2015 ibid.
44. Interview with HIAS director, ibid.

45. Interview with HIAS director, ibid.

46. See Operation Blessing International, "Frequently Asked Questions," <http://www.ob.org/frequently-asked/> (last accessed February 26, 2018). Some of the interviewed refugees believed that OBI was a Christian Zionist organization, and was motivated to help the Israeli government decrease the number of non-Jewish refugees in Israel. Further research on this topic may be warranted, to help clarify OBI's possibly hidden motivations. If OBI had ulterior religious or political motives, then it was perhaps exploiting refugees, encouraging return to promote its own values, rather than refugees' wellbeing and rights. I put this aside for now because I found no actual evidence of these motivations and, even if OBI was completely humanitarian, and only intending to help refugees, there is still a major ethical dilemma as to whether they should have provided such return.

47. HIAS, "History," <http://www.hias.org/history> (last accessed February 26, 2018).

48. HIAS Kenya, "Protection Intervention," <http://hiasafrica.org/interventions/Protection-Interventions/> (last accessed December 6, 2015).

49. Harriett Sherwood, "Israelis Attack African Migrants during Protest against Refugees," *The Guardian*, May 24, 2012, <https://www.theguardian.com/world/2012/may/24/israelis-attack-african-migrants-protest> (last accessed February 26, 2018).

50. Ephraim Yaar and Tamar Hermann, "Peace Index – May 2012," <http://en.idi.org.il/media/602071/Peace%20Index-May%202012(1).pdf> (last accessed October 3, 2014).

51. Law for the Prevention of Infiltration (Crimes and Jurisdiction – Amendment No 3 and Temporary Order) 5772-2012 (Amendment 3).

52. Population, Immigration, and Border Authority of Israel, "A Call for the People of South Sudan," January 31, 2011, <http://www.piba.gov.il/SpokesmanshipMessagess/Documents/2012-2192.pdf> (last accessed February 28, 2011).

53. Interview with Bol, Juba, December 21, 2013; interview with Nathaniel, Juba, December 14, 2013; interview with Vanessa, Juba, December 25, 2013.

54. More accurately, some philosophers claim that cases of third-party coercion are cases of 'morally transformative consent,' but for simplicity I use the term 'valid consent.' See Franklin G. Miller and Alan Wertheimer, "Preface to a Theory of Consent Transactions: Beyond Valid Consent," in (eds) F. Miller and A. Wertheimer, *The Ethics of Consent: Theory and Practice*, Oxford: Oxford University Press, 2009 at 94.

55. Joseph Millum, "Consent Under Pressure: The Puzzle of Third Party Coercion," *Ethical Theory and Moral Practice* 17(1)(2014):113–27.

56. IOM, "About IOM," <https://www.iom.int/about-iom> (last accessed February 26, 2018).
57. Ibid.
58. Michael Barnett, "Humanitarianism, Paternalism, and UNHCR," in (eds) Alex Betts and Gil Loescher, *Refugees in International Relations*, Oxford: Oxford University Press 2011; Jennifer Rubenstein, "The Misuse of Power, Not Bad Representation: Why It Is besides the Point that Nobody Elected Oxfam," *Journal of Political Philosophy* 22(2)(2014):204–30 at 218.
59. Diane Jeske, "Special Obligations," Stanford Encyclopedia of Philosophy 2014 and Francesco Orsi, "Obligations of Nearness," *The Journal of Value Inquiry* 42(2008):1–21.
60. See David Lewis, "Causation," *The Journal of Philosophy* 70(17) (1973):556–67.
61. Ishan Ashutosha and Alison Mountz, "Migration Management For the Benefit of Whom? Interrogating the Work of the International Organization for Migration," *Citizenship Studies* 15(1)(2011):21–38.
62. Barnett and Finnemore 2004 ibid. at 106.
63. Protocol 84 (Hebrew), "Distancing South Sudanese in Israel," Committee for the Problem of Foreign Workers, April 30, 2012; 18th Knesset.
64. Galia Sabar and Elizabeth Tsurkov, "Israel's Policies towards Asylum-Seekers: 2002-2012," Instituto Affari Internazionali, Working Papers 15, 20/5/15.
65. In reality, UNHCR refused to help with return, because the return was not considered voluntary. See Assefaw Bariagaber, *Conflict and the Refugee Experience: Flights, Exile and Repatriation in the Horn of Africa*, Abingdon, UK and New York: Routledge 2016 at 117; and Barbara Hendrie, "The Politics of Repatriation: The Tigrayan Refugee Repatriation 1985-1987," *Journal of Refugee Studies* 4(2)(1991):200–18.
66. David Lewis, "Causation as Influence," *The Journal of Philosophy* 97(4) (2000):182–97. Some may claim a person is merely "contributing" to an event in such cases; regardless, it seems clear that a wrong can take place when one contributes to an unjust event.
67. This claim contrasts somewhat with those made by Lepora and Goodin. They argue, firstly, that for an agent to be complicit in a particular death, the agent must contribute to the death. To contribute to the death, an agent must be essential for the death or potentially essential for the death. To be potentially essential, an agent must have been necessary in a nearby possible world, and the closer the possible world, the more complicit they are. I do not believe that this closest-possible-world approach is entirely plausible. The assassin seems very complicit in the death of the victim, and very much causing his death, even if she would only be essential in a very distant possible world without the thousand backup assassins. See

Chiara Lepora and Robert E. Goodin, *On Complicity and Compromise*, Oxford: Oxford University Press 2013 at 63–5.

68. Rick Gladstone, "Exploited and Extorted, 30 Africans Drown While Trying to Return Home from Yemen," *The New York Times*, January 26, 2018, <https://www.nytimes.com/2018/01/26/world/africa/yemen-african-migrants-drown.html> (last accessed January 29, 2018).

69. Frank Jackson, "What Effects?" in (ed.) Jonathan Dancy, *Reading Parfit*, Oxford and Malden, MA: Blackwell Wiley 1997; Michael McDermott, "Influence versus Sufficiency," *The Journal of Philosophy* 99(2)(2002): 84–101.

70. Barnett and Finnemore 2004 ibid. at 106.

71. Ashutosha and Mountz 2011 ibid.; Frances Webber, "How Voluntary are Voluntary Returns?" *Race and Class* 52(4):98–107.

72. Interview with HIAS-Israel director, Jerusalem, 11 December 2012.

73. Alexander Betts, Gil Loescher, and James Milner, Chapter 4 in *UNHCR: The Politics and Practice of Refugee Protection*, Routledge 2012.

74. Megan Bradley, "The International Organization for Migration (IOM): Gaining Power in the Forced Migration Regime," *Refuge* 33(1) (2017):97–106 at 99.

Chapter 3

MISINFORMATION

In 2009 the director of OBI landed in Juba and met with ministers in the South Sudanese parliament. She then traveled to secondary towns, taking photographs of clinics, markets, and schools along the way. After several weeks she flew back to Israel and showed these images on PowerPoint slides to South Sudanese refugees in a community center, informing them that South Sudan had housing, security, free schools, universal healthcare, and income-generating opportunities.[1]

By 2011 several dozen families accepted OBI's assistance to repatriate. After return, most were without reliable shelter, medical care, regular meals, or school. Most notably, they lacked clean water, and had to drink from contaminated rural wells in villages, or streams that flow through mounds of waste in Juba. Some lived off the unreliable charity of distant relatives, or the occasional kind stranger in teashops that dot the streets of South Sudan. While a small number started small businesses, they mostly failed. An unknown number died from illness or ethnic-based violence, and the majority were displaced within two years.[2]

It is widely acknowledged that, if an agent provides a high-risk offer, she must disclose the known risks of this offer. A surgeon must disclose known risks about surgery, a fireworks manufacturer must disclose known risks about fireworks, and the military must disclose known risks of joining the military. But though known risks must be disclosed, it is not clear what risks must be known. OBI did disclose what it knew, but perhaps it ought to have known more, conducting more rigorous research while in South Sudan.

To establish if this is true, we must establish when agents providing high-risk offers have duties to learn the risks of their offers. In some cases, it seems agents have no such duties. If I book a flight to Somalia, my airline needn't tell me the risks of traveling to Somalia. While some agents do have responsibilities to learn about risks, it is not clear when such responsibilities arise.

This ambiguity has serious implications for repatriation, and has been largely overlooked in broader debates on immigration. These debates overwhelmingly focus on when it is wrong to deport or detain immigrants, rather than on when it is wrong to misinform immigrants.[3] But misinforming immigrants, including refugees, has been common practice throughout the past three decades, as seen in the return of refugees to Uganda, Iraq, Afghanistan, and Chechnya.[4] In these cases, individuals returned who would have stayed had they known the risks. It remains unclear who had a responsibility to disclose the risks, if anyone.

In Section 3.1 I describe "Misinformation Cases." These are cases where repatriation facilitators provide false information on countries of origin. In Section 3.2 I argue that, when certain conditions are met, facilitators are culpable for the resulting misinformed repatriation. In Section 3.3 I discuss "Omission Cases," where facilitators omit information, rather than explicitly misinform. I will argue that omitting information is generally wrong in the same sorts of cases where misinforming is wrong. In Section 3.4 I will describe "Relevancy Cases," where facilitators fail to disclose the risks of repatriating, but where refugees claim they would have repatriated regardless. In some such cases facilitators still wrong those they fail to inform. Finally, there is an "intent question" which cuts across the above three cases. If facilitators are unaware they are misinforming refugees, it seems they are not intentionally misinforming refugees. If there is no intent, perhaps there is no wrong. I shall address this question in Section 3.5 before concluding in Section 3.6.

Before I begin, a brief note on my approach.

I shall primarily focus on whether repatriation facilitators – including members of governmental and non-governmental bodies – are culpable for misinforming refugees. I shall assume an individual is culpable if she has failed to fulfill duties and does so intentionally. An agent does something intentionally if she is aware of what she does,[5] has control over what she does,[6] and uses this control to bring about certain desired aims.[7] For example, if I am aware that I take a watch that I have a duty to not take, and I have control over my hand as it picks up the watch, and I pick it up with the aim of wearing a new accessory, then I have the relevant awareness, control, and aim for intent. In Sections 3.1–3.4, my focus will be on establishing whether facilitators failed to fulfill duties to find information. I shall assume that, if they failed in their duties, they had the relevant intent for culpability. Only in Section 3.5 do I consider the objection that, even if they failed to disclose information, they did not intend such a failure, and so were not culpable.

In focusing on culpability for misinformation, the subject of coercion is relevant. I wish to explore whether, if coercing someone to accept a service is impermissible, there is an obligation to find information on the risks of the service. Of course, there is disagreement over when coercing refugees to repatriate is impermissible, and by extension there may be disagreement over when informing refugees is obligatory. Some believe states should only avoid deporting those fleeing persecution, others believe states should avoid deporting anyone whose life will be at risk, and still others believe states should avoid deporting anyone at all.[8] As in the last chapter, I assume states should not deport anyone fleeing life-threatening circumstances, so long as states have the capacity to accept such individuals. As before, my general theory on misinformation is compatible with other theories, including the stance that only those fleeing persecution should not be deported, and the stance that nobody should be deported. My focus is not on when coercion is wrong but whether, if coercion is wrong due to risks, information on these risks should be disclosed.

3.1 MISINFORMING REFUGEES

Misinformation cases arise when facilitators fail to gather data to determine risks of repatriation. As a result, they provide false information to refugees, and these refugees believe a falsehood they otherwise would not, accepting repatriation they otherwise would not.

Such was the case in 1997 when the German government told Bosnian refugees they would receive housing, employment, and other services upon return, none of which materialized.[9] In 2001 Russian officials persuaded IDPs in Ingushetia that returning to Chechnya was safe, and many returned to insecurity and homelessness, with at least one man shot dead soon after arrival.[10] Two years later UNHCR told Afghan refugees living in Iran that it was safe to return, and refugees returned in light of this information, immediately facing violent attacks on the border.[11] Soon after IOM in Norway told Iraqi refugees that there were income-generating activities in Iraq. They returned as a result, and found few job opportunities, many lacking food and shelter a year later.[12] In Israel, the Ministry of Interior set up a repatriation program in 2012, helping roughly 6,000 asylum seekers repatriate either to Sudan and Eritrea, or accept resettlement to Rwanda or Uganda. It told refugees they would receive asylum in Rwanda and Uganda, but they never did.[13] More recently, in 2017 aid agencies in Kenya told refugees they would receive healthcare, education, and food aid upon returning to Somalia, none of which materialized.[14] They also promised security, as a father of five Ali Haji testifies:

> As opposed to what we were told, what we found here is all about insecurity incidents during the day and gangs preying into our camps to rob us of the little things we were given before.[15]

Individuals like Ali Haji demonstrate that, even if refugees are returning to their own countries of origin, they do not necessarily know a great deal about these countries. This is especially true for refugees who have lived their entire adult lives abroad. Such was the case for Somali refugees living in Kenya, and South Sudanese refugees living in Sudan, Egypt, and Israel. Of the South Sudanese refugees I interviewed who returned from Israel, seven subjects were from Unity State, a region they had last lived in as small children, and a region they knew little about. While some were aware that approximately 140,000 had been displaced in Unity State the year they returned in 2012,[16] an estimated death toll has never been publicized in this region.[17] I also interviewed twenty-three subjects who returned to Upper Nile, three to Abyei, and one to Warap State. All were returning to areas where tens of thousands had been displaced a year prior, and at least hundreds had been killed, but the precise number of displaced and killed remained unknown.[18] Ten returning were from Jonglei, an area with slightly more complete data, but still sparse. One estimate states that 200,000 were displaced in Jonglei, and at least 2,700 civilians killed in 2011 to 2012, but the precise number of deaths was never confirmed.[19] Seven returnees were from the town of Akobo in Jonglei, where between 250 and 1,000 civilians were killed between 2011 and 2012, but the precise number never confirmed. Importantly, the total populations of Jonglei and Akobo have never been counted in a reliable census, so an individual refugee could not have known the odds of being killed after returning.[20]

It was not just information on mortality rates that was missing when refugees returned from Israel. The World Bank and the International Labor Organization offered no unemployment statistics on South

Sudan when most returned,[21] and Médecins Sans Frontières could not provide precise locations of health clinics in South Sudan.

Given how little information was available about risks, I asked subjects why they returned. Most responded that it was precisely because they did not know the risks that they returned, feeling unknown risks of returning were preferable to known risks of remaining. As Vanessa explains on her return to Juba:

> I was in prison for six months in Israel. I didn't like it. If I don't know what it's like in South Sudan, but I know I hated prison in Israel, I would prefer to go to South Sudan . . . it might have been worse, but it might have been better.[22]

Vanessa is from the Dinka tribe, but grew up among Nuer, and speaks the languages of both tribes fluently. Two years after her return, Dinka militias came to her home, believing she was Nuer. She fled, returning two days later to find her furniture and clothes stolen. "When we come home," she explains, "people on the street look at us. They don't ask questions. They don't know what tribe I'm from." Today, she does not regret returning, but others do, wishing they had stayed in Israel, even if this meant being detained. They felt life in South Sudan was far more difficult than expected.

When the OBI director began helping South Sudanese repatriate, she was aware that some might be uninformed. She felt the same when helping Sudanese refugees repatriate, paying for their flights to Juba, and allowing them to travel onwards to Khartoum and Darfur. The government of Sudan has a policy of detaining and executing those who have been to Israel, and many may not have been aware of the risks of execution.[23] The OBI director also felt that she should not be the agent determining if refugees were informed of risks, as she had a conflict of interest: She wanted to impress donors by demonstrating that a large number of refugees were returning, and this may have impacted her ability to objectively determine informed consent. She hired HIAS instead. Because HIAS had a history of lobbying for refugee rights, she felt it could be trusted to critically evaluate if a refugee knew little about Sudan or South Sudan. HIAS interviewed each refugee, and if it felt a refugee knew little about their rights in Israel, and little about Sudan or South Sudan, it would tell this to OBI, who would then refuse to help them repatriate.[24]

This policy was ultimately ineffective, as HIAS staff appeared to know little about Sudan or South Sudan, and so largely failed to determine if individuals were uninformed about the risks of returning. The staff's training manual has only a very short page on the history of Sudan and South Sudan, and some information seems to lack any sources. For example, the manual states, "Although South Sudan . . . might not have the same services as we have in Israel, their family is a significant factor for positive mental health." It was not clear this was the case. Many I interviewed after return found their extended family unhelpful, and often emotionally harmful, largely ignoring them on the road and in their homes. The manual also states, "Many applicants might not be aware of the entire situation in Sudan. Instead, they might only know about the circumstances in their village. This is OK." In reality, this was often not OK, as information about urban centers was essential for refugees unable to find employment or basic services in their rural villages.

To learn about the extent and content of misinformation, I asked refugees who had already returned what information they recalled having prior to their return. I also asked them how they had this knowledge, and whether they felt the information was true after returning. I then coded interviews for general categories of misinformation and the sources of this information.

Table 3.1 describes the findings from these interviews. The rows describe different pieces of information provided to refugees, and the columns describe the sources of this information, including the police, NGOs, the media, and so forth. As noted, thirty-six of 128 respondents recall being told they would be detained indefinitely if they stayed, when this was unlikely for small children and mothers.[25] Sixty-eight subjects recall being told that South Sudan was a safe country. The majority learned this from the media or friends and family, but nine said they were told this by OBI or the UN, neither of which mentioned continuous ethnic-based fighting.[26]

When interviewing subjects, I was aware that some respondents may be misrepresenting what they were told prior to returning, because they were disappointed with their return. While this was a possibility, it is likely that most were telling the truth, as those who were satisfied with their return recalled being told very similar misinformation to those who were disappointed with their return. Furthermore, to confirm the accuracy of responses, I also interviewed the repatriation facilitators themselves, asking staff members what they recall telling

Table 3.1 South Sudanese pre-return information and sources

N: 128	Police	Media	Human rights NGO	Repatriation NGO or UN	Israel Ministry of Interior	South Sudanese officials	Friends and family	Political leaders and protesters from Israel or South Sudan	School or employer	Just assumed	Personal memory
I couldn't work anymore N: 37	3				18		2		9	5	
I would be in prison for life if I stayed N: 36	12			2	16		2	1		2	1
I would be deported N: 14	6	1			5		3	1			
I was told it was the law to go back N: 43	3	2	5	1	3		3	31	3	4	
Education is provided in South Sudan. N: 19			1		1		2		6	13	
Conditions are good in South Sudan N: 68	3	20		9	5	3	20	9	2	33	2
Conditions are bad in South Sudan N: 33		6		2			13			10	3

Note: The total number recorded in the left-hand column does not equal the sum of each row, as many subjects received information from multiple sources.

refugees prior to returning. Though most recall saying nothing, in line with the policy of asking refugees to find information themselves, the OBI director recalled telling parents that their children would be able to access free healthcare,[27] when reliable healthcare was rarely found in secondary towns. This was possibly the most problematic of the misinformation, as post-return illnesses were the most likely cause of death in the first two years, with at least seven dying of malaria within the first three months.[28] Of the forty-eight children whose conditions I could confirm, three died from illnesses, representing over 6 per cent of my sample. The total percentage who died was likely higher, given that I was unable to reach the most remote areas with even poorer healthcare.

In addition to telling refugees there was healthcare, OBI told refugees there was security and food. By 2014, I learned of one returnee killed in crossfire during the war, and four killed because of their ethnicity, including two children, aged three and five, shot at gunpoint. There were most likely more I never heard about, due to survivorship bias in my sample. Displacement was also common, and of the 136 returnees whose conditions I could confirm,[29] thirty-two were of the Nuer ethnic group, and all from this group had fled militias from the Dinka ethnic group. We might suppose that the war was unpredictable ahead of time, but twenty-four of these individuals suffered less from the war than the general poverty in South Sudan, having no income or family support before fleeing to IDP camps. All lived off one meal per day, mostly consisting of corn meal, failing to obtain the basic nutrients necessary for survival according to World Health Organization standards.[30] As of 2014, thirty-seven individuals were still living in South Sudan and not displaced, but nineteen had no income and lacked food security. Twenty-five subjects had left South Sudan, and all except for two were without employment, basic medical care, or food security.

For comparison, I also conducted interviews with individuals who returned, or were about to return, to Ethiopia, Guinea, Nigeria, Togo, Colombia, the Philippines, and Thailand. Their return had been partly facilitated by IOM, which provided me their contact details.[31] As with South Sudanese who returned, I asked respondents what they recall being told prior to returning, who told them this information, and whether this information seemed true after they returned. I then coded the interviews for the types of misinformation, the sources of information, and post-return conditions.

Table 3.2 Misinformation and post-return conditions

	South Sudanese N: 136	Nigeria, Guinea, Ethiopia, Togo, Colombia N: 15	Thailand and the Philippines N: 15
Misinformation about country of origin	69	2	0
Internal displacement after return	32	0	0
Displacement to other countries	27	2	0
Death from illness	3	0	0
Death from violence	5	0	0
Lack of food and medical care	62	4	0
Yet to return	0	7	0

When comparing the data from all groups, including the South Sudanese returnees, I found that those groups which faced the poorest information prior to returning also faced the most risks after returning. As
noted in Table 3.2, a large number of South Sudanese were misinformed
prior to returning, and a large number died or were living in extreme poverty after returning. Those returning to Ethiopia, Nigeria, Guinea, Togo,
and Colombia were slightly less likely to be misinformed, and less at risk
of displacement and being killed. Those returning to Thailand and the
Philippines were never misinformed, and never displaced or killed. Due
to the small sample, there is a limit to how much we can conclude from
this comparison, but even within South Sudan there was a similar cor-
relation between poor information and the risks faced after returning.
Those returning with more information, especially from family members
who had never left South Sudan, were the least likely to be displaced or
without a job once they arrived in their hometowns or villages.

It is not clear why South Sudanese were less informed, but one obvious reason is that South Sudan is a more volatile country compared to
other countries of origin. Due to this volatility, it would have been difficult before 2013 to predict the future of South Sudan, and so difficult

to gain accurate information. However, as noted above, most of the respondents were misinformed not about unexpected events, such as war, but about general poverty, food insecurity, and lack of healthcare, all ongoing prior to 2013.

A more likely explanation for why South Sudanese were less informed is that there was less available information on South Sudan, precisely because it was risky to conduct research in the country. Even in my own research, I was far less likely to visit unsafe and remote areas, such as Bor, where ethnic cleansing was especially widespread in 2011 and 2012, limiting my research to the capital and safer secondary towns.

Given that refugees were given inaccurate information prior to returning, it remains unclear if repatriation facilitators ought to have found more information. Perhaps not; refugees should be the agents responsible for gathering information. But maybe repatriation facilitators have some responsibilities to gather information. Whether they do depends on a number of considerations.

3.2 WHEN MUST FACILITATORS DISCLOSE RISKS?

Whether facilitators have a duty to know about risks is dependent, firstly, on costs. If finding information is costless, then facilitators ought to find this information. This is obvious, but important to state, as NGOs like OBI could have easily disclosed public data on health statistics and education in South Sudan.[32] Similarly, UNHCR in Kenya could have easily presented refugees with its own reports on the conditions in Somalia, helping ensure refugees like Ali Haji were more informed before returning.[33]

When information is not available on countries of origin, governments could permit refugees to spend time in their home countries before returning. This might involve permitting refugees to repatriate for a year or two, and then allowing them to return to the host country if they fail to access security and other basic necessities. For example, in the 1990s Sweden, France, and the UK helped refugees return to Bosnia, and allowed them to re-enter their territories in the event of an emergency.[34] This ensured that, even if refugees were misinformed about risks in Bosnia, they had a way of mitigating risks by returning to host states. On a more limited scale the UN provided refugees in Tanzania transport to Burundi to see what conditions were like, later re-entering Tanzania to report on these conditions to other refugees.[35]

Informally, Lebanon sometimes permits Syrian refugees who returned home to again re-enter Lebanon. One such refugee describes his experience with such a return:

> From the Lebanese border to Aleppo [Syria], I had to pay a $100 bribe ... I had packed a food bag for my sister: tea, coffee, powdered milk, and so on. But once I arrived at Aleppo, my suitcase was empty because at every checkpoint on the road they took something. Our apartment could be rehabilitated with some work, but it is too expensive and there is almost no electricity. Our shop was destroyed and looted.

After seeing that his shop was destroyed and looted, this refugee decided to re-enter Lebanon where he and his family could access employment, school, and a stipend from UNHCR.[36]

Unfortunately, permitting refugees to visit is often impossible or ineffective. It is impossible when humanitarian organizations are the ones facilitating return, and unable to persuade governments to permit refugees to visit. Even when governments permit refugees to visit, this is ineffective when refugees' lives will be at risk even during these short visits, and governments lack information to disclose the risks of short visits. Importantly, short visits are often poor replacements for information on long-term risks. In such cases, it is not clear whether governments and organizations have a duty to find information, given the high costs of obtaining it.

We might suppose organizations do have such a duty, derived from their duty of care. As argued in the previous chapter, NGOs, IOM, and UNHCR were created precisely to help vulnerable populations, and so should do more than what is costless. But governments may claim to have no such duty of care, and merely a responsibility to protect those who choose to stay. This is because governments, unlike many humanitarian organizations, were not created specifically to protect vulnerable populations. They were created, some might claim, to help those within their borders. This merely requires them to treat refugees the same way they treat citizens, providing them with visas, freedom from detention, and equal rights before the law. Just as governments needn't gather and disclose information to residents every time they fly abroad, governments needn't disclose information to refugees every time they repatriate.

Even if governments do not have a substantial duty of care towards refugees in the manner of humanitarian organizations, they may still have a duty to find information for three additional reasons. The first two are relatively weak, but the last is strong.

3.2.1 Harm

One reason concerns harm. If one is able to find information and does not, and this causes harm, perhaps one is culpable for the resultant harm.[37] If I buy fish from a store that buys from a producer that uses slave labor, and buying the fish reinforces slavery, and I could have found this out, then I am partly blameworthy for my ignorance. Officials may similarly be causing harm through their ignorance, misinforming refugees and causing them to repatriate to unsafe countries.

But it is not clear that we are culpable whenever we fail to find information we are able to find, if finding information is very difficult. If I purchase fish, I may have a duty to read available research on labor conditions in foreign countries, but it is not clear that I must fly to these countries in the absence of full data, and conduct my own in-depth study. It is not enough to establish that misinformation causes harm. It is also necessary to establish whether we have a duty to find information to prevent harm.

There is another reason we might suppose governments have a duty to find information.

3.2.2 Ability

In the broader philosophical literature on consent, it is largely presumed that, if information is costly and there is no duty of care, then agents may still have a duty to disclose relevant information they know.[38] If I am selling you my car, and I know it has faulty brakes, I should tell you this, because I have this information and you do not. In the cases of repatriation, there is no such asymmetry of information – all know little about countries of origin – but there is an asymmetry in the ability to obtain new information. Governments have greater resources than refugees, and are more able to find information in areas that are difficult to reach.

This consideration may be relevant, but it would require demonstrating that agents really do have greater duties to find information when it is easier for them to find it. It is not clear they do. If I am a car mechanic selling you a car, and could run a test you are not able to run, it seems unfair to claim that I have a duty to run this test while another car seller, who is not a mechanic, does not. Even if asymmetric knowledge creates a duty to disclose what one knows, it does not follow that asymmetric ability to obtain knowledge creates a duty to know.

There is a more plausible reason why governments have duties to find and disclose information.

3.2.3 *General Duties*

Sometimes we have a duty to know information in order to fulfill more general duties. Drivers, for example, have duties to look in their rear-view mirrors to know if anyone is behind them, fulfilling their general duties to avoid collisions.[39] Drivers might also have duties to inspect their car brakes annually, similarly to avoid collisions with other cars or pedestrians. Sometimes, when we have a duty to know information to fulfill general duties, this information must be disclosed to others. If I have a duty to know whether my car brakes are faulty, and I want to sell you my car, I should tell you if the brakes are faulty. It is not that I must know about the faulty brakes in order to tell you. Rather, I must know about the brakes because I have a duty to avoid collisions, and once I know this information, I have a duty to disclose it in a subsequent sale.[40] If I am negligent, and fail to have my brakes inspected, and then sell you my car without telling you the brakes are faulty, I am partly blamewor-thy for your decision to buy my car without full information. It would seem a poor excuse to tell you, "I didn't know about the brakes!" if I had a previous duty to know about the brakes.

We may apply similar reasoning to repatriation. Governments have general duties to know about ethnic cleansing and genocides in foreign countries, derived from their "Responsibility to Protect" others from great harm, as outlined in the 2005 UN World Summit.[41] States also must know about suffering in other countries to help alleviate global suffering more generally, at least to an extent. For example, govern-ments have a duty to know about famine in South Sudan, because only by knowing about famine can they take efforts to stop it, fulfilling their duties to stop famine. If governments have duties to know information to prevent suffering, and have a duty to disclose what they know, then governments are blameworthy for failing to tell refugees about suffer-ing in their home countries. It is not an excuse for them to claim they did not know about the suffering, for they ought to have known, due to their other general duties.

A government ministry in charge of immigration may also have duties to know about countries of origin to establish who is a refugee.

The Israeli Ministry of Interior, for example, had a duty to find information about South Sudan to establish which South Sudanese asylum seekers were refugees, in order to grant them refugee status in Israel. If the ministry failed to find information to determine who was a refugee, its ignorance was a poor excuse for its failure to disclose risks to refugees wanting to return. It ought to have known the risks, for reasons related to its other duties.

To clarify this point: I am not claiming we have a duty to know information derived from our duties to ensure that others give their informed consent. For it is unclear when we have a duty to ensure informed consent, when finding accurate information is costly. Rather, I am claiming that, when we have duties to know derived from duties unrelated to informed consent, we ought to disclose this knowledge when it will help ensure informed consent. If we don't have this knowledge, we are acting wrongly towards those we fail to inform.

Furthermore, I am not claiming we should disclose all information we have a duty to know to anyone who wants this information. If my jealous neighbor asks about the brakes of my Lamborghini, but has no interest in buying it, I have not wronged her when I tell her the brakes are not faulty when they are. For were I to know my brakes were faulty, I would have no duty to tell my neighbor this fact. Rather, my argument is that, when we have a duty to disclose information we know, it is not an excuse to say we didn't know if we ought to have known.

This reasoning implies there are limits to information that must be sought. State officials have no duty to research ethnic cleansing abroad if such research places their own lives at risk, and so do not wrong refugees if they fail to inform them. In such cases, it may be enough for officials to merely provide a disclaimer, informing refugees that there is insufficient information to know the full risks of returning, because it is too dangerous to conduct research in their home countries. But when it is merely difficult to find information, but safe, officials have a duty to find information, and so misinforming is wrong.

3.3 OMITTING INFORMATION

This raises the question of whether omitting information is permissible. In 2008 the Norwegian government helped Iraqi nationals repatriate, never misinforming them, but never warning them of food insecurity in Iraq.[42] In 2010 the government of Denmark helped Iraqi refugees repatriate, also never misinforming them, but never disclosing risks of violence.[43] More recently, the UK government helped refugees return to Sierra Leone without disclosing the risks of homelessness, common after return, and never warning refugees returning to Sri Lanka about security concerns, with many arrested, detained, and tortured after returning.[44]

In Israel, staff members from OBI and HIAS never told refugees they could not re-enter Israel once they left, as staff assumed refugees had this information.[45] Staff also assumed refugees had information about South Sudan from families, or from their own memories. For this reason, they never disclosed information about violence in Unity State, Jonglei, and other areas,[46] or information on healthcare and food insecurity.[47]

It was not completely unreasonable that OBI and HIAS assumed refugees could rely on their families for information. Amongst those I interviewed, family members were the best sources of information compared to other sources, such as the media, government officials, and NGOs. Of the nine I interviewed who found full employment after returning, eight had been told by family members that there were jobs. However, it was also the case that, of the nineteen who were told by family that there were jobs, eleven found no employment, and lacked reliable shelter. Though families were the best sources of information, they were not very good sources in absolute terms.

One reason we might suppose repatriation facilitators have an obligation to disclose risks is that information can be costly to obtain, but free to disclose. When facilitators have duties to know about conditions in other countries, they may as well disclose this information to refugees, given that the act of disclosing is costless.

But facilitators might respond that failing to provide information is not wrong, or at least less wrong than actively misinforming.[48] To defend this claim, they might raise three arguments.

3.3.1 Causation

The first argument relates to causation. We might suppose acts are especially wrong if they are necessary and sufficient for harmful outcomes. If an agent misinforms a recipient of a service, and as a result the recipient believes a falsehood only because of this misinformation, the misinformation is necessary and sufficient for the recipient's false belief. For example, if I falsely tell you it is safe to go skydiving, and you think it safe because of what I say, and would have otherwise thought it unsafe, my misinformation would be necessary and sufficient for your believing it safe to go skydiving. If you then proceed to go skydiving as a result, the misinformation would also be necessary for your choice to take a major risk. Omissions, in contrast, are less likely to be necessary and sufficient for false beliefs. If I never bother telling you that skydiving is unsafe, and you continue to think it safe, then my omitting information is not sufficient for your false belief: you partly think it safe because someone else told you it was, or because you inferred that it was from other sources of information. The same could be said about repatriation. If a government tells a refugee it is safe to repatriate, and the refugee thinks it safe as a result, and would have otherwise thought it unsafe, the misinformation is necessary and sufficient for the refugee believing it is safe to go home. If the refugee then proceeds to go home as a result, the misinformation would also be necessary for the choice to take a major risk. In contrast, if a government omits information to a refugee, and as a result the refugee continues to hold false beliefs about her home country, the omission is not sufficient for her false beliefs; her other poor sources of information – such as family members, or the media – are also necessary.

I do not believe this distinction is sound, because the act of misinforming is also not sufficient for false beliefs. If I tell you skydiving is safe when it is not, and you hold a false belief as a result, one reason you hold the false belief is that nobody else provided alternative information to correct your false belief. As such, your false belief is the result of both the misinformation I gave you, and information omissions from other sources. Similarly, if a government tells a refugee it is safe to go home when it is not, and the refugee holds a false belief as a result, one reason she holds the false belief is that nobody else provided alternative information to correct her false belief. As such, her false belief is the result of both the misinformation from the government, and information omissions from other sources. Misinforming, in this sense, can be similar to omitting information. Just as omitting information only leads to false beliefs when another source is misinforming, misinforming only leads to false beliefs when another source is omitting information. Omitting information, therefore, can be causally responsible in a similar manner to misinforming.

3.3.2 Positive versus Negative Acts

There is a second reason misinforming may be more wrong than omitting information. It may be that a "positive act" is more wrong than a "negative act." Examples of positive acts include injecting arsenic into a patient or stealing money from an elderly man. They seem more wrong than negative acts, such as letting a person die of arsenic injected by someone else, or failing to return the money that an elderly man lost. Perhaps misinforming is a positive act and so more wrong, while omitting information is a negative act and so less wrong.

To establish if misinforming is a positive act and omitting information a negative act, we must have plausible definitions of what positive and negative acts are. Some argue that positive acts are more causally related to outcomes,[49] but, as noted, acts of omission can have the same causal impact as positive acts. Jonathan Bennett provides a more plausible definition of the positive/negative distinction. He argues that an agent's act is positive if most of the other actions she could have taken would not have led to the same outcome, and an act is negative if most of the actions an agent could have taken would have still led to the same outcome.[50] If a doctor injects arsenic into a healthy patient, most of the other acts the doctor could have taken – stayed at home, gone for a stroll, read a book, danced a jig, and so forth – would not have led to the patient dying. As such, she committed a positive act. In contrast, if the doctor failed to treat an ill patient, then most of the acts she could have done – also stayed at home, gone for a stroll, and so forth – would still have led to the patient dying.

Some have critiqued this conceptualization, raising a counter-example: Martha is preparing to assassinate a man named Victor. Martha knows that a second assassin is waiting across the street and will kill Victor if she does not. She could kill the second assassin, and let Victor live, but she doesn't, instead shooting Victor. Bennett's theory would seem to implausibly hold that Martha merely lets Victor die in a negative act, because most of the other acts she could have done – gone for stroll, read a book, danced a jig, and so forth – would have led to the same outcome of Victor dying, this time from the second assassin. This seems odd: surely, if Martha pulled her trigger and killed Victor, she is guilty of a positive act, rather than a mere omission.[51]

I do not believe this counter-example undermines Bennett's theory. Though Martha could commit many other actions that would still result in Victor dying, she could not commit many other actions that would result in the increased probability, in her mind, of Victor dying. When she pulled the trigger, she could not have known for certain that the second assassin would have pulled his trigger had she not pulled hers first. In this sense, had she not pulled the trigger, and instead gone for a stroll, read a book, or danced a jig, then the outcome would have been different in her mind. It would have been a world with a lower probability of Victor dying. Similarly, an agent misinforming the recipient of a service increases the perceived probability that the recipient will be misinformed, because she cannot know that someone else will provide misinformation if she does not. If so, then misinformation is a positive act, because most of the acts the misinformer could have done – walked, read, danced, and so forth – would not have led to the perceived increased probability of the recipient holding a false belief. In contrast, if an agent omits information, then most of the other acts she could have done – walked, read, danced – would have still lead to the same probability of a misinformed recipient.

While the above explains the distinction between positive and negative acts, it does not imply that misinforming is always a positive act and omitting information a negative act. Sometimes omitting information can be a positive act. HIAS kept records of the interviews it conducted, which it provided to me. There are moments in the transcripts where a refugee says she is returning to South Sudan to access education, and it is not clear if HIAS responded that access to education was unlikely. If HIAS never responded, and instead remained silent, this moment of silence could be interpreted as a communicative act, signaling to the refugee that her beliefs are correct. Had HIAS not sat in silence and listened attentively, and instead never spoken to the refugee at all, then the refugee may have sought out further information. If this is true, then HIAS's silence would be a positive act: Most of the acts HIAS could have done instead, including going for a walk or dancing a jig, would not have led to the outcome of a false belief. Its attentive and silent listening would be a form of information omission that serves as a positive act, and as egregious as misinforming.

3.3.3 Easy versus Hard

Repatriation facilitators might present a final defense of the claim that omitting information is not as wrong as misinforming. Some acts are especially wrong because they are easy to avoid, and other acts are less wrong because they are hard to avoid. It is especially wrong to inject arsenic into a patient because it is easy to avoid doing this: just keep the arsenic at home. It is less wrong to fail to cure a patient of arsenic poisoning: avoiding this omission requires treating the patient. The same can be said regarding information. It is especially wrong for facilitators to misinform refugees because it is easy to avoid misinforming: they can simply keep their mouths shut. In contrast, it is less wrong to omit information because it is hard to avoid omitting information: this requires finding information. For this reason, omitting information is less wrong.

Though it is often hard to avoid omitting information, because it is hard to find information, this is not always the case. Sometimes information is not hard to find. When HIAS failed to tell refugees about ethnic-based killings in Unity State and Jonglei, it could have easily changed its actions by searching the internet for "death toll in Unity State" and "death toll in Jonglei," relaying this information without great effort. Importantly, even if providing accurate information would have been difficult, HIAS could be blameworthy for the acts that, though costly to avoid, would be a cost expected of them to bear, given their unique position, or their commitment to ensure informed returns. More generally, if governments and organizations ought to have information, and ought to disclose information they know, then we can expect them to bear the costs of finding information. If they don't, they may be acting wrongly, even if slightly less wrongly than actively misinforming.

3.4 RELEVANCY

Until now, the examples I raised concerned facilitators failing to inform, leading refugees to return when they would have otherwise stayed. There are instances where facilitators fail to inform, but refugees would have repatriated even if better informed. In such cases, the misinformation seems irrelevant, and so perhaps not wrong.

Consider the case of Stephen, a father of three living in Tel Aviv. He wished to repatriate, and was told by the government that South Sudan was safe. He knew this was not true, having lived in South Sudan relatively recently, but returned nonetheless, boarding a flight for Juba with his wife and children shortly after. Within a year he had opened a cleaning and maintenance company, and one day in December 2013 went to work cleaning at the Sudanese People's Liberation Movement's (SPLM) annual congress.

Towards the evening, he heard gunshots from soldiers who had opened fire on each other. He dropped to the ground, crawled to the entrance, and ran home. The next morning, peering out his window at sunrise, he saw eleven small children and two young men taken out of their houses by soldiers, lined up, and shot. He told his wife and children to exit with him through their back door, and they ran to the UN IDP camp. He later went back to his home to rescue his two dogs and equipment, worth tens of thousands of dollars. His dogs were there but his equipment was not. He returned to the camp, sat down in his tent, and managed to tap into the UN's electricity source, creating an impromptu phone-charging station for other camp residents. The residents were paying him a few pounds a day for the service in 2014, but the money was barely enough to survive.[52]

Even after losing his business and fleeing to the camp, Stephen said the Israeli government's ignorance of South Sudan did not bother him, because he himself knew the risks, and returned regardless. He does not regret his choice and so, perhaps by chance, the government is not guilty of the wrong of misinformation.

Consider, also, the case of Yasmin. Unlike Stephen, she had no accurate information before she returned, and upon reaching her home village in Aweil she was surprised and disappointed to find no reliable clean water, education, or safety for her children. She says that she would have returned even if she had been given more information. She runs a restaurant today, and is happy to be close to her family.[53]

There are two reasons we might suppose that neither Stephen nor Yasmin were wronged.

3.4.1 Moral Luck

In both of these cases, there is a question concerning moral luck. On the one hand, we might believe that repatriation facilitators – the government in Stephen's case and OBI in Yasmin's case – failed to ensure informed consent because they failed to provide accurate information. Even if Stephen and Yasmin would have returned regardless, neither facilitator knew this, and so the facilitators should have worked harder to find and disclose risks. But though it seems the facilitators should have acted differently, we might believe in moral luck. Moral luck is the idea that, if an agent acts in a manner expected to cause harm, but by luck does not, she is off the hook: by luck she did no wrong. Imagine, for example, that I sell you my car without telling you the brakes are faulty, but by chance you do not care about the faulty brakes, fixing them promptly yourself. By luck I did no wrong. Though I did not provide you full information, you gave your informed consent, as the information I failed to provide was irrelevant to your decision. In the case of repatriation from Israel, by luck facilitators did no wrong because Stephen happened to know about the risks and Yasmin happened to not care. Though Stephen and Yasmin were not given full information, they gave their informed consent.

Even if we believe in moral luck, there are reasons to believe that Yasmin, in particular, was wronged. She says today she would have returned, but this may be because she cannot change her past decision, and so feels she may as well be happy. Had Yasmin been told information while still in Israel, she may not have returned even if, today, she says she would. This is because, more generally, individuals are sometimes happy with past decisions they cannot escape,[54] as when someone is happy in their current town they cannot leave, or happy they bought a car that cannot be returned. As such, our current happiness for our past decisions are not good indicators of whether we would have consented in the past, had we been better informed in the past. This is less of a concern for Stephen, because we know that he would have returned even if the government had given him more information, because he had this information and still returned.

3.4.2 Hypothetical Consent

Let us say, though, that we trust Yasmin. She says she would have returned even if she had been informed, and so we should assume she really would have returned even if she had been informed. If this is true, we might claim she was not wronged. For she gave "hypothetical consent" at the time she returned. Hypothetical consent is provided when someone would have consented had she been aware of risks. Such consent is often sufficient for an intervention to be permissible. For example, a coma patient is not wronged if she undergoes treatment, so long as she would have consented to the treatment had she capacity and awareness of risks. Even if actual consent is preferable, hypothetical consent still indicates a lesser wrong, or no wrong, because at least the intervention promoted the aims of those who would have consented.[55] When Yasmin gave her hypothetical consent, her aims of being close to her family were reached, and so she experienced no wrong.

There are two responses to this reasoning. The first response begins with the premise that taking away someone's control is wrong even if this promotes her aims. Imagine a doctor asks a patient if she consents to surgery, and the patient tells the doctor she does not. The doctor then thinks for a few hours, returns to the patient, and tells her, "After thorough deliberation, I have taken into account what you prefer, and also taken into account the risks of surgery, and concluded that I will not force you to undergo surgery." Such an attitude seems wrong, as the doctor is in control of the final decision.[56] A similar phenomenon occurs with misinformation. Imagine the doctor never warns a patient of the risks. Even if the patient would have consented to surgery regardless, the patient lacked control when accepting surgery without full information. This is because, if she did not know about the risks of the surgery, she could not weigh the risks against the benefits, and so could not come to a decision herself. If she lacked control when misinformed, she was wronged even if this had no impact on whether the surgery occurred. The same can be said about Yasmin: When OBI failed to warn her about the risks, she lacked control over her decision, given that she could not weigh the costs and benefits herself. She lacked control even if she would have chosen repatriation regardless, and even if repatriation helped her reach her aims.

Some may reject this line of reasoning, claiming individuals do not lack control if their choices are consistent with their desires and aims. At the very least, a lesser wrong has occurred. Even if this is true, and hypothetical consent indicates no wrong or a lesser wrong, there is reason to believe that Yasmin did not even give her hypothetical consent.

When considering if a person would have hypothetically consented, it is necessary to establish an appropriate counterfactual world. To do so we must consider what we value. I assume we value information, and so if a person is in a coma, we ask what they would have consented to in a counterfactual world where they were both conscious and fully informed. But if we value information, we don't only value information on a given service, such as a given medical treatment. We also value information on the character of the service provider. When I consent to surgery, I want to know both about the risks of the surgery, and to know my surgeon is informed about the risks herself. If my surgeon tells me an operation has no risks, and after the operation I learned it did, I would feel wronged. I would think, "Had I known the surgeon was providing me misinformation, I would have chosen a surgeon more forthcoming about risks, even if I still would have chosen to undergo the same operation."

If so, then the relevant counterfactual in hypothetical consent is a world where a person is both informed and aware others are misinforming them. For example, if my grandmother is in a coma, and I know her surgeon is poorly informed about surgery, I might ask, "Would grandma have consented to surgery with this poorly-informed surgeon?" If she would not, then she failed to give her hypothetical consent, even if she would have consented to surgery with a different surgeon. This test for hypothetical consent captures the range of information she likely values: the information on the risks of the surgery itself, and information on the type of agent the surgeon is. We care about the type of agent a service provider is because we want to know if they are fulfilling their responsibilities, and whether they are the sorts of individuals we want to support. If my grandmother were awake she would likely want to signal to others the incompetence of her surgeon, and so she would not have consented to surgery with this surgeon.

This has implications for Yasmin. Even if Yasmin would have returned had she been fully informed, this does not mean she would have returned via OBI had she known OBI was misinformed. Indeed, some refugees refused to return via OBI precisely because they were upset about the misinformation provided. A man name Bok, frustrated by OBI's PowerPoint slides, paid for his own flight and managed his own logistics. He did not want to support an NGO that failed to warn about risks.[57]

In Stephen's case, we needn't ask what he would have done had he known he was misinformed. In reality, he knew he was being misinformed, and this did not bother him enough to refuse the government's repatriation services. In Yasmin's case, we do not know if she would have returned had she known that OBI was misinforming her. She may say today that she would have returned, but we cannot know what she would have truly done at the time. We must take her memories at face value for this consideration as well. And the more we rely on memories, the less we are certain that information really was irrelevant.

In general, we cannot travel back in time to a counterfactual world and see how refugees would have acted had they been informed. As such, it is difficult to establish what information was irrelevant. To be safe, repatriation facilitators should ensure information is available to all, and should be held accountable for failing to provide information that may have been irrelevant.

3.5 INTENT

When repatriation facilitators speak with refugees, they rarely know they are misinforming. If they are not aware they are misinforming, and awareness is necessary for intent, they do not intend to misinform. If intent is necessary for blameworthiness, they are not blameworthy for misinformed repatriation.

This is not to claim that all agree that intent is important for blameworthiness. According to some philosophers, an agent can be blamed for lacking morally important motives if this leads to harmful outcomes, even if she is not aware of these harmful outcomes, and so does not intend these outcomes.[58] If I lack a motivation to help the poor, and so fail to help them, I may be blameworthy for my failure to help them even if I am not aware of the poor and so not intending to fail to help them. Similarly, if officials lack a desire to help refugees, and so misinform them of risks, they may be blameworthy for misinforming them even if they are not aware they misinform them, and so do not intend to misinform. Other philosophers argue that intent is not necessary for blameworthiness because only foreseeability matters. Foreseeability refers to the likelihood that one's actions will causally contribute to an outcome, regardless of whether one intended this outcome.[59] A repatriation facilitator is blameworthy if a reasonable person could foresee that failing to find information would increase the probability of an uninformed repatriation.

But many philosophers do view intent as necessary for blameworthiness, or at least increasing blameworthiness. To have intent, certain conditions must be met, including having control over one's actions,[60] and being aware of what one is doing. For example, for me to intentionally steal a watch I must be aware I am picking up a watch that is not my own; were I to pick up a watch I thought was my own, I would lack the necessary awareness for intent. In cases where one lacks awareness of information and then misinforms as a result, one is not aware one is misinforming, and so one is not intentionally misinforming. Another condition for intent is having a particular aim in mind.[61] If one intends to omit information by keeping one's mouth closed, one has the aim of not uttering this information. It is not clear repatriation facilitators have any such aims when keeping their mouths closed, and so do not intentionally fail to inform.

Such was potentially the case for HIAS staff members in Israel. Staff members were not aware they were misinforming or omitting information, and had no particular aim in their actions. A similar claim could be made about UNHCR. When UNHCR helped Afghan refugees in Iran return home in the 2000s, it never warned refugees about the risks, and soon after return refugees faced regular attacks from warlords and Taliban resurgent groups.[62] The UN agency was not aware of these risks, because it never interviewed those who returned,[63] and so was not intentionally failing to inform refugees of the risks. When UNHCR officials in Kenya handed out pamphlets to Somali refugees, pamphlets that had not been updated for years,[64] UN officials were perhaps not aware that the information was out of date, and did not aim to misinform refugees. When the German government told Bosnian refugees they would receive housing upon return, it did not know it was misinforming refugees because it never conducted post-return evaluations. While governments may be acting wrongly when unintentionally misinforming, perhaps they act more wrongly when intentionally misinforming. The latter is a form of deception or recklessness, rather than a mere oversight.

Even when facilitators do not intentionally misinform, they may still be blameworthy. This is because an agent can be blameworthy for unintentionally misinforming, if they are misinforming because of an earlier intentional act. A doctor can be blamed for unintentionally failing to disclose risks if the reason she did not know the risks was because, earlier, she intentionally failed to read the latest medical journals.[65] When I asked the director of HIAS in Israel why he never disclosed all risks, he responded that he was not aware of all risks because he never conducted research on South Sudan, as he assumed refugees already had sufficient information.[66] He therefore unintentionally omitted risks because he intentionally did not find out about these risks. The government also founded a repatriation program in 2012 and, as noted above, it had helped over 6,000 refugees depart Israel by 2015.[67] The Israeli civil servant heading the scheme never warned refugees of the risks of repatriation and resettlement, such as the risks of homelessness, displacement, and execution by Sudanese authorities. This was because he, like HIAS, was not aware there were risks to disclose. He was not aware there were risks because he intentionally never bothered to learn about risks, feeling this would be "patronizing"[68] to refugees who were capable of informing themselves. As with HIAS, he unintentionally omitted information because he earlier intentionally never found information.

Some might claim that, even if the HIAS director and the civil servant intentionally failed to find information, they were not blameworthy if their intentions were good or neutral. The HIAS director failed to find information merely because he thought refugees were capable of finding information themselves. The civil servant failed to find information merely because he thought this was patronizing. Neither intended to encourage an uninformed return.

Even if both facilitators had good intentions when failing to find information, their good intentions could potentially be traced back to even earlier acts, both with wrongful intentions. The HIAS director believed refugees had their own access to information, but he intentionally never validated his belief: he never bothered to find out if it was true that refugees had access to accurate information. And we do not know why he failed to find out if his belief was valid. If his intentions were to encourage return, then his ultimate intentions were wrongful, and his omitting information blameworthy.

Unlike the HIAS director, the civil servant's intentions were not necessarily based on false beliefs about refugees' knowledge. Many refugees really may have felt patronized if they learned that the government was gathering information on their country, rather than relying on refugees' own knowledge. If the civil servant's intentions were not based on false beliefs, he cannot be blamed for intentionally failing to find out if his beliefs were correct. But even if his reasons were to avoid being patronizing, reasons can be derived from other reasons. His reasons for avoiding being patronizing may have been to facilitate unsafe returns, so that more would return. If so, then his ultimate intention was not to avoid being patronizing, but to encourage unsafe returns.

The above analysis is limited by the fact that we cannot know the intentions of other agents. It is impossible to read the minds of NGO directors and civil servants to learn about their reasons for actions. Nonetheless, we can still find evidence of wrongful intent, if not decisive certainty. The policy of the Israeli government was to promote civil servants based on how many refugees left the country under their watch. As such, the civil servant had an interest in more refugees repatriating, to meet his annual targets. OBI similarly had such an interest in more returning to impress donors who expected their donations to contribute to repatriation. HIAS may have seemed more neutral, but it received money from OBI for its work, and may have felt pressure from OBI to claim a refugee was informed to meet OBI's targets. Even if we cannot know the intentions of staff members and civil servants, we can at least conclude that no annual targets should be established, removing one reason to intentionally misinform.

3.6 CONCLUSION

When the director of OBI traveled throughout South Sudan and took photographs along the way, she could have read independent reports on the country, and interviewed more refugees who had already returned. Had she done this, she could have told refugees in Israel that there were few clinics, schools, or reliable policemen in South Sudan. Instead, she assured her audience that the South Sudanese government was prepared to help them, and that conditions were stable. When organizations like OBI unknowingly misinform, they may be acting impermissibly if they have a duty to work hard to disclose accurate information. They have such a duty if they were created to help vulnerable populations, and can better help them by finding accurate information.

This much is obvious. What is less obvious is whether governments have duties to find information if they have no special duties to help vulnerable populations. To address this question, I addressed a broader question of when and whether agents must disclose information to others. I argued that, even if agents have no duties to find information to ensure informed consent, they must still disclose relevant information they already know. And if there is information they ought to know, based on their other duties, they risk wronging those they fail to inform. If I ought to know my car brakes are faulty to avoid collisions, and fail to know my brakes are faulty, and so sell you my car without telling you they are faulty, I commit a wrong. This is because the information I omitted was the sort I would have needed to disclose had I known it, and I ought to have known it. If states have general duties to help prevent poverty and atrocities abroad, and have a duty to determine who is a refugee, they have a duty to gather information on poverty and atrocities abroad. If states have a duty to know about atrocities abroad, then failing to know about the atrocities is a poor excuse for failing to warn refugees repatriating home.

In some cases, refugees are misinformed and return, but say they would have returned even if better informed. In such cases, it is not clear if refugees were wronged, because the misinformation was irrelevant for their decisions to return. To determine if misinformation really was irrelevant, it is not enough to consider if refugees would have consented had they been informed; we must consider if they would have consented had they known they were being misinformed at the time of the service. This is because, when we consent to a high-risk service, we have a right to know if the service providers are ignorant of key facts, to know if we can trust them. Of course, some refugees may claim they would have returned even if they knew facilitators were ignorant of key facts. But these refugees may be happy with their decision because they cannot change their current circumstances. If they failed to give their informed consent prior to returning, then they were wronged even if they do not mind today.

In many such cases, repatriation facilitators are unaware of the risks of repatriation, and do not intentionally provide false or no information. OBI genuinely believed that repatriation was safe. Even if facilitators do not intentionally fail to inform refugees of risks, they may still be blameworthy for intentionally failing to gather information on risks.

To avoid misinformed repatriation, facilitators should institute a number of policy changes. They should ensure that resources are available for more rigorous research on the consequences of repatriating. This would entail learning about the conditions of refugees who have already returned. Today, UNHCR lacks the capacity to conduct such post-return research, as does IOM.[69] This may be because UNHCR and IOM earmark their budgets for repatriation itself, paying for the transport of hundreds of thousands of refugees annually. They should focus less on maximizing the number who return and more on maximizing information before return. This would involve interviewing a substantial sample of past returnees, selected as randomly as possible, to determine how many were likely displaced, killed, or unable to access basic necessities after repatriating.

Such research should not only include a large number of subjects, but should account for survivorship bias. It is not enough to call refugees and interview those who answer their phones, because those who are killed will not answer, and those who fled are less likely to answer. To counteract such bias, facilitators should interview friends and family members of returnees to find out if they have been killed. Facilitators should also interview returnees without cell phone access in refugee camps and rural areas, ensuring that those who fled are included in the sample. They should then communicate their findings to refugees considering returning.

In communicating such findings, facilitators should clarify the limitations of their research, including survivorship bias that is difficult to completely mitigate. For example, if an organization explains that 2 per cent of returnees in a sample were killed, it should explain that the mortality rate amongst this sample is likely lower than amongst the total population of returnees. In addition to communicating biased sampling, facilitators should avoid biased communicating. Today, when organizations provide information on their websites, they publish attractive images of refugees' countries of origin, and photographs of smiling returnees alongside stories of their success.[70] Organizations rarely describe details of those less successful, instead using vague phrases such as, "People in Afghanistan have reported concerns about security."[71] To encourage refugees to consider all information, facilitators should resist including stories of only successful refugees, and include stories and statistics on those displaced or killed. More generally, facilitators should spend more time warning refugees of potential problems, rather than opportunities. Given that repatriation is generally irreversible and potentially unsafe, precaution should be a primary goal.

One of the reasons that facilitators fail to find information is that some have an interest in more returning. In general, agents finding information on services should not be the agents with interests in more accepting these services. Within medicine, for example, researchers running trials to know the risks of a treatment should not be the same researchers profiting from this treatment. Similarly, civil servants researching the risks of repatriation should not be those promoted based on how many repatriate. Nor should humanitarian organizations researching the risks of repatriation be the organizations who receive funding for repatriation. If there is to be a method of promoting or funding, it should be based on how satisfied refugees feel after returning to their countries of origin.

Repatriation facilitators have yet to adopt the above policies. As a result, many refugees returning soon regret their choice, finding themselves again displaced, or without reliable food, water, or asylum. Just as preventing coerced returns is essential, so is ensuring informed returns.

NOTES

1. Interview with Bol, Juba, December 21, 2013; interview with Nathaniel, Juba, December 14, 2013; Interview with Vanessa, Juba, December 25, 2013.
2. Yuval Goren (Hebrew), "Aid Organizations: Over 22 Refugees Expelled to South Sudan Die within the First Year," June 5, 2012, <http://www.nrg.co.il/online/1/ART2/477/197.html> (last accessed February 25, 2018).
3. Alexander Betts, "Survival Migration: A New Protection Framework," *Global Governance* 16(2010):361–82; Matthew Gibney, *The Ethics and Politics of Asylum*, Cambridge: Cambridge University Press 2004; Javier Hidalgo, "Resistance to Unjust Immigration Restrictions," *Journal of Political Philosophy* 23(4)(2015):450–70; David Miller, "Immigration: The Case for Its Limits," in (eds) A. Cohen and C. Wellman, *Contemporary Debates in Applied Ethics*, Malden, MA: Blackwell Publishing 2005 at 193–206.
4. Yevgenia Borisova, "Scared Refugees Regret Returning Home," *Moscow Times*, April 27, 2001, <http://old.themoscowtimes.com/sitemap/free/2001/4/article/scared-refugees-regret-returning-home/253777.html> (last accessed July 29, 2017); Helen Carr, "Returning 'Home': Experiences of Reintegration for Asylum Seekers and Refugees," *British Journal of Social Work* (2014):1–17; Arne Strand, "Review of Two Societies: Review of the Information, Return and Reintegration of Iraqi Nationals to Iraq (IRRINI) Program," Chr. Michelson Institute, 2011, <http://www.cmi.no/publications/publication/?4155=between-two-societies-review-of-the-information> (last accessed February 25, 2018); Anisseh Van England-Nouri, "Repatriation of Afghan and Iraqi Refugees from Iran," *International Journal on Multicultural Societies* 10(2)(2008):144–69; Martha Walsh, Richard Black, and Khalid Koser, "Repatriation from the European Union to Bosnia Herzegovina: The Role of Information," in (eds) Richard Black and Khalid Koser, *The End of the Refugee Cycle? Refugee Repatriation and Reconstruction*, New York and Oxford: Berghahn Books 1999 at 121.
5. One version of this condition is that, for an agent to intentionally φ she must believe that she φ-es. There are other versions of this condition, but nothing in my argumentation hinges on the precise form of awareness that is necessary for intent. For a broader discussion on awareness and intent, see Elizabeth Anscombe, *Intention*, second edition, Oxford: Blackwell 1963 at 49–57; Ulrike Heuer, "Intentions and the Reasons for Which We Act," *Proceedings of the Aristotelian Society* 114(3)(2014):291–315; Kieran Setiya, *Reasons without Intention*, Princeton: Princeton University Press 2007.
6. Heuer 2014 ibid. at 297–300.
7. Holly Smith, "Non-Tracing Cases of Culpable Ignorance," *Criminal Law and Philosophy* 5(2)(2011):115–46.

8. These are just some of the possible stances. See Matthew Gibney, *The Ethics and Politics of Asylum*, Oxford: Oxford University Press 2004; Javier Hidalgo, "Resistance to Unjust Immigration Restrictions," *Journal of Political Philosophy* 23(4)(2015):450–70; David Miller, "Immigration: The Case for Its Limits," in (eds) A. Cohen and C. Wellman, *Contemporary Debates in Applied Ethics*, Malden, MA: Blackwell Publishing 2005 at 193–206.

9. Martha Walsh, Richard Black, and Khalid Koser, "Repatriation from the European Union to Bosnia Herzegovina: The Role of Information," in (eds) Richard Black and Khalid Koser, *The End of the Refugee Cycle? Refugee Repatriation and Reconstruction*, New York and Oxford: Berghahn Books 1999 at 121.

10. Yevgenia Borisova, "Scared Refugees Regret Returning Home," *Moscow Times* April 27, 2001, <http://old.themoscowtimes.com/sitemap/free/2001/4/article/scared-refugees-regret-returning-home/253777.html> (last accessed July 29, 2017).

11. David Turton and Peter Marsden, "Taking Refugees for a Ride? The Politics of Refugee Return to Afghanistan," Afghanistan Research and Evaluation Unit, December 2002, <https://www.ecoi.net/en/file/local/1104372/1329_1211899193_taking-refugees-for-a-ride-ip.pdf> (last accessed February 26, 2018); Anisseh Van England-Nouri, "Repatriation of Afghan and Iraqi Refugees from Iran," *International Journal on Multicultural Societies* 10(2)(2008):144–69.

12. Strand 2011 ibid.

13. Galia Sabar and Elizabeth Tsurkov, "Israel's Policies towards Asylum Seekers, 2002–2014," Istituto Affari Internazionali Working Paper May 15, 2015.

14. Agence France-Presse, "Somali Refugees Regret Returning Home from Kenya," June 27, 2017, <http://m.news24.com/news24/Africa/News/somali-refugees-regret-returning-home-from-kenya-20170627> (last accessed July 28, 2017).

15. Associated Press, "'It Was a Deception:' Ex-Somali Regret Returning Home," Fox News, December 27, 2016, <http://www.foxnews.com/world/2016/12/27/it-was-deception-ex-somali-refugees-regret-coming-home.html> (last accessed July 28, 2017).

16. BBC, "Sudan's South Kordofan: 'Huge Suffering from Bombs,'" June 14, 2011, <http://www.bbc.co.uk/news/world-africa-13767146> (last accessed February 28, 2018).

17. BBC, "South Sudan Profile," January 17, 2018, <http://www.bbc.co.uk/news/world-africa-14019202> (last accessed February 26, 2018); Landmine and Cluster Munition Monitor, "South Sudan: Casualties and Victim Assistance," <http://www.the-monitor.org/custom/index.php/region_profiles/print_theme/2342#_ftn3> (last accessed July 24, 14).

18. BBC, "South Sudan: Cattle Raid in Warap State 'kills 74,'" January 30, 2012, <http://www.bbc.co.uk/news/world-16786869> (last accessed February

26, 2018); IOM, "South Sudan Annual Report 2012," <https://www.iom.int/files/live/sites/iom/files/Country/docs/IOM_South_Sudan_Annual_%20 Report_2012.pdf> (last accessed February 26, 2018); Norwegian Refugee Council/Internal Displacement Monitoring Center, "Global Overview 2012: People Internally Displaced by Conflict and Violence – South Sudan," <http://www.refworld.org/docid/517fb0526.html> (last accessed February 28, 2018).

19. Judith McCallum and Alfred Okech, "Drivers of Conflict in Jonglei State," *Humanitarian Exchange Magazine* 57, May 2013, <https://odihpn.org/magazine/drivers-of-conflict-in-jonglei-state/> (last accessed February 26, 2018).

20. According to the Sudanese 2008 consensus, the population was 1.2 million, but this has been disputed. See South Sudanese National Disarmament, Demobilization, and Reintegration Commission, <http://www.ssddrc.org/states/jonglei.html> (last accessed March 4, 2012).

21. World Bank, "Unemployment, Total (% of Total Labor Force) (Modelled ILO Estimate)," <http://data.worldbank.org/indicator/SL.UEM.TOTL.ZS> (last accessed June 15, 2015).

22. Interview with Vanessa, Juba, December 25, 2013.

23. Maeve McClenaghan and Patrick Galey, "Returning to Sudan: Migrants Leaving Israel Face Persecution," The Bureau of Investigative Journalism, January 6, 2014, <https://www.thebureauinvestigates.com/stories/2014-01-06/returning-to-sudan-migrants-leaving-israel-face-persecution> (last accessed February 28, 2018).

24. HIAS Interview Form provided by HIAS in December 2012.

25. Interview with Sigal Rozen, Tel Aviv, December 9, 2012.

26. Al Jazeera, "'Hundreds dead' in South Sudan Cattle Raids," August 22, 2011, <http://www.aljazeera.com/news/africa/2011/08/201182220946583842.html> (last accessed February 26, 2018); Jared Ferrie, "More Than 200 Die in South Sudan Tribal Feud, Official Says," CNN, March 12, 2012, <http://edition.cnn.com/2012/03/12/world/africa/south-sudan-violence/> (last accessed March 14, 2012); Una McCauley, "Separated Children in South Sudan," *Forced Migration Review* 24 (2005):52–5; MSF, "Patients and Families Killed Outside of MSF Compound," November 29, 2007, <http://www.msf.org/article/patients-and-family-members-killed-inside-msf-compound> (last accessed March 15, 2012); MSF, "South Sudan: Violence against Healthcare," July 1, 2014, <http://www.msf.fr/actualite/publications/south-sudan-conflict-violence-against-healthcare> (last accessed February 26, 2018); Small Arms Survey, "Fighting for Spoils: Armed Insurgencies in Greater Upper Nile," November 2011, <http://www.smallarmssurvey-sudan.org/fileadmin/docs/issue-briefs/HSBA-IB-18-Armed-insurgencies-Greater-Upper-Nile.pdf> (last accessed March 15, 2012).

27. Interview with OBI director, Jerusalem, October 6, 2010.

28. Goren 2012 ibid.
29. These included the 128 subjects who I interviewed.
30. See a list of recent guidelines from the World Health Organization, as well as datasets on food security by country, <http://www.who.int/nutrition/publications/en/> (last accessed April 24, 2018).
31. IOM worked alongside a local NGO called the Center for International Migration and Integration (CIMI). Interview with CIMI director, Jerusalem, September 22, 2011; interview with CIMI employee 1, Jerusalem, September 23, 2011; interview with CIMI employee 2, Berlin, March 3, 2011.
32. Tim Brown, "South Sudan Education Emergency," Forced Migration Review July 2006: 20–1, <http://www.fmreview.org/sites/fmr/files/FMRdownloads/en/FMRpdfs/EducationSupplement/13.pdf> (last accessed February 26, 2018); Giorgio Cometto, Gyuri Fritsche, and Egbert Sondorp, "Health Sector Recovery in Early Post-Conflict Environments: Experience from Southern Sudan,"*Disasters* 34(4)(2010):885–909; Andrew Green, "Healthcare in South Sudan at a Crossroads,"*The Lancet* 379(9826)(2012):1578.
33. UNHCR, "UNHCR Positions on Returns to Southern and Central Somalia," May 2016, <http://www.refworld.org/docid/573de9fe4.html> (last accessed January 22, 2018).
34. Richard Black, "Return and Reconstruction in Bosnia-Herzegovina: Missing Link, or Mistaken Priority?" *SAIS Review* 21(2)(2001):177–99.
35. UNHCR, "Burundi: Repatriation from Tanzania – Numbers Remaining under 300,000," Briefing Notes, May 18, 2004, <http://www.unhcr.org/40a9e0a21.html> (last accessed September 19, 2015).
36. Fabrice Balanche, "A Half-Million Syrian Returnees? A Look behind the Numbers,"Policywatch 2826, The Washington Institute, July 7, 2017, <http://www.washingtoninstitute.org/policy-analysis/view/a-half-million-syrian-returnees-a-look-behind-the-numbers> (last accessed January 21, 2018).
37. Steven Lukes, *Power: A Radical View*, second edition, London: Macmillan 2005 at 53–4.
38. Franklin Miller and Alan Wertheimer, "Preface to a Theory of Consent Transactions: Beyond Valid Consent," in (ed.) Franklin Miller and Alan Wertheimer, *The Ethics of Consent: Theory and Practice*, Oxford: Oxford University Press 2009: 79–106 at 96.
39. Holly Smith, "The Subjective Moral Duty to Inform Oneself before Acting," *Ethics* 125(1)(2014):11–38.
40. In other words: It is not that I have duty to know about the brakes in order to tell you; I had a duty to know and, as it happens, this information is the sort that I should disclose if I know about it.
41. United Nations, "The Responsibility to Protect," Outcome Document of the 2005 United Nations World Summit, A/RES/60/1, para. 138–40,

<http://www.un.org/en/preventgenocide/adviser/responsibility.shtml> (last accessed March 1, 2012).

42. Strand 2011 ibid.

43. Maria Helene Bak Riiskjaer, "Circular Repatriation: The Unsuccessful Return and Reintegration of Iraqis with Refugee Status in Denmark," Research Paper 165, New Issues in Refugee Research at 7.

44. Helen Carr, "Returning Home: Experiences of Reintegration for Asylum Seekers and Refugees," *British Journal of Social Work* 44(1)(2014): 1–17.

45. Interview with a former employee of HIAS and OBI, Tel Aviv, April 28, 2012.

46. Al Jazeera 2011 ibid.; Ferrie 2012 ibid.; McCauley 2005 ibid.; MSF 2007 ibid.; MSF 2014 ibid.; Small Arms Survey 2011 ibid.

47. Training manual provided by HIAS in December 2012.

48. James Edwin Mahon, "Kant and Maria von Herbert: Reticence vs. Deception," *Philosophy* 81(2006): 417–44.

49. Frances Howard-Snyder, "Doing vs. Allowing Harm," in (ed.) Edward N. Zalta, Stanford Encyclopedia of Philosophy (Winter 2011 Edition), <http://plato.stanford.edu/archives/win2011/entries/doing-allowing/> (last accessed March 3, 2012).

50. Jonathan Bennett, *The Act Itself*, Oxford: Oxford University Press 1998, ch. 6–8.

51. Howard-Snyder 2011 ibid.

52. Interview with Stephen, Juba, January 4, 2014.

53. Interview with Yasmin, Aweil, March 30, 2012.

54. Others have raised this empirical fact to argue that our current levels of happiness or preference-fulfillment are not always good metrics for determining if a particular state of affairs is just, or for determining if our past decisions were good decisions. I am making a more modest claim, and simply pointing out that we can be happy with our past decisions even if we did not consent to these decisions. For a broader discussion on the role of current preferences in moral theorizing, see Joseph Fishkin, *Bottlenecks: A New Theory of Equal Opportunity*, Oxford: Oxford University Press 2014 at 16; R. Jay Wallace, *The View from Here: On Affirmation, Attachment, and the Limits of Regret*, Oxford: Oxford University Press 2013 at 66.

55. When I write "hypothetical consent" I do not refer to the consent a reasonable person would give. I refer to the consent an individual would likely give were they more aware of the relevant facts. If a non-reasonable person would likely consent, because they are unreasonable, then this person has given hypothetical consent. This is similar to a version of hypothetical consent addressed by Enoch in a recent article on the subject. See David Enoch, "Hypothetical Consent and the Value(s) of Autonomy," *Ethics* 128(1)(2017):6–36.

56. Daniel Groll, "Paternalism, Respect, and the Will," *Ethics* 122(4)(2012): 692–720.
57. Discussion with Bok, Juba, January 1, 2013.
58. Michael Slote, *Morals from Motives*, Oxford: Oxford University Press 2001; Holly Smith, "Non-Tracing Cases of Culpable Ignorance," *Criminal Law and Philosophy* 5(2)(2011): 115–46.
59. For versions of this approach, see Jonathan Bennett, *The Act Itself*, Oxford: Oxford University Press 1998; and Frank Jackson, "What Effects?" in (ed.) Jonathan Dancy, *Reading Parfit*, Oxford and Malden, MA: Blackwell Wiley 1997.
60. D. Justin Coates and Neal Tognazzini, "Blame," in (ed.) Edward N. Zalta, Stanford Encyclopedia of Philosophy (Spring 2016 Edition), <http://plato.stanford.edu/entries/blame/> (last accessed February 26, 2018).
61. Holly Smith, "The Subjective Moral Duty to Inform Oneself before Acting," *Ethics* 125(1)(2014):11–48 at 14.
62. Anisseh Van Engeland-Nourai, "Repatriation of Afghan and Iraqi Refugees from Iran: When Home is No Longer Home," *International Journal on Multicultural Societies* 10(2008)(2):145–68 at 158.
63. Helen Morris and Machiel Salomons, "Difficult Decisions: A Review of UNHCR's Engagement with Assisted Voluntary Return Programs," UNHCR Policy Development and Evaluation Services July 2013.
64. Human Rights Watch, "Kenya: Involuntary Refugee Returns to Somalia," September 14, 2016, <https://www.hrw.org/news/2016/09/14/kenya-involuntary-refugee-returns-somalia> (last accessed January 7, 2018).
65. Holly Smith, "Non-Tracing Cases of Culpable Ignorance," *Criminal Law and Philosophy* 5(2)(2011):115–46.
66. Interview with HIAS-Israel director, Jerusalem, December 11, 2012.
67. The majority of these refugees were not officially repatriating, but accepting resettlement to Uganda or Rwanda. None of these refugees, to the best of our knowledge, obtained refugee status in these two countries, and so in practice they would either return to their home countries, or pay smugglers to take them to another country until they found asylum. See Lior Birger, Shahar Shoham, and Liat Bolzman, "'Better a Prison in Israel Than Dying On the Way': Testimonies Of Refugees Who 'Voluntarily' Departed Israel to Rwanda and Gained Protection in Europe," January 2018, ASSAF and the Hotline for Migrant Workers, <http://assaf.org.il/en/sites/default/files/Testimonies%20report%20-%20Jan%202018%20ENG.pdf> (last accessed March 8, 2018); Galia Sabar and Elizabeth Tsurkov, "Israel's Policies towards Asylum Seekers, 2002–2014," Istituto Affari Internazionali Working Paper, May 15, 2015.
68. Interview with AVR official, Tel Aviv, August 7, 2013.
69. Helen Morris and Machiel Salomons, "Difficult Decisions: A Review of UNHCR's Engagement with Assisted Voluntary Return Programs,"

UNHCR Policy Development and Evaluation Services July 2013; Frances Webber, "How Voluntary are Voluntary Returns?" *Race and Class* 52(4): 98–107 at 101.

70. IOM, "Assisted Voluntary Return and Reintegration: At a Glance," 2015, <https://www.iom.int/sites/default/files/our_work/DMM/AVRR/AVRR-at-a-glance-2015.pdf> (last accessed February 26, 2018); Barak Kalir, "Between 'Voluntary' Return and Soft Deportation," in (eds) Zana Vathi and Russell King, *Return Migration and Psychosocial Wellbeing*, New York: Routledge 2017: 56–72 at 56; Refugee Action, "Stories of Return," <www.choices-avr.org.uk> (last accessed April 15, 2015).

71. Refugee Action, "Afghanistan," <www.choices-avr.org.uk> (last accessed April 15, 2015).

Chapter 4

REGRET

As Mol boarded his fight in 2012, he was fully informed of risks, but by 2013 he regretted taking them. That year, nine days before Christmas, six armed men followed him home. As he reached his front gate to his Juba home, they approached him from the side.

"What tribe are you?" they asked him.
"Why are you asking me?" he responded.

One of them grabbed him, but he managed to pull away, and ran to a UN IDP camp nearby.[1]

Twenty-nine years earlier, Mol was a young boy studying in an elementary school in Maiwut, a small town in southern Sudan. One morning, militias arrived at his school and he fled out the back door, later taking a bus to Khartoum, a train to Wadi Halfa, a boat to Egypt, and a Jeep to Israel. He settled in Tel Aviv and was given temporary protection from deportation, but no work visa. Though he managed to survive by finding a job on the black market, in 2012 he was nervous he would be detained, and so asked OBI for help returning, undergoing an interview with HIAS shortly after. Unlike some refugees, he was warned by HIAS that there was food insecurity and violence in South Sudan.[2] He also knew that most past returnees regretted their decision to return home, and that he might feel regret as well.

He nonetheless accepted OBI's free flight and $1,500, arriving in Juba shortly after. He opened a small shop, made a decent income, and was happy with his decision to return until, nine days before Christmas, six men forced him from his home. As of 2014 he still lived in an IDP camp near a military base, where soldiers occasionally fired at camp residents. He had no access to food, as the camp only provided food aid to children, and he feared venturing outside because his ethnicity is clear from Nuer tribal scars on his forehead. When I visited him, latrines in the camp were overflowing, dysentery spreading, and Médecins Sans Frontières evacuating.[3] Today, if Mol could, he would go back in time, reject the help of OBI, and instead live in Israel, even if this meant living in detention.

The case of Mol is distinct from the cases I have addressed thus far. Though Mol was coerced to return, there is little evidence that OBI or HIAS could do anything to improve his circumstances in Israel by the time he left. Moreover, he was well-informed prior to his return, aware not only of the risks in South Sudan, but of the risks of regretting his choice. His case raises the distinct question of whether repatriation should continue if regret is widespread. While we might suppose it should, so long as refugees are informed of risks, perhaps it should not, to prevent future refugees from feeling similar regret.

This dilemma was prevalent in Israel. Of the twenty-eight who returned from Israel prior to 2012, eight of the twenty adults regretted their decision to return. Of the sixty adults I interviewed who returned during or after 2012, a total of thirty-five regretted their decision. Nineteen said this was because they lacked basic necessities, twelve because of ethnic-based killings, and four because of general violence. Many of these individuals were not informed about risks, but some were. Samuel described such regret in vivid detail:

> I knew about the fighting in South Sudan, but was afraid of being in prison in Israel, and returned in 2012. I was at home in Juba, on Monday, when soldiers started shooting at 10:00 pm. They shot at my friends who stayed with me. Two were killed. I put on a pair of shoes – any shoes, it did not matter – and ran to the IDP camp. Today, I cannot leave, as I am in a prison. I think, "in Israel prison would have been better because my enemy is not outside of the prison doors."

The regret felt by refugees returning from Israel is similar to the regret found in other parts of the world. In 2010 thousands of refugees returning to Iraq regretted their decisions to return via UNHCR, wishing they had remained in Iran.[4] In 2001 IDPs returning from Ingushetia to Chechnya regretted their return home, as did refugees returning from Pakistan to Afghanistan in 2015 and from Kenya to Somalia in 2017.[5]

More recently, some refugees returning from Lebanon to Syria have expressed regret, such as Dr. Hassan Ammar:

> I worked as a doctor in Arsal [Lebanon] . . . Jabhat al-Nusra was the main opposition group operating in Arsal . . . They didn't really protect us from the menace of the Lebanese army and Hezbollah . . . So I am here in Idlib [Syria] now, miserable . . . [It was a mistake coming here to Idlib, there is no work.] I lost everything and the ride in the bus was from hell.[6]

If most refugees feel similar to how Dr. Ammar felt, and this predicts regret amongst future returnees, it is not clear if repatriation should be provided

To address whether repatriation should be provided when regret is widespread, we must consider the broader question of whether regret is relevant in determining what services are provided. Imagine, for example, that a hospital found that most patients regretted accepting a given treatment, or a sports team learned that most athletes regretted joining a team, or a university learned that most students regretted beginning a Ph.D. program. The hospital, team, and university may be able to predict that future patients, athletes, and students will feel similar regret. It is not clear whether they should deny their services to prevent this future regret.

In this chapter I shall address the question of whether, both in cases of repatriation and beyond, regret is a reason to deny a service. When I write "service" I refer to a resource, action, or opportunity provided by one agent to another, where no coercion is used, and the point of the service is to give someone an option she otherwise would not have. When I write "reason" I mean a weighty pro tanto moral reason. A "pro tanto reason" provides partial justification for an act. For example, if most people who I teach skydiving to regret their decision, and I can predict that future recipients will feel similar regret, this likely regret provides partial justification for denying you my skydiving lessons. Though there is partial justification, it might still be permissible if there were countervailing considerations, such as you desperately wanting to skydive and being aware of the risks. In certain contexts a pro tanto reason can turn into a decisive reason. When an agent has a decisive reason to do X, then she ought to do X. Imagine I cannot decide whether to help you skydive: on the one hand I know skydiving is fun, on the other hand it is risky. If I know that you will likely regret your decision, the likely regret may be a decisive reason to deny you the lessons. In other words, a decisive reason is a deciding factor when we are otherwise uncertain what to do.

The claim that regret can be a reason to deny a service is controversial. When we predict an individual will feel regret, we are predicting they will experience a reduction in wellbeing. It is these outcomes alone, we might suppose, that give us reason to deny a service, regardless of regret. Mol's likely displacement was reason enough to deny him repatriation. Section 4.1 refutes this claim: Regret can be an independent reason to deny a service, separate from reasons related to welfare-reduction.

Section 4.2 argues that regret is a particularly weighty reason to deny a service when certain properties are present. In Section 4.3 I address cases where refugees are likely to regret both returning and remaining, so it is not clear whether repatriation should continue.

Before I begin, a brief description of what I mean by "regret."

Regret, as I define it, is the feeling that one no longer endorses one's earlier decision because one feels the outcome from the decision is less preferable than what would have occurred otherwise. I put aside cases where individuals regret their decision but not the outcome. A soldier might regret his decision to kill an innocent person to save two innocent lives, feeling this was morally wrong, but not regret the outcome due to the lives saved. I also put aside cases where individuals regret the outcome but not their decision, as when a refugee says it's regrettable civil war broke out in South Sudan, but not regretting her decision to return home because she feels civil war was preferable to life in Israel. In all of the cases I raise, individuals regret their decision and the outcome. We can predict such regret as likely when the vast majority of past recipients of a service regret their choice because of the outcome, and there is reason to believe this regret will likely arise in the future. If, for example, 80 per cent of past recipients of a choice wish they had chosen otherwise, because they prefer the life they would have likely lived, and future recipients hold similar characteristics to past recipients, we can often predict there is an 80 per cent chance that any given future recipient will later feel similar regret. My focus is on the moral status of this future regret.

In focusing on future regret, I focus on individuals experiencing no coercion from the service provider, and who are informed about the risks from the service provider. I put aside cases where individuals are forced to accept a service they regret, or are not told about risks and so regret their decision. Recipients, in all of my examples, are fully aware of the risks, including the risks of regretting their choices.

Why would individuals make choices they know they will likely regret? One reason is that the potential pay-offs are substantial, as with the lottery. Another reason is that recipients cannot quite imagine what it would feel like experiencing this regret, and so take the plunge, later wishing they had not. Individuals may also accept services that take an extended amount of time such that, for every day that lapses, accepting the service is rational and regret unlikely. I might accept a box of chocolates every day, because one box on one day will have minimal harm, and give me joy as I bite into each praline, until I later suffer from health complications, regretting my accumulative decisions.[7]

Finally, a person may accept a service they know they will regret if they have preferences now which they know will change. I might accept tequila at 8:00 pm, knowing I will regret it tomorrow, because at 8:00 pm I prefer drinking tequila and regretting it tomorrow to not drinking tequila and feeling no regret tomorrow. Tomorrow, of course, I will feel differently. It is perhaps unclear if my accepting the tequila is rational, or whether feeling regret tomorrow is rational.[8] Regardless, we often make such decisions and feel such regret. It remains unclear when others should deny us services to prevent this regret from transpiring.

As noted above, my focus is primarily on voluntary services. Though I focus on voluntary services, I assume that a recipient can give their voluntary consent even if coerced by a third party into their decision, so long as they are not coerced by the agent providing them the service. Mol was coerced by the Israeli government into repatriating, as the government would detain him if he stayed, but I assume his consent was valid if OBI was doing no coercing itself and could not stop the coercion. He nonetheless also made a decision he would likely regret. It is not clear what the moral status of this regret was.

Some might suppose that, because Mol was choosing between two objectionable options, he did not truly regret his choice. He only regretted the state of affairs in Israel where he was forced to choose between detention and unsafe repatriation.

While it is true he regretted the state of affairs in Israel where he had only two choices, he also regretted the one choice he did make.[9] More generally, one can regret a state of affairs and the choice made within this state of affairs. A patient diagnosed with cancer can later regret having had to choose between death and life-extending treatment, while still regretting accepting the life-extending treatment because of its painful side effects. This regret for a single choice is important: In many tragic or unjust scenarios, third parties must decide whether to offer an additional objectionable choice, likely to be regretted, or do nothing at all, constraining choices now.

4.1 REGRET AS ONE REASON TO DENY A SERVICE

I propose the following claim: *If a service-provider can predict that an individual will regret accepting a service, and feel no or less regret if they reject the service, preventing regret is one reason to deny the service.*

My claim can be derived from two broad values. First, there is value, all else being equal, in helping individuals live the lives they prefer living. If an individual will later regret their decision to accept a service, and this regret will extend into the remainder of their lives, we can help them live the life they prefer by denying the service. It is true that future preferences are difficult to establish. But when predictions of future regret are strong and long lasting, this future regret ought, at times, to take priority over current short-term preferences.

There is a second value that underpins my general claim, related to control. In general, if a person lacks control over their past decisions, it is better if they are satisfied with their past decisions. Imagine that on October 1 I accept surgery for the afternoon of October 10, and on the morning of the 10th I suffer from locked-in syndrome, unable to communicate whether I still wish to receive the surgery. If I still wish to receive the surgery, and do receive the surgery, it seems that no harm is done: I gave my consent on October 1, and still prefer to have the surgery. In contrast, if I wake up on the 10th and am both locked-in and change my mind, it seems a significant harm occurs as the surgeon inserts the scalpel into my body. It seems that lacking control when my preferences have changed is more disturbing than lacking control when my preferences have not.

When an individual makes an irreversible decision, they are not locked in, but they do they lack control over this earlier decision, given that they cannot change the past. All else being equal, it seems better if this person has not changed their mind about their past decision, given that they cannot control this past decision. If we know ahead of time that a person will likely change their mind about their past decision, and so regret their decision, we have one reason to deny them a service which makes regret possible.

If we have one reason to deny a service that makes regret possible, we have reason to predict whether regret is likely. Determining how we predict regret would require a broad empirical discussion beyond the scope of this book, but one mechanism is to compare those who accept an intervention and those who do not. If the vast majority who accept an intervention regret their choice, but those who reject the intervention do not, and future potential recipients hold similar characteristics to past recipients, this is evidence that regret will be widespread amongst future recipients.

Sometimes, the majority of individuals who accept a service do not regret their decision, but the majority of a sub-group do, and we can predict that future members of this sub-group will experience similar regret. Of the nineteen adults I interviewed who returned from Israel prior to 2012, only seven regretted their decision, but all seven were living in rural areas or without family connections, and all those who felt no regret were living in urban areas or had family connections. This suggests that future refugees returning to rural areas or without family connections may feel similar regret, even if most refugees will feel no regret. Similarly, out of all those I interviewed, the majority returning after 2012 felt regret, suggesting that future individuals returning after 2012 would feel similar regret.

Of course, the above methods alone will not demonstrate that there is a causal relationship between the service and the regret. It may be that those accepting the service are more prone to feelings of regret for reasons unrelated to the service. It would therefore help to supplement this evidence with random control trials (RCTs). Today, limited RCTs have tested the extent that patients are likely to feel regret after the first year of a medical intervention,[10] and more long-term RCTs might be administered. If the vast majority of patients who are randomly given treatment regret their decision to accept treatment, but those randomly denied treatment do not wish they had received this treatment, then this is further evidence that the treatment contributes to regret, creating one reason to deny the treatment to future patients.[11]

RCTs can also determine whether the majority in certain sub-groups regret their decision to accept a service, even if the majority of all recipients do not. We might learn, for example, that the majority of individuals who are younger than twenty-five and suffering from migraines regret a given medical intervention, even if the majority of all recipients do not. Under some conditions, we may be able to use this data to predict that future recipients who are under twenty-five and suffering from migraines are likely to feel similar regret.

The same holds true for the NGO that helped Mol repatriate. OBI could have run a type of RCT for repatriation. This would involve gathering the names of all refugees seeking repatriation, and only helping a randomly selected segment from this group to repatriate, refraining from helping the rest. OBI could then ask those who repatriated if they regreted their decision, and ask those denied repatriation if they wished they had been selected to return. If the vast majority of all or a subgroup regret their decision, while those randomly denied repatriation prefer to have not repatriated, this is evidence that repatriation leads to regret, creating one reason to deny repatriation.

The above claims are relatively modest. They do not establish when regret is a very weighty reason to deny a service, a question I shall address in the next section. They merely establish that future regret is one reason to deny a service, to be weighed against countervailing considerations. They nonetheless face a number of objections.

4.1.1 The Fairness Objection

The first I call the *Fairness Objection*. I claimed above that, to determine if regret is likely, we ought to use RCTs, randomly selecting who is provided the service and who is not. Some might feel it is unfair to force some refugees to stay in detention, rather than help all repatriate who wish to. Others may feel it is unfair to provide repatriation to some, who will then likely live in poverty and insecurity in their home countries, rather than relative security in a host country.

While it is true that such RCTs may be frustrating for those who are not assigned to their preferred group, they are still justified. They are justified if they give us pertinent information on what the effects of an intervention are. Such is the approach taken in medicine. Many medical subjects prefer a pill with an active ingredient, rather than a placebo, but it is often necessary to randomly assign some a placebo to learn what the effects of the active ingredient are. One potential effect of an active ingredient is regret. The same is true for other services: while many may prefer a service, it is often necessary to randomly deny the service to some to learn what the effects of the service are, including whether regret is likely. Even if the service is ultimately provided despite regret, at least recipients will be aware of the likelihood of regret, ensuring their decisions are more informed.

There is another version of the *Fairness Objection*. It may be unfair to deny a service that most regret if some will feel no regret. Those who feel no regret may desperately want this service, and benefit a great deal from its provision. Consider the case of Aken, who arrived in Israel in 2006. For six years for fourteen hours a day she scrubbed hundreds of rooms in hotels in Tel Aviv, eventually saving tens of thousands of dollars before asking OBI for a ticket to South Sudan. She boarded the flight to Juba in 2010 and established a successful company importing dresses from Egypt, never regretting her decision to return.[12] Nor did Nyebol, who saved up far less money before leaving Israel in 2010, and going to Aweil, a small secondary town in the northern region of South Sudan. She quickly bought a small stone house and modest cooker and began selling meals of ground meat, vegetable sauce and warm bread, today making a decent profit while feeling no regret.[13] Importantly, some felt no regret despite the risks to their lives after return. Recall Stephen, from the previous chapter, who knew about the risks of returning, returned regardless, and opened a small cleaning company before fleeing to an IDP camp in 2013. By 2014 he still believed he made the right decision, preferring war in South Sudan to detention in Israel.[14]

While it is true that a minority will feel no regret, it is also true that we cannot know which minority will feel no regret. If we cannot know which individuals will feel no regret, but we can predict that a proportion will feel regret, then we can often predict that any given individual will have a particular probability of feeling regret. For example, if 80 per cent of returnees consistently feel regret, we can often predict that any one individual will have an 80 per cent likelihood of feeling regret. If there was an 80 per cent chance that Aken, Nyebol, and Stephen would feel regret, there was a reason to deny them repatriation given the probabilities known prior to their return. Moreover, even if we think there was no reason to deny them repatriation, given that in reality they did not feel regret, this does not undermine the general claim that regret is one reason to deny a service. Regret is one reason which can, at times, be outweighed by countervailing considerations. One countervailing consideration could be the value of helping the minority return who will be happy with their decision.

4.1.2 The Other Reasons Objection

Some may feel that regret is not even one reason to deny a service, let alone a reason that can be outweighed by countervailing consider- ations. They might raise the *Other Reasons Objection*. In cases where a person feels regret, they are feeling regret about some change in their life, whether it be a reduction in welfare, freedom, or happiness. It is these facts that give reasons to deny the service. Regret creates no addi- tional reason to deny the service.

There are three versions of this objection. The first draws upon the principle of autonomy. In general, one condition for autonomy is that one has sufficient welfare and an adequate range of options.[15] For example, if one is forced to live in a refugee camp one's whole life, or forced to live without adequate food, then one lacks autonomy. It is wrong, therefore, to provide services that significantly reduce welfare or the number of options.[16] It is wrong, therefore, for a repatriation facilita- tor to help refugees return to a country where they will likely be forced to live in IDP camps, or forced to live without security. In cases where we intuitively feel that regret is a reason to deny a service, our intuitions are responding to the reduction in welfare or options, and not to the regret felt.

In some cases, this reasoning may hold. But in cases where a per- son's autonomy will be constrained regardless of whether they accept a service, regret may remain a deciding factor. Mol was choosing between detention in Israel, where he would be unable to travel more than a mile, and returning to South Sudan, able to travel but risking his life. In such a case, we cannot claim that Mol's autonomy would be undermined from returning relative to leaving, because his autonomy was undermined either way. In such a case, his future regret tips the balance against help- ing him return, creating a reason that would otherwise not exist.

Some may insist that, in the case of Mol, life in an enclosed camp in Israel was objectively better for him than life in an IDP camp in South Sudan. Staying would protect his welfare and autonomy more than repa- triating, and this was reason enough to deny repatriation. Regret was irrelevant. Even if one accepts this for Mol, there are many other refugees living in insecurity and poverty in countries of asylum, forced to remain in refugee camps, who are choosing to repatriate to countries with the same levels of insecurity and poverty. Indeed, most refugees repatriating are returning from insecure poor host countries to insecure poor home countries.[17] If these refugees will face similar conditions in remaining and returning, we cannot claim their reductions in welfare and autonomy explain why return is wrong. If we feel it is wrong to assist with return when regret is likely, it seems the regret itself explains this intuition.

There is a second variety of the *Other Reasons Objection*. Some might claim that, though there is reason to deny a service when regret is likely, the regret is not an independent reason to deny a service. When individuals feel regret, they regret something that has happened, such as losing their freedom, or security, or subjective happiness. Regret is just the additional psychological response to such outcomes, rather than an independent consideration. To establish if regret is an independent consideration, we must consider cases where there is regret without any of the painful outcomes associated with regret. In other words, a truly interesting thesis would pull apart regret from other considerations, and this is only possible when considering cases where a person feels regret despite their life going better, such as a refugee who regrets repatriating despite their security and income improving, or an athlete who regrets joining a team despite facing no injury and having improved health. If we imagine such cases, we would unlikely be convinced that regret is a reason to deny a service, given that the lives of the relevant agents have improved.

I do not believe, however, that we can only establish if regret creates a reason to deny a service by isolating it from other properties, such as welfare harms. This is because, more generally, I do not believe we can only establish if a property creates a reason for action by isolating it from other properties. A property can constitute a reason in itself even if only arising when interacting with other properties. If I promise to lend Katie my pen, this promise gives me a weighty reason to lend her my pen, even if this reason is contingent on other properties, such as her still wanting to borrow my pen, her needing to borrow my pen, or her being aware that I promised to lend her my pen.[18] Regret is similarly an independent reason to deny a service, even if contingent on the presence of other properties, such as welfare reductions.

If this is true, then to prove regret is a reason separate from welfare reductions, I needn't isolate regret from these welfare reductions; it is enough to isolate these welfare reductions from regret. This is possible by comparing pairs of cases where welfare is identical for two individuals, and regret is present for one individual and not the other. If we compare two refugees, two athletes, and two patients, and the first of each pair will experience both regret and a welfare reduction after a service, and the second will experience no regret but the same welfare reduction after the service, it seems we have reason to deny the service to the first and not the second. If one refugee returning to South Sudan will experience insecurity and regret, while another refugee is returning to this same insecurity but will feel no regret, it seems the NGO has more reason to deny repatriation to the first refugee than the second. Regret is a distinct reason to deny a service, even if contingent on other properties.

There is a final version of the *Other Reasons Objection*, derived from an argument by Krister Bykvist. We are often faced with choices that we know we will regret, but which we also know will make us happier. Imagine I have a choice to either stay single or get married. If I stay single, I will be happy but regret my choice, feeling marriage was preferable. If I marry, I will be miserable but not regret my choice, still feeling marriage was preferable. It seems my future regret as a single person is not a good reason to get married, because I will be miserable as a married person. Instead, Bykvist argues, we ought to consider how strongly we will later want our future state of affairs, and not whether we will prefer this state of affairs to the life we could have lived. If I will be happier as a single person I should stay single, even if I will prefer being married and so regret not having married.[19] If Bykvist is correct, then when providing a service to others, their future attitudes about their circumstances are what matter, rather than future attitudes about the life they could have lived.

Bykvist's example is helpful for demonstrating that future regret is often a very poor consideration for how we ought to act now. Nonetheless, it does not demonstrate that future regret is never a reason at all. It merely demonstrates that, when we will be miserable with a choice, this future misery creates a countervailing reason to avoid this choice. It remains the case that, when we are faced with two choices with equal predicted misery, future regret is a consideration for how we ought to proceed. Similarly, when we can predict that someone will feel regret when accepting our service, but equally miserable either way, their likely regret is a reason to deny them the service.

4.1.3 Future Preferences Objection

There is a third objection, which I call the *Future Preferences Objection*. It comes in two forms. The first relates to reasons. Some argue that we have little reason to determine what we provide others based on their future preferences. This is because we have little reason in our own lives to make choices based on our future preferences, as our future preferences are not our current preferences, and so what we have reason to want later is not what we have reason to want now. This argument is often made by using an example from Derek Parfit, involving a fourteen-year-old girl who decides to conceive, even though she is extremely ill-prepared to do so. She knows that, once her child is born, she will love her child, and feel it is preferable the child was born. The child, of course, will feel this as well.[20] Neither will regret the decision. This prediction of future non-regret, it is argued, seems like a poor reason for the girl to conceive at such a young age. Though she will later have reasons to affirm her past decisions, these reasons arise from an attachment to her child, and she did not have this attachment prior to conceiving. If future preferences for past actions are poor reasons for these actions at the current time,[21] we should not deny services to others based on predicting their future preferences.[22]

I am not certain that the fourteen-year-old's future affirmation about giving birth gives her no reason to conceive. She may simply have other reasons to not conceive which outweigh this reason: It is better to create a world with children raised by mature parents, who are able to provide sufficient resources and care.[23] But even if one believes that the fourteen year old has no reason at all to conceive, despite her future affirmation, future regret may still give her an additional reason to not conceive. This is because, even if future affirmation for past actions is irrelevant for how one acts at the current time, future regret may remain relevant for how one ought not act at the current time. Imagine an adult who, unlike the fourteen-year-old girl, knows she will not love her child in the future, and knows she will regret having the child, later wishing she could go back in time and never give birth. This woman has a very strong additional reason not to conceive because of her future regret.

There is a second version of the *Future Preferences Objection*. We might suppose that there is value in having autonomy, and having autonomy requires having control over one's life. One is in control even if one's preferences change, and this change leads to subsequent regret.[24] Imagine an eighteen year old makes a choice that impacts her life at thirty, such as getting a tattoo. When she gets the tattoo she has control over her life, so long as her preferences and choices at eighteen are made with full capacity and information.

Even if there is value in having control, control at one point can limit control at another. When this occurs, it seems important to minimize regret during the period of limited control. Imagine an eighteen year old consents to a full-body tattoo which she cannot easily remove. She has control when accepting the tattoo, but her control is limited as a result, given that she cannot change her earlier choice. In such a scenario, it seems her likely regret is one relevant consideration for whether the tattoo parlor ought to provide her the tattoo. This reason may not be very weighty – an issue I shall address in the next section – but it is a reason nonetheless.

4.1.4 Implications Objection

There is a fourth objection to my claim, the *Implications Objection*. It comes in two forms. The first relates to paternalism. If we ought to sometimes deny services to prevent regret, because this fulfills individuals' future preferences, this implies we ought to sometimes require services to prevent regret, because this fulfills individuals' future preferences. We ought to force individuals to accept surgery they will regret not accepting, or force individuals to join a sports team they will regret not joining, or force refugees to return home who will regret remaining. This seems unacceptably paternalistic. It would seem wrong to require a patient to accept surgery even if they will later prefer having had surgery, and wrong to require an athlete to join a team or a refugee to return home, regardless of whatever preferences they will later have.

There are two responses to this objection.

The first begins with a premise: Committing an act constraining options requires a weightier justification than omitting an act constraining options. Tying a person to a chair requires a weightier justification than failing to help a person stand up from a chair.[25] If one accepts this distinction between omissions and commissions, it follows that forcing a person to accept a service requires a weightier justification than denying a person this service. If this is true, then the justification for denying a service may be insufficient for forcing someone to accept a service. If this is true, then claiming we should deny a service to prevent regret needn't imply we should force someone to accept a service to prevent regret.

Some might reject the above explanation, arguing that there is no morally relevant distinction between committing an act and omitting an act.[26] Others may feel that, if an agent has a history of providing a service, suddenly withdrawing the service is more similar to committing an act, comparable to tying a person to a chair. If one holds either of these views, there is a second response to the *Implications Objection*.

In general, there is a distinction between our reasons for providing services and our reasons for not providing services. If a surgeon is providing surgery, or an NGO repatriation, their reasons for providing the surgery or repatriation are because this is what recipients desire, and possibly because this improves recipients' lives. In contrast, surgeons and NGOs have many more reasons for not providing surgery or repatriation: they could engage in other activities instead, such as reading a book, dancing a jig, or helping other vulnerable populations in need. As such, their reasons for denying a service needn't be as substantial; they have plenty of other reasons already. As such, preventing regret may be a decisive reason to deny a service when combined with these many other reasons for denying the service. These other reasons are not present when forcing someone to accept the service. It is therefore wrong to force someone to accept a service merely to prevent regret.[27] Therefore, my claim that we have reason to deny a service to prevent regret needn't imply that we should force someone to accept a service to prevent regret.

There is a second version of the *Implications Objection*. If the reason future regret matters is that a person's future preferences matter, this implies that we have less reason to deny a service if a person will develop adaptive preferences. If OBI learned that past refugees persuaded themselves that life was fine to avoid the frustration of regret, OBI would have one less reason to deny repatriation. Similarly, if there was a magic pill refugees could swallow to rid themselves of regret, OBI would have less reason to deny repatriation.

This is not entirely odd. We often think it preferable to help individuals take high-risk choices if their preferences will remain the same later on. This is true even if their preferences are stable because they adapt their preferences to their surroundings, or use various tools – such as exercise or meditation – which encourage them to maintain their preferences across time. If we know that an individual lacks the psychological disposition to keep their preferences stable, or lacks the tools to do so, it is not odd to deny them a service to prevent regret. Indeed, this is the approach that many organizations already take. For example, in 2006 I chose to join the military, requesting a particular unit, and the recruitment officer asked me a series of questions intended to gauge whether my current preferences to join this unit would likely remain stable across time. The officer accounted not only for my natural dispositions, but whether I was likely to take actions – such as exercise and meditation – that would ensure my preferences did not dramatically change. Of course, the reason the recruitment offer wished to ensure I would not regret my choice was because she wanted to ensure I would be a reliable soldier, rather than because she cared about preventing regret for my own sake. But it is not implausible to imagine a similar system intended to predict regret for the individual's own sake.

Importantly, one may accept this reasoning without holding that adaptive preferences or magic pills make a harmful service right. If an individual is living a safe life, we should often deny a service that will endanger their life even if the person will learn to prefer this dangerous life because she has no other choice. I am merely claiming that, if regret is likely, this future regret is an additional reason to deny a service, a reason that does not arise if an individual will feel no regret due to adaptive preferences.

4.2 REGRET AS A WEIGHTY REASON

Though regret is one reason to deny a service, it is not necessarily a very weighty reason, to be adopted into the policies of organizations and states. The extent that regret is a weighty reason will depend on six relevant properties.

4.2.1 Time

The longer the regret will likely last, the greater the reason to deny the service to prevent regret. For example, certain medical interventions have led to relatively long-term regret, with patients still wishing they had never accepted an intervention a year later, and the regret increasing over the course of the year.[28] Follow-up studies may find that these patients continue to feel regret for years to come. Certain repatriation programs have led to similar long-term regret, with the majority of refugees repatriating to Baghdad regretting their choice years later.[29] Importantly, sometimes repatriation leads to no regret initially, but pronounced regret for an extended time later on. When I initially interviewed another refugee named Bol in 2014, he did not express any regret about returning, but later began feeling that detention in Israel would have been better than displacement in South Sudan. He continued to feel this way when I spoke with him in Kenya in 2018.[30]

The most extreme case will involve individuals feeling regret for their rest of their lives. While this may seem rare, it is not so rare if we acknowledge that, even if an individual will likely feel regret, they needn't feel distress. A person may prefer the life they could have lived while feeling happy, learning to cope with distress through meditation, music, education, and spending time with friends. Such was the case with Bol, who copes with his regret by focusing on his studies in Nairobi and his position as a leader in the Nuer community. Just as a person who has experienced an involuntary medical intervention needn't feel distress the rest of their lives, even if they prefer to have not had the intervention, a person who feels regret needn't feel distress the rest of their lives, even if they prefer to have chosen differently.

4.2.2 All-Things-Considered

The second relevant property is that the regret is "all-things-considered." For an agent to know she feels all-things-considered regret, she would need to consider all life events that resulted from her decision and compare these to every event that would have happened, had she decided differently. She would then need to conclude that the life she would have lived was preferable to the life she was living. Imagine, for example, that a woman stated that she regretted having an abortion.[31] For a woman to truly know she felt such regret, she would need to consider all life events that resulted from the abortion, such as the job she obtained and the relationships she built, and compare these to every event that would have happened had she decided differently, such as the job she would not obtain and the relationships she would not build. If a woman chooses to have an abortion, she usually cannot know if the life she is living now would be very similar or different to the life she would have lived, had she decided differently. Without knowing how life would be different, she would struggle to know if she regretted her choice. If a woman rarely knows if she regrets her past choice, then it is usually wrong for others to deny her a choice based on future regret.

Though it is difficult to know if one feels all-things-considered regret, it is possible to be fairly certain one feels such regret. In rare cases, a person is fairly certain that nearly all possible lives they could have lived, had they chosen differently, would have been better than the best possible life they can now live as a result of the choice they made.[32] In the case of refugees repatriating, there is some evidence this was the case. Of those I interviewed, nearly all considered the very worst life they could have in Israel, including in detention, and felt this would have been preferable to the best life they could now live in South Sudan. They felt that the food and medicine they would have in Israel were more valuable than the freedom they gained from returning.

Now, in reality, the best life with a service is never certainly worse than the worst life without a service. Without a service, tragedy could have occurred. Had Mol not repatriated he may have been deported, killed, or died of natural causes in Israel. Assuming these outcomes were not preferable for him compared to whatever would happen if he returned, the worst possible life without repatriation was not better than the best life with repatriation. There is also the possibility that Mol, now that he has repatriated, will later find refuge in another country. Refuge in another country may be better than the worst life he could have lived in Israel. Moreover, even if he must remain in South Sudan, he may adapt his preferences to his environment, and prefer the life he has to the life he could have had in Israel.

To account for this possibility, we can view this property as scalar: the greater the recipients will feel that the best life with the service will be worse than the worst life without the service, the greater the reason to deny the service. Imagine that we can predict that Mol will feel, after returning, the following three thoughts: *(a) the best life after repatriation must involve resettlement to a safer country; (b) all other outcomes are worse for me than the worst life in Israel; (c) there is only a 1 per cent chance of resettlement to a safe country occurring.*[33] There would be a weightier reason to deny repatriation than if he held the first two thoughts, but also felt there was a 2 per cent chance he could obtain resettlement to a safe country. Conversely, imagine that after returning Mol will feel, looking back at his life in Israel, that there was a 1 per cent chance of either dying in the near future or being deported had he remained in Israel,[34] and dying or deportation in Israel are worse than the best possible outcome in South Sudan. If this feeling could be predicted ahead of time, there would be a weightier reason to deny repatriation than if he will later perceive a 2 per cent chance of dying or being deported had he remained in Israel.

Note that the relevant property above is not the actual probabilities of certain outcomes arising, but the probabilities recipients will perceive after accepting the service. We might imagine Mol thinking, after returning, that he has a 2 per cent chance of being resettled when he has in fact a 10 per cent chance of being resettled. His level of regret is based on a false understanding of the odds of his life becoming much better. Even though his regret is based on a false understanding of the odds, we ought to care about such regret. This is because we ought to care about preferences based on a false understanding of the world, assuming the service provider provides accurate information of the world. Imagine a doctor warns a patient that the risks of paralysis from surgery are 1 per cent, but the patient insists there is a 60 per cent chance of paralysis from the surgery; if the patient rejects the surgery, the doctor ought to respect her preferences. Similarly, imagine a doctor warns the patient that the risks of paralysis are 1 per cent, but the patient will feel regret after the surgery because she will feel it has caused her a 60 per cent chance of developing paralysis at some point in her life. There is a weightier reason to deny the surgery than if the patient will feel there is only a 1 per cent chance she will develop paralysis over the course of her life.

4.2.3 Greater All-Things-Considered Regret from Accepting the Service

In some cases individuals will likely feel all-things-considered regret if they accept a service, but would have felt the same regret had they rejected the service. This might occur if individual's subjective probabilities change as a result of decisions made. A refugee in detention might feel the probabilities of being safe if she returns are high, such that if she were to reject repatriation she would feel regret, but if she repatriated she would perceive the probabilities of protection to be low, such that if she were to accept repatriation she would feel regret. Even when a refugee's perception of probabilities remain the same, her preferences can still change as a result of choices made. A refugee currently in detention may prefer detention to displacement, feeling the worst life with detention is better than the best life with displacement, such that if she remained she would feel regret, but if she returned she would change her mind upon being displaced, feeling the best life in detention would be better. If preferences for outcomes can change based on choices, individuals can feel regret regardless of what they choose.

When individuals will feel the same regret regardless of whether they accept a service, there is a weaker reason to deny the service. Though denying the service would prevent regret – if an individual is denied a service, she cannot regret her choice because she has no choice – it would still lead to individuals feeling that the best life they can live now is worse than the worst life they would have lived, had they access to the service. They will remain in a state where they lack control and their preferences are not met, failing to promote the value of preference-fulfillment described in the previous section. Regret is therefore a weightier reason to deny a service when the all-things-considered regret in accepting the service is greater than the all-things-considered regret in rejecting the service.

4.2.4 Epistemic Transformation

Some might feel that, even if the above three properties are present, individuals should still be provided services they will likely regret. So long as individuals give their informed consent to accept the service, the service gives them control, providing an option they otherwise would not have.

If what matters is that individuals have control, and they have control when giving informed consent to a service, there is a fourth relevant property: regret is a weightier reason to deny a service the less individuals can give informed consent. Individuals cannot give informed consent if they are uninformed, as when the service provider never discloses risks. This might occur if the service provider cannot gather information about the service, including the risks of regret. I assume such scenarios are irrelevant for our discussion: if there is no information about likely regret, we cannot know if there is reason to deny the service to prevent regret. Moreover, I assumed in the introduction to this chapter that recipients are warned of risks, unlike in cases addressed in Chapter 3.

Even if recipients are warned of risks, there is another way they may not be fully informed. They may be accepting a service that is "epistemically transformative."[35]

According to L. A. Paul, an epistemically transformative experience arises if one gains knowledge one cannot gain without the experience.

All experiences are epistemically transformative to an extent. The apple I ate this morning tasted slightly different than other apples I have eaten, and so I could not have known its taste before it touched my tongue. Some choices are more transformative, such as eating a durian fruit for the first time. Some choices are so transformative that a dominant element of one's life will change, and this change is both impossible to understand prior to the choice, and necessary to understand in establishing one's preferences.[36] A woman who has seen only black and white, and is deciding whether to experience the color red, is faced with such a choice,[37] as is a teenager deciding whether to enlist, a deaf individual deciding whether to gain hearing, and a potential parent deciding whether to have children. In such cases, the teenager, deaf individual, and potential parent cannot establish whether they prefer enlisting, hearing, and having children unless they understand what it is like to enlist, hear, and have children, but they cannot understand what these experiences are like until they experience them first-hand. They are therefore faced with an insurmountable information-constraint.[38] In such cases, they cannot make an entirely informed choice because they cannot entirely understand the nature of the risks they are accepting, even if they are informed in words what these risks are. Though they cannot make an entirely informed choice, they nonetheless can consider how much they value new experiences and discoveries for their own sake, as distinct from the subjective goodness or badness of the outcomes. Because each person values new experiences to a different degree, only each person can decide what she ought to do.[39]

Based on the above analysis, governments and organizations should generally not deny services based on their epistemically transformative character. It is true that recipients of the services cannot entirely understand the decisions they are about to make, but each individual is able to decide whether they are willing to accept a decision whose meaning they cannot comprehend.

Nonetheless, special reasons to deny such services arise if regret is likely. If individuals will likely regret a choice, they will later fail to live the life they want to live, and be unable to change their earlier decisions. Given this likely outcome, there are reasons to ensure recipients are especially well-informed about the choices they are about to make. Being especially well-informed requires an especially clear understanding of the service one is accepting. Such a clear understanding is impossible for services that are especially epistemically transformative, as they will change one's life in a manner impossible to comprehend ahead of time. This creates one reason to deny the service likely to be regretted, a reason not arising with regretted services that are not epistemically transformative or with epistemically transformative choices that are not likely to be regretted.[40]

Mol's choice to repatriate was epistemically transformative. Though he was informed about malnutrition in South Sudan prior to this return, and informed of widespread racism against Nuer citizens, he struggled to comprehend the meaning of such malnutrition and racism until actually experiencing these phenomena. This is because he had last lived in South Sudan as a very young boy, and had access to food and security as a young boy, having moved to Khartoum before violence reached his village. Similar experiences were common amongst others who repatriated, such as Bol:

> You know, I should have stayed in Israel. It would have been better to stay in Israel, even in detention . . . Before I returned I had heard about what it was like in South Sudan. I heard about insecurity and the problems. But hearing is not experiencing.[41]

Refugees like Mol and Bol were told about the facts of life in South Sudan – such as persecution and malaria – but struggled to understand the meaning of living with persecution and malaria, having lived their adult lives abroad. When individuals take a plunge into a life that includes elements impossible to understand, and these elements are crucial to understand in forming preferences, they struggle to give truly informed consent. If truly informed consent is necessary for services involving all-things-considered regret, there is a weightier reason to deny epistemically transformative services that lead to all-things-considered regret.

Not all cases of refugee repatriation are epistemically transformative. When refugees are returning to a country they have lived in recently, or for an extensive period of time, they may be returning to conditions they have experienced in the past, and so the experience will not be transformative. But such conditions are increasingly rare. Many refugees returning from Uganda to Rwanda in the 1990s had last lived in the country as small children, having fled in the 1950s and 1960s. Younger refugees returning from Pakistan to Afghanistan in the 2000s had little recollection of the country, having fled prior to the rise of the Taliban. Refugees currently returning from Kenya to Somalia are arriving in towns and villages they have never seen, their parents having fled before they were born.[42] If they cannot give their truly informed consent, the high likelihood of regret may be a decisive reason to deny repatriation.

4.2.5 Transformative Rejections

Of course, even if an individual is accepting an epistemically transformative service, rejecting the service might be equally transformative. Refugees who reject repatriation may find themselves in detention for the first time, an experience whose meaning they cannot comprehend beforehand, and they may feel similar all-things-considered regret to those accepting repatriation.

To account for the potential ways that rejecting a service can be transformative, we ought to add a fifth relevant property: regret is a weightier reason if those rejecting the service will unlikely feel all-things-considered regret at rejecting the service, or unlikely feel their decision was epistemically transformative. Were we to learn that both providing and denying the service were all-things-considered regretful and transformative, there would be a weaker reason to deny the service, as individuals will still be experiencing something incomprehensible and contrary to their future preferences.

In contrast, when individuals accepting and rejecting the service feel similar all-things-considered regret, but only one group is accepting an option that is epistemically transformative, there would be greater reason to deny the option that is transformative. This might occur if refugees are choosing between a life in detention they have already experienced, and a life in a country of origin they have never seen. In such a scenario, if regret is likely for both choices, only the second choice is transformative, and so only the second choice is not fully informed. In such a scenario, there would be a weightier reason to deny repatriation than if both remaining and returning were equally transformative. Similarly, we might imagine refugees who have lived in their country of origin recently, but will experience detention if they remain, and they have never experienced detention before. In such a scenario, if regret is likely for both returning and remaining, only remaining is transformative, and so only remaining is not fully informed. In such a scenario, there would be a weaker reason to deny repatriation.

4.2.6 Causality

There is a final relevant property, relating to causal explanation: The more the service explains the regret, the weightier the reason to deny the service to prevent regret. In cases where the recipient will likely feel regret because of the service alone, and this regret is not dependent on other choices, there is an especially weighty reason to deny the service.

There is some evidence that Mol's all-things-considered regret was largely explained by the repatriation he accepted. While still living in Israel, Mol could not apply for refugee status, and so was forced to work on the black market, and then forced to face detention. He had only two choices: live in detention, or repatriate. When he returned, his only source of income was the money he returned with, his only option of employment was to start a business, and his only place to live was Juba, given the lack of customers in secondary towns. He was then forced to flee to an IDP camp. In a life of few options, repatriation was the only choice that resulted in the outcome of all-things-considered regret. And it is this choice alone that was made possible by OBI. As such, he received help to make a choice that was largely responsible for the all-things-considered regret he felt.

This is not always the case with repatriation. Unlike Mol, some refugees can apply for refugee status, but choose not to. Had they applied, and gained refugee status, they would have gained residency and possibly citizenship. Had they gained citizenship, they could have left and re-entered the safe host country fairly easily. Had they repatriated after this, their repatriation would be reversible, and less likely to be regretted. If in reality they chose to not apply for refugee status and also chose to repatriate, their all-things-considered regret would be from a series of choices, and not just repatriation. Helping with repatriation in such cases is not as problematic. Repatriation would be only one of many choices that, in combination, lead to the regret felt.

Some might suppose that this property is rarely ever found. This is because it is rare that someone feels regret from a single choice alone, or even from a small number of choices. Mol almost certainly made many choices after he repatriated that he regretted, and so the regret he experienced after repatriating would be the result of both repatriation and these subsequent choices. For example, if Mol repatriated, regretted his decision, and then opened a small stand in the IDP camp which he regretted as well, he would feel regret from both repatriating and this subsequent decision. Indeed, there will likely be many decisions he makes in life that lead to the feeling that his life could be better had he decided differently, and so no one decision that will lead to the regret he feels.

Though Mol will likely make other decisions that lead to regret, it is unlikely he will make other decisions that lead to regret that is all-things-considered, and from an epistemically transformative experience. This regret is rare, and so if one does feel such regret from a service, there will likely be an extended period of time where the service alone explains this regret. In the case of Mol, even if he were to regret opening a stall in the IDP camp, he would not feel all-things-considered regret, where the worst life without the stall would have been better than the best life with the stall. If only the choice to repatriate entailed such strong regret, and no other choice explains this strong regret, then repatriation explains this strong regret. The more repatriation explains this strong regret, the greater reason to deny repatriation.

This sixth property is not limited to cases of repatriation. Imagine a segment of the population, despite leading the healthiest of lives, is diagnosed with cancer, and undergo treatment to extend their lives by two years, leading to painful side effects and regret. Imagine they feel regret from the particular choice to accept the treatment, never having made another choice that contributed to the regret felt. In such cases, the doctor providing the treatment would be contributing a great deal to the regret felt, as the regret would arise from the treatment alone, and no other prior or subsequent choices. The hospital would have a weighty reason to discontinue the treatment, assuming the other five properties were present. Similarly, imagine students regret their choice to enroll in a costly degree program, later feeling that their lives would be all-things-considered preferable had they never enrolled, and no other choice explains this all-things-considered regret they feel. If this regret were epistemically transformative, and they wished the degree had never been an option at all, this would give the university an especially weighty reason to discontinue the degree program, or limit it to students less likely to feel all-things-considered epistemically transformative regret.

It is worth noting that, even in cases where regret is an especially weighty reason to deny a service, because there is a strong presence of all six properties, there may still be competing considerations. When these competing considerations are sufficiently weighty, regret may not be a decisive reason to deny the service.

This might be the case if those who will not regret their choice will help the worst off as a result of their choice. Some refugees who repatriated from Israel started their own businesses, felt no regret, and employed other South Sudanese nationals who would otherwise have no employment. Such benefits may justify continuing repatriation services, even if most who repatriate regret their decision. Moreover, we may feel that regret is not a decisive reason to deny a service if, in the distant future, the recipients will ultimately feel no regret. If recipients will likely be satisfied with their decision in the final years of their lives, feeling they ultimately made the right decision, this future satisfaction may create a countervailing reason to support the service, even if regret in the interim period is long lasting.

This same conclusion is relevant outside the sphere of repatriation. Consider policies surrounding contraceptive sterilization. Today, many states deny sterilization to individuals younger than twenty-five,[43] as those younger than twenty-five are statistically more likely to regret their decision.[44] Even if there is a weighty reason to deny sterilization, this reason may not be decisive due to competing considerations. One competing consideration is related to reproduction: the right to control one's reproductive organs to not have children may be especially weighty, such that preventing regret may be insufficient to override this right.[45]

Though regret is not always a decisive reason to deny a service, it is still a weighty reason, and this can have implications for cases where competing considerations are relatively weak. Such is the case, I believe, with repatriation: the interests in refugees returning to unsafe countries is not a weighty enough consideration to trump the importance of preventing of regret, at least when the six properties I described are present. Similarly, athletes' interests in joining a team do not necessarily trump the value of preventing regret, and it is not clear that patients' interests in extending their lives by two years trump the value of preventing regret. Of course, establishing when other interests trump the value of preventing regret will require a broader discussion, but such a discussion is necessary precisely because regret matters.

Until now, I have limited my discussion to individuals who will feel regret in addition to experiencing reductions in welfare and freedom. When Mol repatriated he was forced into an enclosed camp without reliable food and water, and regretted his decision for these reasons. I believe that regret also matters when welfare or freedom will be improved. Imagine a refugee who repatriates from a detention center to Gambella in Ethiopia, never having tasted Ethiopian food or Ethiopian espresso, never having lived in a hot tropical climate, never having slept under a mosquito net, and never having worked as an interpreter, his profession upon arrival. His life is improved according to certain objective criteria – he has more food and mobility – but he regrets his choice nonetheless, a choice leading to a life he could not fully understand prior to repatriating. If an NGO could predict that he would likely feel this way prior to return, I believe the NGO would have a reason to deny him repatriation. This is because, if regret is likely, we ought to demand a higher level of informed consent, impossible to obtain with epistemically transformative services.

Some may reject this last claim, and argue that regret is only a weighty reason to deny a service if welfare or freedom will be reduced. If this true, then we might add this as a final, seventh relevant property. It remains the case that, even if regret is only a reason to deny a service when welfare and freedom are reduced, regret is a reason distinct from these outcomes. Were we to compare two refugees, two athletes, and two patients, and the first was likely to feel regret because her welfare was reduced, and the second unlikely to feel regret despite her welfare being reduced, there would be a reason to deny repatriation to the first and not the second. Regret is a distinct reason, and ought to be taken seriously by organizations and states.

4.3 REGRET-EITHER-WAY

Even if we accept that regret is a weighty reason to deny a service, a dilemma remains for what I call regret-either-way cases. These occur when most accepting a service feel regret that is epistemically transformative and all-things-considered, but those declining the service feel the same level of regret as well. Therefore, both continuing and discontinuing the service will likely lead to unfulfilled preferences later on. In such cases, I argued in the previous section, there is weaker reason to deny the service compared to cases where individuals will only feel regret if they accept the service. Nonetheless, it is still not clear what those providing the service ought to do.

For example, when the Israeli government completed a mass detention center for asylum seekers in 2013, thousands were either detained or denied work visas, leading thousands to return.[46] Though many regretted their choice to return, many who stayed in Israel regretted staying, feeling they were wasting their youth either homeless in Tel Aviv, or in a cold detention cell in the middle of the Israeli desert.[47] In such cases, it is not clear if NGOs should help with return. They will cause regret if they do, but if they don't, individuals will still prefer the life they could have lived.

A similar issue may be prevalent in other countries of asylum. Some Iraqi refugees feel regret at having arrived in Germany, because of unemployment, xenophobic attacks, and being forced to live in cramped quarters with strangers. They wish to return home as a result.[48] If many regret returning, a sub-set of refugees may both regret remaining and returning. Importantly, they might regret remaining and returning to the same degree. This would be the case if both those accepting and those rejecting return feel all-things-considered regret to the same extent, and the outcomes are both transformative to the same extent.

A similar dilemma arises outside the sphere of repatriation. Imagine a woman in her early twenties wishes to undergo sterilization, and evidence demonstrates that she will likely feel regret if she does, and regret if she does not due to the distress of potentially having a child she does not want.[49] Were a hospital to deny her sterilization to prevent regret, it would prevent the regret of unwanted sterilization, but would cause her to feel her preferences have not been met. It is not clear what the hospital ought to do, just as it is not clear what repatriation facilitators ought to do.

Some might claim that it is irrational for someone to feel regret either way. Either a woman will regret sterilization, feeling the best outcome with sterilization is worse than the worst outcome in remaining fertile, or she will regret remaining fertile, feeling the best outcome remaining fertile is worse than the worst outcome with sterilization. Similarly, either a refugee will regret returning, feeling the best outcome in returning is worse than the worst outcome in staying, or she will regret staying, feeling the best outcome in staying is worse than the worst outcome in returning. How could both possibly be true?

I believe they can. As humans, our preferences change depending on what we are experiencing, and so we can regret a choice because we chose it. For example, some people get married because they cannot imagine life without their partner being better than life with their partner. After several years of experiencing life with their partner, they begin feeling that the worst life without their partner would be better than the best life with them. If they get divorced, they may again change their mind, pining for their ex-spouse precisely because they are gone, again feeling the worst life with their ex-spouse would be better than the best life without them. While marriage is reversible – a person can marry and divorce multiple times – many choice pairs are not. When a person must select one of two irreversible choices, she may face angst and indecision, knowing that all-things-considered regret is inevitable. When we are tasked with helping others reach one of two likely regret-table decisions, it is similarly unclear what we ought to do.

A similar question arises when we cannot contact past recipients, and so cannot establish the extent of regret-either-way. For example, the UN struggles to contact those who have repatriated to rural areas, or who have migrated to other countries after repatriating. More worry-ingly, the UN may have the most difficulty contacting those most feel-ing regret, because those most feeling regret have no access to a cell phone in an IDP camp. It is not clear if repatriation should continue if the UN cannot determine whether refugees returning feel greater regret than those remaining.

The above dilemmas can be avoided by appealing to considerations of freedom and safety. If refugees will face detention if they stay, in addition to regretting their choice either way, then return should be facilitated because at least they will be free. If refugees will face persecution if they return, in addition to regretting their choice either way, return should not be facilitated because at least they will be safe. Similarly, if refugees' regret is uncertain, because they cannot be contacted, return should be facilitated to avoid detention, or not facilitated to protect safety.

However, this is unhelpful if refugees will face detention if they stay and lack safety if they return, possibly regretting either outcome. In such cases, there is another relevant consideration. Sometimes, one choice is reversible while another is not. For example, a woman rejecting steriliza-tion can always accept sterilization later, but if she accepts sterilization now she cannot reject sterilization later.[50] Repatriation often has this asymmetry. Many refugees can return later if they do not return now, but cannot live in the host country if they do return now.[51] When such asymmetry arises, facilitators should not necessarily block refugees from repatriating if they cannot predict regret, or if regret is likely to occur either way.[52] But facilitators should nudge refugees to stay rather than return. This can be instituted by requiring that refugees wait a specified amount of time before their transport is provided, or by emphasizing the extreme dangers of returning and the advantages of staying.

The idea of nudging individuals to accept a reversible decision over an irreversible one has been applied in spheres outside repatriation. It has been noted by Wang et al. that, when a person posts on Facebook, they are posting a largely irreversible post, and many posts are life-altering, involving an offensive joke or an incriminating photo, undermining a person's career, reputation, and friendship network. Because of this risk, Wang et al. suggest that users first be asked if they are certain they wish to post a comment. The authors emphasize that this is justified to mitigate regret,[53] and I believe the reason it mitigates regret is that, if users post now they cannot reverse the act, but if they do not post now they can always post later.

While only nudging is justified in most cases, completely denying a service may be justified if, one day in the future, a choice will become reversible. In such cases, service providers should wait until this day arrives before helping. Such was the case for Theodore, a South Sudanese refugee who arrived in Israel in 2007 and lacked any legal status in Israel by 2012. Had he returned he would be unable to re-enter Israel, but he had a child with his Israeli partner, qualifying him for residency status in the future.[54] Once he gained this status, he would be able to enter and exit Israel at will, and repatriating would no longer be irreversible. Refugees like Theodore should not be assisted with repatriation until they gain residency status, making repatriation reversible. Under such a policy, refugees would be able to avoid the all-things-considered regret that comes from irreversible decisions, while still accessing repatriation later on.

In many cases, irreversible choices will likely remain irreversible. Many refugees will be unlikely to gain legal status to exit and enter their host country at will. In such cases, we cannot wait until their choices become reversible if they never will. The irreversible nature of their choice is not a reason to deny it, even if regret is possible.

4.4 CONCLUSION

When an individual consents to a service, we might provide it, believing it is her choice to make. But a choice at one time can conflict with preferences at another. Mol later regretted leaving Israel, feeling his life would have been better had he remained, and such regret was perhaps predicable: the UN warned of likely violence and poverty, and past returnees expressed similar regret to what Mol felt. When regret for a life-altering service is predictable, regret is one reason to discontinue the service.

In cases where someone will likely feel regret from both receiving and rejecting the service, the service should be denied if it is irreversible, assuming it will become reversible in the future. When the service will not become reversible in the future, it should be provided but still discouraged: those given the service should be told the benefits of its rejection and the disadvantages of its acceptance.

Repatriation facilitators today rarely explore whether their assistance leads to regret. If regret is ever a reason to deny a service, they ought to interview past returnees, asking them if they regret their choice to return. Most refugees will unlikely experience all-things-considered regret. But some may feel regret similar to that of Mol. We should know about such experiences, accounting for preferences refugees have later, when assisting them now.

NOTES

1. Interview with Mol, Juba, December 30, 2013.
2. Thousands of civilians had been killed between 2011 and 2012 because they were Dinka, Nuer, Bari, or Shilluk, depending on the region one was in. See Human Rights Watch, "Southern Sudan: Abuses on Both Sides of Upper Nile Clashes," April 19, 2011, <https://www.hrw.org/news/2011/04/19/southern-sudan-abuses-both-sides-upper-nile-clashes> (last accessed April 25, 2011).
3. After I left in January 2014, they returned.
4. UNHCR Briefing Note, "Iraqi Refugees Regret Returning to Iraq, Amid Insecurity," October 19, 2010, <http://www.unhcr.org/uk/news/briefing/2010/10/4cbd6c9c9/unhcr-poll-iraqi-refugees-regret-returning-iraq-amid-insecurity.html> (last accessed 26 February 2018).
5. Yevgenia Borisova,"Scared Refugees Regret Returning Home," *Moscow Times*, April 27, 2001, <http://old.themoscowtimes.com/sitemap/free/2001/4/article/scared-refugees-regret-returning-home/253777.html> (last accessed July 29, 2017); Agence France-Presse, "Somali Refugees Regret Returning Home from Kenya," June 27, 2017, <http://m.news24.com/news24/Africa/News/somali-refugees-regret-returning-home-from-kenya-20170627> (last accessed July 28, 2017); Josh Smith, "Limited Options Leave Afghan Refugees Reluctant to Return Home," Stars and Stripes, January 2, 2015 <https://www.stripes.com/news/middle-east/afghanistan/limited-options-leave-afghan-refugees-reluctant-to-return-home-1.322129#.WXuNBdPyvre> (last, accessed July 28, 2017).
6. Martin Chulov, "Thousands of Refugees and Militants Return to Syria from Lebanon,"*The Guardian*, August 14, 2017, <https://www.theguardian.com/

world/2017/aug/14/thousands-refugees-militants-return-syria-from-leb-anon-hezbollah> (last accessed January 19, 2018).

7. Warren Quinn's example of the self-torturer is a case of similarly rational regret. See Warren Quinn, "The Puzzle of the Self-Torturer," in *Morality and Action*, Cambridge: Cambridge University Press 1993 at 198.

8. For a related discussion on the rationality of similar decisions, see Michael Bratman, "Toxin, Temptation, and Stability of Intention," in (ed.) Jules L. Coleman, *Rational Commitment and Social Justice: Essays for Gregory Kavka*, Cambridge: Cambridge University Press 1998 at 59–83.

9. Interview with Mol, Juba, January 4, 2013.

10. Maria Margarita Becerra Perez, Matthew Menear, Jamie C. Brehaut, and France Legare, "Extent and Predictors of Decision Regret about Health Care Decisions: A Systematic Review," *Medical Decision Making* 36(6) (2016):777–90.

11. Another possibility is to run natural experiments. In some cases, individuals cannot access a service due to random acts of nature which nobody could control. If those who accessed the service feel regret, but those who could not access the service and wanted the service feel no regret, then this is further evidence that the service will cause regret. See Thad Dunning, *Natural Experiments in the Social Sciences: A Design-Based Approach.* Cambridge University Press 2012.

12. Interview with Aken, Juba, March 21, 2012.

13. Interview with Nyebol, Aweil, March 30, 2012.

14. Interview with Stephen, Juba, January 4, 2014.

15. Joseph Raz, *The Morality of Freedom*, Oxford: Oxford University Press 1988 at 373.

16. Raz 1988 ibid. at 408

17. Jeff Crisp, "The Politics of Repatriation: Ethiopian Refugees in Djibouti, 1977–1983," *Review of African Political Economy* 30(1984):73–82; US Department of State IDIQ Task Force Order No. SAWMMA13F2592, "Field Evaluation of Local Integration of Former Refugees of Tanzania," April 15, 2014, <http://www.state.gov/documents/organization/235057.pdf> (last accessed March 1, 2015).

18. For more examples demonstrating this point, see Shelly Kagan, "The Additive Fallacy," *Ethics* 99(1)(1988):5–31 at 18.

19. Krister Bykvist, "Prudence for Changing Selves," *Utilitas* 18(3)(2006): 264–83.

20. Derek Parfit, *Reasons and Persons*, Oxford: Oxford University Press 1984 at 357–61.

21. Kate Greasley, "Abortion and Regret," *Journal of Medical Ethics* 38(2012):705–11; R. Jay Wallace, "Justification, Regret, and Moral Complaint: Looking Forward and Looking Backward on (and in) Human Life,"

in (eds) U. Heuer and G. Lang, *Luck, Value and Commitment: Themes from the Ethics of Bernard Williams*, Oxford: Oxford University Press 2012.

22. Elizabeth Harman, "'I'll be Glad I Did It' Reasoning and the Significance of Future Desires," *Philosophical Perspectives* 23(2009):177–99.

23. R. Jay Wallace, *The View from Here: On Affirmation, Attachment, and the Limits of Regret*, Oxford: Oxford University Press 2013 at 96–108.

24. Richard Arneson, "Autonomy and Preference Formation," in (eds) Jules L. Coleman and Allen Buchanan, *In Harm's Way: Essays in Honour of Joel Feinberg*, New York: Cambridge University Press 1994: 42–75; Paddy McQueen, "The Role of Regret in Medical Decision-Making," *Ethical Theory and Moral Practice* 20(2017):1051–65 at 1057–8; Raz 1988 ibid. at 371.

25. Of course, if helping her sit up would be absolutely costless, and I idly stand by as she struggles to get up, my actions are awfully similar to an individual who restrains her, forcing her to remain in the chair. But I take it that my actions still require a more substantial justification if I restrain her, rather than merely fail to help.

26. Bennett, for example, rejects the idea that there is something morally distinct about doing an act versus allowing an act. See Jonathan Bennett, *The Act Itself*, Oxford: Oxford University Press 1998 ch. 6–8.

27. This is consistent with the claim that preventing regret may be one pro tanto reason to force someone to accept a service. This reason is simply insufficient on its own to justify doing so.

28. Further clinical trials are required to establish just how long this regret lasts, but we should not assume that it will not last based solely on the possibility that individuals will adapt their preferences. See Perez et al. 2016 ibid.

29. UNHCR Briefing Note 2010 ibid.

30. Interview with Bol, Juba, December 21 2013; interview with Bol, Nairobi, February 7, 2018.

31. Greasley 2012 ibid. at 708 and 710.

32. When I write "better" I mean preferable. When I write "best possible life" I mean "most preferable possible life." I shall use the words "better" and "best" in these senses for the remainder of the chapter.

33. Indeed, the odds of him resettling to a truly safe country are likely less than 1 per cent, given his very limited resources to travel, the lack of food security in neighboring countries, the low rates of resettlement, his inability to resettle directly from South Sudan, and the greater challenges of resettling as a single male. See UNHCR, "Figures at a Glance," 2016, <http://www.unhcr.org/en-us/figures-at-a-glance.html> (last accessed December 9, 2017); Annelisa Lindsay, "Surge and Selection: Power in the Refugee Resettlement Regime," *Forced Migration Review* 54(2017):11–13.

34. The chances of Mol dying within Israel were extremely low, given the excellent medical care and food security he would obtain, and his odds of deportation were extremely low, given that the courts in Israel have consistently blocked government attempts to deport refugees to South Sudan. At most, the government is able to detain asylum seekers indefinitely. See Ilan Lior, "Israel Seeking to Get around Court Ruling and Go on Coercing Refugees into Deportation," *Haaretz*, August 31, 2017, <https://www.haaretz.com/israel-news/.premium-1.809855> (last accessed December 9, 2017).
35. L. A. Paul, "Transformative Choice," in *Transformative Experience*, Oxford: Oxford University Press 2014 at 1–51.
36. Paul 2014 ibid. at 1–51.
37. Frank Jackson, "Epiphenomenal Qualia," *Philosophical Quarterly* 32(1982): 127–36.
38. Paul 2014 ibid. at 115.
39. Paul 2014 ibid. at 115.
40. No such reason to deny the service would arise with epistemically transformative services that are not likely to be regretted because, if there is no regret, there is less of a need for a high level of informed consent. The epistemically transformative nature of the service is less problematic.
41. Interview with Bol, February 11, 2018.
42. Awa M. Abdi, "In Limbo: Dependency, Insecurity and Identity Amongst Somali Refugees in Dadaab Camps," *Refuge* 22(2)(2005):6–14; Agence France-Presse, "Somali Refugees Regret Returning Home from Kenya," June 27, 2017, <http://m.news24.com/news24/Africa/News/somali-refugees-regret-returning-home- from-kenya-20170627> (last accessed July 28, 2017); Ahimbisibwe Frank, "'Voluntary' Repatriation of Rwandan Refugees in Uganda: Between Law and Practice-Views from Below," *Journal of Identity and Migration Studies* 11(2)(2017):98–120; Lindsey N. Kingston, "Bringing Rwandan Refugees 'Home': The Cessation Clause, Statelessness, and Forced Repatriation," *International Journal of Refugee Law* 29(3)(2017):417–37; Sarah Pour Rohani and Sima Pour Rohani, "Afghan Immigrants in Iran and Citizenship," *Journal of Public Administration and Governance* 4(4)(2014):18–28; US Committee for Refugees and Immigrants, "USCR Country Report Rwanda: Statistics on Refugees and Other Uprooted People," June 2001, <https://reliefweb.int/report/burundi/uscr-country-report-rwanda-statistics-refugees-and-other-uprooted-people-jun-2001> (last accessed February 10, 2018); Anisseh Van England-Nouri, "Repatriation of Afghan and Iraqi Refugees from Iran," *International Journal on Multicultural Societies* 10(2)(2008):144–69.
43. Engender Health, Chapter 4 in *Contraceptive Sterilization: Global Issues and Trends*, 2002, <https://www.engenderhealth.org/files/pubs/family-planning/factbook_chapter_4.pdf> (last accessed December 4, 2017).

44. Kathryn M. Curtis, Anshu P. Mohllajee, and Herbert B. Peterson, "Regret Following Female Sterilization at a Young Age: A Systematic Review," *Contraception* 73(2)(2006):205–10; S. D. Hillis, P. A. Marchbanks, L. R. Tylor, and H. B. Peterson, "Poststerilization Regret: Findings from the United States Collaborative Review of Sterilization," *Obstetrics and Gynecology* 93(6)(1999):889–95; Denise J. Jamieson, Steven C. Kaufman, Caroline Costello, Susan D. Hillis, Polly A. Marchbanks, Herbert B. Peterson, and the US Collaborative Review of Sterilization Working Group, "Comparison of Women's Regret after Vasectomy versus Tubal Sterilization," *Obstetrics and Gynecology* 99(6)(2002):1073–9.

45. More specifically, the right to control your organs to not have children may be weightier than the right to control your organs to have children, which is why denying sterilization is wrong, even if a person will later wish they could have children. However, it might also be the case that individuals can sufficiently control their reproduction if given other forms of reversible contraceptives, rather than sterilization. If we learned to create a form of reversible contraception that was as effective, safe and convenient to use as sterilization, then there may be a weightier reason to deny sterilization to prevent regret.

46. Galia Sabar and Elizabeth Tsurkov, "Israel's Policies Towards Asylum Seekers, 2002–2014," Istituto Affari Internazionali, Working Paper May 15, 2015 at 11–13; and Ruvi Ziegler, "'No Asylum For Infiltrators': The Legal Predicament of Eritrean and Sudanese Nationals in Israel," Immigration, Asylum, and Nationality Law 29(2)(2015): 172–191.

47. Ilan Lior, "Prison Service Confiscates Heaters from Asylum Seekers Detained in Holot," *Haaretz* 10 January 2015; Gideon Levy and Alex Levac, "Seekers Find Asylum with Crammed Rooms and No Heat," *Haaretz* 1 February 2014.

48. Rebecca Collard, "Meet the Iraqi Refugees Who Are Going Back to Iraq," Time, March 31, 2016, <http://time.com/4278325/iraq-refugees-return/> (last accessed January 21, 2018).

49. McQueen raises similar type of cases with women who accept sterilization. McQueen 2017 ibid. at 1062.

50. This is not always the case; some sterilization is reversible. However, it is not guaranteed. See K. Jayakrishnan and Surneet N. Baheti, "Laparoscopic Tubal Sterilization Reversal and Fertility Outcomes," *Journal of Human Reproductive Sciences* 4(3)(2011):125–9; and A. Ramalingappa and Yashoda, "A Study on Tubal Recanalization," *Journal of Obstetrics and Gynecology of India* 62(2)(2012):179–83.

51. Theophilus Kwek, "Between Home and a Hard Place: Paying Refugees to Return," The Diplomat, October 27, 2017, <https://thediplomat.com/2017/10/between-home-and-a-hard-place-paying-refugees-to-return/> (last accessed February 15, 2018).

52. This is because providing individuals the service can protect their autonomy. Protecting an individual's autonomy entails letting them choose whether they will accept the service or not, even if they may ultimately regret their decision. Patty McQueen makes a similar claim. She argues that autonomy can be a reason to provide a service even if regret is likely. While she does not specify when autonomy is a reason to provide a service when regret is likely, it seems clear that autonomy is a reason to provide a service when regret will occur either way, or when the extent of regret cannot be determined. See McQueen 2017 ibid. at 1056–8.

53. See Yang Wang, Pedro Giovanni Leon, Xiaoxuan Chen, Saranga Komanduri, and Gregory Norcie, "From Facebook Regrets to Facebook Privacy Nudges," *Ohio State Law Journal* 74(2013): 1308–34.

54. Interview with Theodore, Jerusalem, July 17, 2014.

Chapter 5

PAYMENTS

In 2007 Sweden offered $7,150 to families who agreed to return to Afghanistan.[1] A year later the Ghanaian government, working with the UN, gave refugees $100 to return to Liberia.[2] Soon after, Denmark began offering $18,700 to anyone returning to Iraq, Iran, and Somalia.[3] In 2010 the British National Party promised, if elected, to give $78,000 to migrants or refugees who agreed to leave the country.[4] The BNP was never elected, but in 2011 the UK government handed over $3,500 in cash to families agreeing to return to Zimbabwe.[5] In 2013 the Israeli government followed suit, providing $3,500 to thousands of asylum seekers who agreed to repatriate. Those who refused were provided a slightly different offer: $3,500 to accept a one-way ticket to Uganda, Rwanda, or Ethiopia, where they would be unable to obtain any legal status. Three years later Germany began paying $7,000 to Afghan nationals returning home,[6] and Australia promised $20,000 to Rohingya returning to Myanmar.[7]

In all of these cases, and many more,[8] a large proportion of those returning were owed asylum and protection from deportation.[9] Given that they were owed asylum, it is not clear if paying them to leave was morally permissible. Perhaps it was, because only forcing refugees to leave is wrong, but perhaps it was not, given the dangers of returning.

Payments for repatriation are not new, but there are few studies describing such payments, nor analysis as to whether they are ethical.[10] This chapter both describes payments, and considers whether they ought to be given.

Section 5.1 describes "Motivation Payments," when governments hope to motivate refugees to unsafely leave the country. I argue that such payments are only morally permissible if refugees can again access the host country after leaving. In Section 5.2 I address "Coercion Payments." These occur when refugees are coerced to return, because they are forced to endure insecurity, detention, or enclosed camps if they remain. Humanitarian organizations, eager to help, provide money to refugees who decide to return. Such was the case in the 2000s, when the UN provided $400 to thousands of refugees repatriating from Kenya to Somalia[11] and to hundreds of thousands of refugees repatriating from Pakistan to Afghanistan.[12] If refugees are accepting money to return because remaining is unsafe, it is not clear if organizations should be providing such money. I argue that organizations should provide money if refugees will likely face detention or insecurity regardless, and if providing money does not causally contribute to government coercion. In Section 5.3 I address an objection: refugees ought to be given funds to expand their choices, even if the funds motivate them to forego asylum, and even if returning contributes to government coercion. I argue that payments may, indeed, be justified for this reason, but only in cases where the funds are substantial enough to ensure long-term safety.

Before addressing the above claims, a clarification is in order. As in previous chapters, I assume that states ought to grant asylum to survival migrants, including those fleeing poverty or general violence, rather than only those fleeing persecution. As before, one can reject this assumption while still accepting my general conclusions about payments. If you think that only those fleeing persecution have a right to remain, or only those fleeing violence, then assume my analysis is limited to such individuals. I aim not to establish who has a right to asylum, but whether those with a right to asylum ought to be paid to leave.

5.1 MOTIVATING REFUGEES TO LEAVE

Motivation Payments occur when states offer refugees full protection, and motivate them to decline this protection by providing money on the condition they leave. It is unclear if such money is ethical.

Consider, for example, a case involving Gatluak, a refugee who fled southern Sudan as a boy during the Second Sudanese Civil War in the 1980s. As an adult he eventually took a boat to Egypt and crossed into Israel with the help of smugglers. In Israel he was denied the right to apply for refugee status, but was provided a temporary visa as part of general protection granted to all southern Sudanese. His life in Israel was satisfactory, as he was free to work in a hotel, could access medical care, and experienced no coercive pressure to leave. When South Sudan became an independent country in 2011 Gatluak feared returning due to his ethnic identity, and because he lacked family to ensure basic food security after returning. He nonetheless returned in 2012 when offered $1,500 by the Ministry of Interior. Six months later he was living on a concrete patio outside a police station in Juba, without shelter, savings, job skills, family or daily meals. When I visited him that year, strangers were providing him limited food, medicine, and water. He did not know how long their charity would last, and had no access to state services.[13] I was unable to reach him when the South Sudanese Civil War broke out in 2013. Based on my interviews with other former refugees who returned, he was likely displaced, and possibly killed.

We might suppose that Gatluak's choice to return was not voluntary because he did not have true protection in Israel, lacking any refugee status. We might also suppose we cannot know if he was a genuine refugee, precisely because his claim was never assessed. But Motivation Payments are also provided by states assessing claims and providing asylum. In the 1990s Australia recognized tens of thousands of Afghan asylum seekers as refugees, providing them access to social services, work visas, and healthcare, later offering each family $10,000 to repatriate in 2002, leading 3,400 refugees to return.[14] Similarly, in the 1990s the German government assessed the claims of all Bosnian asylum seekers, and recognized them as refugees, later using money to motivate them to repatriate to a country where they faced extreme poverty and discrimination.[15] Sweden, when providing payments to Afghan refugees, similarly assessed their claims and provided them refugee status before paying them to repatriate.[16] In all of these cases states were offering protection, but also paying refugees to decline such protection. It is not clear if such payments were ethical.

The UN's official position is that such payments can be ethical if conditions have substantially improved in refugees' countries of origin.[17] The UN also endorses payments when, though conditions remain unsafe, there is evidence that conditions are improving, and refugees' status will soon be revoked. For example, the UN approved of payments to refugees returning from Ghana to Liberia in 2008, and to refugees returning from Pakistan to Afghanistan in 2014.[18] However, the UN remains silent on cases where return is clearly unsafe and will remain unsafe, and governments still wish to encourage return using monetary incentives. Furthermore, even when conditions have improved, it remains unclear whether payments are ethical if conditions are still dangerous enough to warrant continued protection.

Before considering when such monetary incentives are ethical, it is worth establishing if there is any empirical evidence that money motivates return. In the cases noted, refugees may be responding only to fear of future detention, or a belief that conditions have improved in their countries of origin. If money itself does not motivate return, there are no true Motivation Payments.

There is some evidence that money did motivate refugees to leave Israel. I analyzed Israeli labor statistics on payments provided to Eritrean, Sudanese, and South Sudanese refugees agreeing to repatriate or accept resettlement to Rwanda and Uganda. In the months refugees received more money to leave, more tended to leave, even when detention rates were the same as in other months, and conditions in countries of origin remained the same.[19] For example, in October 2013, the government paid all asylum seekers $1,500 if they left the country, and also began detaining asylum seekers. There were 180 who left. While the number decreased when the High Court of Justice ordered asylum seekers released in November, from the beginning of December the government passed new legislation to detain refugees, and also increased the grant money to $3,500, such that detention policies were similar to October, but the payments greater. That December 295 returned compared to October's 180, a significant increase.

There was also evidence that the government used money to encourage return precisely when detaining refugees was legally difficult. In March 2013, the UN and Israeli High Court of Justice pressured the government to stop detaining refugees and the government immediately increased the payments from $100 to $1,500. Between March and August 2013 the government found other ways to detain refugees, using a series of by-laws to circumvent the court's instructions, and never also raising the payments. The High Court ordered the end of these by-laws in September, requiring the government to again release refugees, and the government soon began talks to increase the payments again. When the government stalled and never actually released any refugees, the High Court forced the government to release refugees in October, and the prime minister rapidly approved an increase in payments from $1,500 to $5,000.[20]

The above does not prove that money motivated return, as other unknown variables – such as the rate of policing, or refugees' changing access to information – may also explain the variation in return rates. Nonetheless, this provides supporting evidence that money motivated return, and similar evidence was found in studies on repatriation from Pakistan to Afghanistan, where refugees were provided $100 to repatriate;[21] from Tanzania to Burundi, where refugees were provided $41 to repatriate;[22] and from the UK to Zimbabwe, where refugees were paid $3,500 to repatriate.[23] In all of these cases, there were either positive correlations between payments and return rates, or governments stated that payments were to increase return rates.

If payments motivate refugees to leave, and are intended to motivate them to leave, are they morally permissible? To answer this question, we might first consider whether refugees are accepting payments voluntarily. If they are not, they are victims of forced return, and may be wronged for this reason.

In general, there is broad consensus that individuals' choices are voluntary if four criteria are met: individuals must be fully informed; they must have full capacity;[24] they must not be coerced into their decisions; and they must have at least one alternative that ensures an acceptable level of welfare.[25] For an example where the last condition is not met, imagine a starving person accepting a job at slave wages. Their choice is involuntary, as both working and not working involve unacceptably low levels of welfare. Refugees are similarly involuntarily repatriating when choosing between life in detention and starvation upon return, or starvation in a refugee camp and persecution upon return.[26]

Though choices are not voluntary when both the choice and alternatives are unacceptable, a single choice can be voluntary if this choice is acceptable and all alternatives are not. Katy Long has persuasively demonstrated this point, using the example of a destitute person who has no choice but to accept a job they feel is fulfilling, and which meets their welfare needs.[27] The person's choice seems voluntary because they have one acceptable option. Following Long's reasoning, a choice is also voluntary if one is leaving behind a life with a high level of welfare, and choosing a life without basic necessities, such as a businesswoman voluntarily choosing to quit her pleasant and well-paying job and move to a desert island. Her choice seems voluntary because she has at least one acceptable alternative.

Based on the above criteria, refugees who accept money and return are doing so voluntarily if they are returning to a country where their lives will be safe and their conditions reasonably acceptable or if, though returning is unsafe, they have the option of staying in the host country with reasonably acceptable conditions. In the case of Israel, these conditions were arguably met for Gatluak, though not for all refugees in the country. These conditions were also met for some refugees returning from Australia and Sweden to Afghanistan in 2002 and 2007, as some refugees returning could access full rights if they remained.

Therefore, the minimal conditions for voluntariness can be met with payment schemes. But even if returns are voluntary, there is another reason to believe the payments are unethical. In general, voluntary offers can be unethical if they demean the recipients of the offers, or create negative externalities for others.[28] When governments pay refugees to repatriate, this may reinforce the stereotype that refugees are unwanted members of society, whose exit is worth whatever money the government is willing to pay. Payments also send a demeaning message to refugees: "We do not want you so much," the payments imply, "that we are willing to sacrifice money so that you repatriate." The greater the money offered, the stronger this message. For this reason, the British National Party – a fringe party and openly xenophobic – was willing to give $78,000 to each asylum seeker returning, far more than any other party or government in the world. Refugees have no alternative but to be exposed to this demeaning treatment, whether they accept the money or not.

I believe this is a strong reason to deny payments some of the time. When the government pays only African refugees to leave, as part of a racist immigration policy, the payments are impermissible because of their demeaning nature alone. I shall elaborate on this reasoning in Chapter 8. However, when all refugees are paid to leave, and there is no racist intention, I do not believe the demeaning nature of the payments creates a decisive reason against their provision. Refugees can turn down the offer, and send a strong counter-message back: "We want to stay so much that we are willing to reject your money in order to stay." The greater the money offered, the stronger this counter-message. Rejecting payments can strengthen the expressed commitment of refugees to stay, publicizing how dangerous it is to leave.

There is a second, stronger reason to believe payments are impermissible. In general, offers are impermissible if they involve great physical harm. For example, if I agree to lend you money, and you agree to give up your right hand if you do not pay me back, no judge should force you to give up your right hand if you cannot pay me back. In contract law, judges do not uphold such "unconscionable contracts" partly because it is wrong for the state to encourage self-harm, given that states were created partly to protect residents within their borders. Were the state to encourage self-harming activity, it would also be forcing citizens to pay taxes into a system that made such encouragement possible, and there is a limit to what the state should force citizens to do.[29] Self-harming contracts are also involuntary in one sense: When an individual accepts money on the condition they accept harm in the future, their future selves will be forced to accept this harm. There is a limit to the harm our future selves should be forced to accept, even in light of previous consent.

Payments to repatriate are types of "unconscionable contracts." In Israel, refugees arrive at the office of a civil servant, sign on a dotted line, their legal status is revoked, and they receive $1,500 in an envelope once boarding a flight. If they attempt to re-enter the country, they will likely be deported, because they earlier received money to forgo future protection.[30] Throughout this process, refugees are encouraged to risk their lives, rather than continue to accept protection, and the public is forced to pay taxes into a system that enforces this contract.

We might claim that, in cases where refugees cannot re-enter the host country, it is not payments that are wrong, but the enforcement of the agreement. If refugees who tried to re-enter Israel were deported, then this was a form of *refoulement*, the illegal forced removal of refugees according to international law. The problem is the wrongful rejection of genuine refugee claims, and this would be wrong whether there were payments or not. However, even in cases where refugees are merely paid to repatriate, but not blocked from re-entering, they may still face immediate danger after return, and be unable to apply for a visa, travel back to the safe country, and again apply for refugee status. When civil war broke out in South Sudan, almost half of my respondents fled to an IDP camp, and could not leave the camp safely because of their Nuer identity. They also lacked money to pay for a private vehicle to pick them up, take them swiftly to the airport, and flee the country by air. If the risks of return are significant, then the government is still encouraging self-harming activity, even if it is merely paying for repatriation, rather than paying for the revoking of all future refugee rights.

The above reasoning suggests that payments are morally permissible for those not at risk from return. Some refugees return to countries with considerably improved conditions, or have private means for ensuring protection. Others are returning to unsafe countries but have practical and legal mechanisms to later re-enter the host country if they find themselves in danger.

This last condition may be realized if refugees are paid to leave with re-entry visas and evacuation services in the event of a crisis, similar to the evacuation provided to citizens abroad. The risks to return would be limited, and so such payments permissible. As noted in Chapter 3, a close version of this policy was implemented in the 1990s, when the governments of Sweden, France and the UK provided funds to Bosnian refugees to travel to Bosnia, and allowed them to re-entry to these states' territories if they were unhappy with their return.[31] On a more limited scale, UNHCR organized "go-and-see" visits for Burundian refugees in Tanzania, providing them payments to repatriate, along with transport to again re-enter Tanzania if they so wished.[32]

Many of these programs did not allow refugees to change their mind more than once: They could repatriate, re-enter the host country once, and if they repatriated a second time they were not offered a visa to again re-enter the host country. A better policy would allow refugees to exit and enter the host country at will, and access emergency evacuation if necessary. Such payments would merely incentivize return, without significantly sacrificing refugees' safety.

5.2 PAYING REFUGEES FORCED TO LEAVE

In many cases refugees will likely face serious risks if they return, but if they stay they will be detained, destitute, confined to camps, or likely deported in the future. In such cases, humanitarian organizations often provide their own funds to refugees hoping to return. These organizations clearly provide payments for involuntary returns, given that refugees are choosing between two unacceptable alternatives, but perhaps they should provide payments if refugees are unlikely to be offered full rights regardless. It may be better to encourage individuals to return via a repatriation program than to remain in detention or enclosed camps, possibly violently deported.

Such was the case in the mid-2000s in Tanzania, when anti-refugee sentiment increased, prompting the government to confine Burundian refugees to camps, denying them the option of working in urban areas, and forcing many into detention-like conditions. The UN, hoping to help alleviate these conditions, offered refugees funds to repatriate, even as evidence grew that they would be unlikely to find food security in Burundi with the money offered.[33] In 2002 UNHCR made a similar decision in Pakistan and Iran, where over three and half million Afghan refugees were living at the time, many detained, denied visas, and threatened with deportation.[34] UNHCR offered refugees willing to return $50, a significantly large proportion of the average annual income for refugees. It later managed to raise enough money to pay $400 to each refugee repatriating, hoping to eventually pay each family $3,000.[35] Its payments were a critical factor in explaining at least some refugees' reasons for returning, and critics argued that the UN was complicit in mass forced returns.[36]

The same dilemma arose in Kenya, where the UN began paying Somali refugees $200 if they returned home, and an additional $200 once they arrived. Some refugees explained that they agreed to return because it was better to accept money now than be deported later. One mother-of-five explained, "Since our future is unclear, I do not want to be put on a lorry and sent back, so I will take the money." A 70-year-old grandfather similarly stated:

> What will happen if we don't voluntarily return? Will we be forced back in a few months? We are feeling a lot of pressure. If we will be forced back anyway, it would be better to take the benefits now rather than just get kicked back later.[37]

Around the time Somali refugees began leaving Kenya, Eritrean and Sudanese refugees began leaving Israel, either returning home or accepting a one-way ticket to Uganda or Rwanda.[38] At first, the government was the only body to provide funds to refugees leaving, and most NGOs refused to cooperate, feeling refugees were accepting funds because they feared detention or deportation. Evidence suggests that refugees were indeed accepting funds for these reasons. According to the labor statistics, more refugees accepted funds to leave when detention increased, and fewer left when detention decreased, even when payments remained the same.[39] For example, in August 2013 the government passed a new "Anti-Infiltration Law" allowing the Ministry of Interior to arrest refugees, and 170 left the country. When the High Court of Justice nullified the law in September, only eighty-nine left, even though payments remained the same. When no one was actually released by October 2013, the number of those leaving increased again, from eighty-nine to 180, even while payments remained the same as in September.

Some refugees, though destitute or in detention, were afraid to leave and remained homeless or detained. As the Israeli government seemed unwilling to change its policy, some NGOs eventually offered refugees an additional payment of €800 to those returning home, feeling this was preferable to no help at all. One of the first refugees to receive such funds was Tigisti, her husband Massawa, and their two children.[40] All were included in the 38,000 individuals whom UNHCR considered likely refugees,[41] despite the Israeli government denying them this status. Tigisti decided to return because, though UN officials were resettling some refugees to Europe and North America, she did not know if she would be included in this resettlement. When her husband was detained in 2013, NGOs tried to help him obtain a visa, but failed, instead offering the family €3,200 to repatriate. After returning she and her family fled to Ethiopia where they gained asylum-seeker status but no work visas to support themselves.[42] Given that her return was involuntary and unsafe, and given that she would not have returned had it not been for the funds, it is not clear if the NGOs ought to have provided these funds.

The dilemma becomes more complex when we consider cases of asylum seekers who have yet to prove they are refugees. Consider, for example, the case of Daniel. In the 1980s Daniel's land was confiscated by the government of Ethiopia, forcing him to migrate to Sudan, where he joined a church, found work as a bus driver, and married, but faced harassment from authorities. He eventually moved with his wife to Egypt, where they gave birth to their daughter, but faced similar harassment from authorities, deciding eventually to pay smugglers to take them into Israel in 2006. Once there, they found jobs in hotels, and a school for their daughter, but in 2012 they separated and Daniel was forced to raise his daughter alone. When anti-immigration protests spread, he was detained and his daughter placed in foster care.

Government officials told him he could re-join his daughter if they returned to Ethiopia, and he at first refused, demanding access to a Refugee Status Determination process. He finally agreed to repatriate when an NGO offered him €800 for this purpose. After returning he and his daughter lacked medical care, food security, reliable shelter, and access to Daniel's ancestral land.[43]

We might at first suppose that, in the case of both Tigisti and Daniel, NGOs should not have provided money for return. Tigisti and her family were faced with only two unreasonable options, and so their choice was involuntary. They were therefore victims of *refoulement*, the illegal forcing of refugees back to their countries of origin. Daniel was not necessarily a refugee, but he was denied the right to apply for refugee status, and so was wrongfully forced to return before given this right. If his return was unsafe, he too was faced with only unreasonable alternatives, and so his choice was involuntary as well.

Even if Tigisti and Daniel's choices were involuntary, NGOs might defend their actions with one of two arguments. As argued in Chapter 2, it is not wrong to help a person with an involuntary choice if there is no other choice available. If I am shot by a sniper and run to the hospital, I can give valid consent to a doctor for risky life-saving treatment, even though my options are all unacceptable due to the sniper. Refugees may be capable of giving valid consent to humanitarian organizations, even though they have no reasonable options, so long as organizations can do little else to help. If they can help – such as by trying to stop government detention – they should, but if they try and fail then payments are justified. Similarly, in cases where refugees and asylum seekers are denied access to food and shelter, organizations are justified in providing funds to repatriate if there is nothing else they can do. Though refugees are involuntarily accepting money, it would be even more involuntary for refugees to lack the resources to return. This reasoning has been expressed by the UN, which states that humanitarian organizations should assist refugees to obtain their legal rights but, if this fails, assisting with return may be ethical if the "life or physical integrity of refugees in the country of asylum is threatened."[44]

The above argument, however, is not quite enough to justify the payments. Humanitarian organizations could make return possible without actively encouraging return by offering thousands of dollars for the opportunity. Though refugees may be deported, this is not certain, and so encouraging return risks undermining potential protection in the future.

Humanitarian organizations may present a second argument defending payments. Encouraging refugees to return is justified because returning is better than waiting. Waiting involves possible deportation, even if deportation is not certain. If Daniel had remained in detention, immigration officials would likely one day open his cell door, force him and his daughter into a van, drive them to the airport, and handcuff both to their seats as the plane lifted off. Deportations throughout Europe involve psychiatrists forcibly sedating refugees on flights and officials physically sitting on refugees until they cannot breathe, move, or fight back.[45] If deportation is traumatic, it would be better to return without resistance, and money encourages such non-resistance.

Though payments may encourage a safer return compared to forced deportations, there is a good reason organizations should still avoid payments. As noted in Chapter 2, organizations should avoid causally contributing to coercive policies. When organizations encourage refugees to return from detention, they may encourage the government to detain even more refugees.

Such a causal phenomenon may have been at play in some of the cases raised in Chapter 2. In 1994 and 1995, when UNHCR began facilitating the repatriation of Rohingya refugees from Bangladesh to Burma, it provided limited aid to the most vulnerable, and various forms of aid upon return. The Bangladesh government may have significantly increased its pressure on refugees to return precisely because it knew that aid would be provided.[46] And, in general, if facilitating return frees up places in detention, then encouraging return by providing payments would free up places even more, contributing to the further detaining of refugees.

Such payments may also make petitions against government policies very difficult, by making it difficult to prove that return is coerced. If refugees quietly accept cash in an envelope, the public may believe the return is voluntary and safe, when it is not. This may undermine advocacy efforts, further fueling detention policies. In contrast, if refugees stay in detention they send a message to the public that they are afraid to return and, if they are eventually deported, the public and judicial system will be aware that they were forced to return.

Payments to repatriate may similarly discourage refugees from protesting for a change in policy. Activist refugees in Israel, who strongly

opposed payments schemes, would organize hunger strikes in detention, long marches through the desert, and incessant media campaigns
documenting precisely why they left Eritrea, Ethiopia, Sudan, and South
Sudan.[47] They focused on encouraging others to lobby the government
so their claims could be heard. These politically active refugees felt that
repatriation funds undermined legitimate resistance. This phenomenon was especially clear in 2012. That year, a month before the planned
deportation of all South Sudanese nationals in Israel, hundreds of refugees protested regularly against the deportation. Soon after, represen-
tatives from OBI began offering money to return, explaining to refugees
that deportation was likely.[48] The campaign to prevent deportation
slowly died down, as more returned, and fewer remained in detention.
As the campaign died down, the detention rates steadily increased,
leaving fewer behind to protest and encouraging even more to return.
As more returned, more detention cells became available, allowing the
government to detain even more refugees.

More evidence is needed to fully establish whether payments causally contribute to coercion in the way described. If they do, humanitarian organizations have a weighty reason to discontinue payments. Not
only will denying payments help mitigate coercion, but it needn't force
refugees to stay in detention or face a traumatic deportation. Refugees
can still avoid such traumatic deportation by acquiescing to deportation
without money. Immigration authorities informed Daniel that his flight
would be paid for by the government, and he could board the flight without handcuffs any time. Organizations, in paying him to return, did not
substantially increase his options; they merely encouraged acquiescence
to a silent return, potentially undermining advocacy in the process.

The above reasoning suggests it would be ethical for humanitarian
organizations to provide payments in either one of two scenarios. The
first is where individuals will be safe if they return, either because conditions are generally safe, or because they are receiving enough money
to pay for security and necessities after return. Such a return would be
voluntary because the choice would entail an acceptably high level of
welfare upon return, even if the alternative is unacceptable detention in
the host country.

The second scenario is when, though return is unsafe, refugees will
continue to lack rights regardless of whether they are paid money to
repatriate and, in being paid money, this does not causally contribute to
the coercion of others. Money needn't contribute to coercion if it does

not undermine advocacy efforts, and if the government has unlimited means of coercion. If the government has enough cells in detention centers to detain all refugees in the country, encouraging one refugee to return would not free up a cell to detain a new refugee. The government might also, rather than detain all, simply deny work visas to all, forcing all into destitution, such that if one person left, this would have no effect on the overall level of destitution. Such is possibly the case when the Kenyan government denies work visas to Somali refugees,[49] such that when a given Somali refugee repatriates to Somalia, this has potentially no effect on the overall level of destitution amongst Somali refugees in Kenya.

In the case of Daniel, the first scenario did not arise, as return was unsafe. The second scenario might have arisen if he would likely remain in detention regardless, and there was space in detention to detain all asylum seekers and refugees. Helping him return, in this hypothetical case, would not contribute to the detention of others, and would help him and his daughter avoid a traumatic deportation or a life of destitution in Israel. In reality, however, the second scenario unlikely arose: there were a finite number of detention cells in Israel, and encouraging him to return freed up his detention cell, leading to the detention of others.

Similarly, in the case of Tigisti there is evidence that neither scenario arose. Return was unsafe and there was a strong chance she and her family would eventually secure refugee status, either in Israel or another safe country. The UN in Israel recognized them as likely refugees and the High Court of Justice had called for ending indefinite detention of Eritreans. Growing international pressure on Israel also led some Western governments to accept refugees for resettlement from Israel. NGOs should not have encouraged her and her family to acquiesce to returning, given that protection was likely. Even if they ultimately would be deported, at least the deportation would be public, unlike quietly returning with money. A public deportation can serve as evidence in a court petition against the government's actions, and help contribute to greater protection for others in the future.

Some may find the implications of my last point disturbing. By denying payments to refugees, organizations would be creating a scenario where some refugees will not agree to return and may ultimately face deportation, possibly experiencing police brutality in the process. To deny refugees payments would seem to be using them as a means, discouraging them from returning quietly for the purpose of creating a traumatic return, all to help bring about a change of policy. Encouraging refugees to repatriate, in contrast, addresses the welfare of refugees as individuals with their own needs, rather than objects for a larger scheme.

Though it is true that refusing to give money is for a larger scheme, it is not true that refusing such money is wrongly using refugees. For we generally do not wrongly use others when denying them an option, unless we have a duty to provide the option. If I refuse to buy someone cigarettes, out of concern for others who would be harmed from second-hand smoking, I am not using the person as a means, because I have no duty to buy them cigarettes. Similarly, if organizations have no duty to pay refugees to return, they are not using refugees when refusing to provide money to leave.

Some might claim that organizations do have a duty to pay refugees to leave, so long as these organizations are *personal advocates*. As noted in Chapter 2, a personal advocate assists those who cannot assist themselves. A lawyer is a personal advocate, and has a duty to defend her client in the best way possible, even if successfully defending her client causes others to be wrongfully accused. Organizations can permissibly provide payments to help refugees who cannot help themselves, even if this contributes to the coercion of others.

While it is true that some organizations serve as personal advocates, many do not; IOM and UNCHR claims to be providing repatriation for the benefit of all, rather than only the individuals they help return. More importantly, personal advocates still have some duties towards others; significant harm towards others provides them reason to discontinue their services, just as a lawyer has reason to discontinue representing clients if this significantly increases wrongful accusations. If the making of payments by organizations significantly undermines efforts to end coercion, they have a weighty reason to end such payments.

5.3 CHOICE

We have, at this point, reached two conclusions: Governments should avoid payments that encourage return, unless they also provide re-entrance visas; and humanitarian organizations should avoid payments that encourage return, unless return is safe and does not significantly contribute to government coercion. These two conclusions imply that, when payments are wrong, governments and organizations are still permitted to allow refugees to repatriate without money.

If this is true, some may raise the following objection: If some refugees will return regardless, perhaps it is best to provide money, giving them options to start a business, go to school, or migrate to another region in their home country. Even if refugees would not really have returned on their own, and are indeed motivated to return because of money, they will have more choices if they are given money, and there is value in having more choices.

Consider the case of Bessie. In 2009 she fled an East African country, went to Egypt, and paid smugglers who promised to take her to Israel. As she began her journey across the Sinai, she was kidnapped and tortured, but managed to flee to Israel, where she was given a year of residency, and a room at a center for victims of human trafficking. She wished to return to her country of origin with some investment money, a choice made possible when she was offered €800, enough money to help her survive during the first year after repatriation in her home village. She used the money for rent, school for her children, and to start a chicken farm. The chickens she bought eventually died, she lost her life savings, and she regretted her decision, but she is still happy she had the opportunity to leave Israel with money. Though the money ultimately did not help her reintegrate and access sufficient welfare, she feels it increased the chances she would, giving her one choice she otherwise would not have.[50]

The idea that money enhances choices is widely accepted by a number of repatriation programs. The UK program was called "Choices,"[51] and emphasized that funds assist refugees to start businesses or receive job training, an option they otherwise would not have. In Pakistan, the UN emphasized that refugees should have the choice of returning to Afghanistan with funds, rather than no assistance at all, even if they faced insecurity after returning.[52] The UN made similar claims when helping refugees return from Tanzania to Burundi.[53]

Though money may provide an extra choice, it can also diminish choices in the long run. If a refugee is unlikely to access sufficient welfare after returning, they will lack various choices associated with welfare, including the choice to leave a given village, send one's children to school, and access sufficient nutrition. A year after Bessie returned, she lacked the full range of employment choices open to her in Israel, and the resources to leave her home village. As a result, she also lacked the resources to ensure she could access an adequate range of food, shelter, and education for her children. Similarly, two years after South Sudanese refugees repatriated, most of my respondents were confined to IDP camps without resources to leave. Their choices were severely constrained compared to their co-nationals in Israel. If organizations and governments will not send money to those who have already returned, and those who return will later need money to access mobility and basic necessities, then funds may diminish rather than expand choices.

Some may feel that, even if money diminishes choices in the long run, the value of choices is that it provides individuals control over their lives, and there is value in giving refugees control over how they repatriate. Money can provide such control. But even if there is value in permitting individuals to control their own lives, there seems less value in actively providing resources for control if this undermines welfare in the long term, and especially if this contributes to regret later on. If I provide an individual cigarettes, they have more control over their lives because they can choose to smoke, but it seems my assistance is of little value if regret is likely, and if smoking will contribute to cancer later on.

This suggests that providing money for repatriation is ethical if it enhances control and protects long-term choices associated with security and welfare. We might imagine a refugee returning with her husband and four children, and each family member receiving $78,000, as promised by the BNP in the UK. Such funds would total almost half a million dollars, providing refugees the choice to decide where to live, what they eat, and when to move again. It is nonetheless not enough to claim any amount of money increases choices. Money can enhance choices at one time, but constrain them at another.

5.4 CONCLUSION

Immigration control involves not just force, but incentives. One major incentive is the money refugees receive when agreeing to return home. If it is wrong for governments to endorse physically unsafe contracts, it is wrong for governments to provide payments to encourage unsafe repatriation. In cases where the government is detaining refugees or threatening them with deportation, organizations should avoid providing payments that significantly contribute to these policies. Organizations should limit payments to those who are not foregoing safety, and whose return does not significantly contribute to the detention of others. While it is true that all payments may enhance choices to an extent, repatriation can undermine choices when refugees lack basic necessities after returning home.

Given these conclusions, governments and organizations should consider changing their current practices, adopting the following policy changes.

5.4.1 Re-Entry Visas

In cases where return entails significant risks, states should only provide funds if they also provide refugees the option of living in the host country later on. States ought to either provide residency visas prior to returning, or agreements where refugees can be re-admitted with the same legal status they had prior to leaving. Such a policy was implemented in the 1990s and 2000s when the French, German, and British governments provided funds to Bosnian refugees repatriating, allowing them to re-enter France, Germany, and the UK if they felt unsafe after returning.[54] An even stronger policy would also include evacuation services for refugees who find themselves displaced after returning, and unable to reach safety. Were states to deny refugees re-admission and evacuation, refugees may fail to gain a visa to board a flight to safety, forcing them to pay smugglers and endangering their lives. Such was the case when Israel paid South Sudanese refugees to return, and some faced persecution, with one paying smugglers to try reaching Egypt, Sudan, and Israel. His experience entailed significant risks. Such risks could have been avoided had he been given a visa to safely and legally re-enter Israeli territory.

5.4.2 Post-Return Research

To ensure that repatriation does not lead to long-term destitution and persecution, states should also conduct post-return research. After a significant number of refugees and asylum seekers have returned, states should interview a random sample of such returnees, and conduct an in-depth study on the mortality rate, rate of displacement, and other risk factors related to their return. If the vast majority of returnees are living in safety and security, it may be justified to provide funds to encourage return without the corresponding promise of allowing later re-entrance. Repatriation would be far more permanent, but at least safe. However, this policy must ensure absolute safety for returnees, including access to food security, healthcare, and reliable protection from the police and military.

5.4.3 Encouraging Voluntariness

In cases where refugees are in detention or enclosed camps, and their return is coerced, humanitarian organizations should avoid immediately providing payments for return. They should first do everything possible to try and secure a fair Refugee Status Determination process for those in detention and enclosed camps, and help them obtain access to freedom, work visas, and social services. Organizations should only provide repatriation funds to those whose lives will certainly not be at risk, or for those likely to face deportation if they stay, and only if this does not significantly contribute to further deportation, detention, or destitution amongst other refugees. They should not provide payments to populations likely to gain refugee status if they refuse repatriation, as was the case with Tigisti, or for those whose departure will contribute to others being detained, as was the case with Daniel.

Though organizations should not provide money for return in these cases, they may still provide money to those who have already returned. So long as organizations do not widely publicize that they are helping refugees after return, such assistance needn't encourage repatriation, while still helping protect returnees in their countries of origin. For example, a small NGO in Israel began paying for the school fees of children whose families had already returned to South Sudan. Such assistance, because it was relatively limited, and only provided to those most in need after return, did not have a major impact on encouraging future repatriation. Indeed, the NGO actively discouraged South Sudanese from returning, even while assisting those who felt compelled to repatriate to avoid detention. Such policies focused on post-return aid as the need arose, rather than pre-return funds to encourage return.

The above three policies would create a more ethical repatriation, but there remain serious dilemmas. It is not clear if payments are always morally permissible when provided to migrants returning to safe countries. Such payments may be wrong if only some ethnic groups are offered money to leave, in order to cater to the interests of racist voters. We may also feel uncomfortable with officials approaching our friends, classmates, and colleagues, telling them they can have cash if they leave, after having established themselves in our neighborhoods, schools, and businesses. Payments do not become ethically unproblematic when return is safe. But they are especially problematic when return is unsafe. Facilitators should avoid encouraging such unsafe returns, and reconsider their current practices.

NOTES

1. UNHCR, "Sweden, Afghanistan, UNHCR Sign Deal on Voluntary Return of Afghans," June 23, 2007, <http://www.unhcr.org/468bb4542.html> (last accessed February 26, 2018).
2. Naohiko Omata, "'Repatriation is Not for Everyone': The Life and Livelihoods of Former Refugees in Liberia," New Issues in Refugee Research, UNHCR Working Papers 213, 2011.
3. *The Telegraph*, "Denmark Offers Immigrants £12,000 to Return Home," November 10, 2009, <http://www.telegraph.co.uk/news/worldnews/europe/denmark/6533845/Denmark-offers-immigrants-12000-to-return-home.html> (last accessed February 26, 2018).
4. Jon Smith, "BNP Would Offer £50,000 to Leave the Country," *The Independent*, April 29, 2010, accessed November 17, 2014 <http://www.independent.co.uk/news/uk/politics/bnp-would-offer-pound50000-to-leave-the-country-1957668.html> (last accessed November 17, 2014).
5. Frances Webber, "How Voluntary are Voluntary Returns?" *Race and Class* 52(4)(2011):98–107.
6. Anthony Faiola, "Germany Learns How to Send Back Migrants: Pay Them," *Washington Post*, March 19, 2016, <https://www.washington-post.com/world/europe/germany-learns-how-to-send-back-migrants--pay-them/2016/03/19/0685dc96-e552-11e5-a9ce-681055c7a05f_story.html?utm_term=.a238f163b615> (last accessed July 28, 2017).
7. Oliver Holmes and Ben Doherty, "Australia Offers to Pay Rohingya Refugees to Return to Myanmar," *The Guardian*, September 19, 2017, <https://www.theguardian.com/world/2017/sep/19/australia-offers-pay-rohingya-refugees-return-myanmar> (last accessed February 15, 2018).
8. Maria Helene Bak Riiskjaer and Tilde Nielsson, "Circular Migration: The Unsuccessful Return and Reintegration of Iraqis with Refugee Status in Denmark," Research Paper No. 165 2008; Richard Black, Michael Collyer, and Will Somerville, "Pay-to-Go Schemes and other Non-Coercive Return Programs: Is Scale Possible?" Improving US and EU Immigration Systems, Migration Policy Institute 2011, <https://www.migrationpolicy.org/pubs/

pay-to-goprograms.pdf> (last accessed February 26, 2018); Sarah Whyte, "Abbott Offers Asylum Seekers $10K to Go Home," *The Sydney Morning Herald*, June 21, 2014, <https://www.smh.com.au/politics/federal/abbott-offers-asylum-seekers-10k-to-go-home-20140620-3ajr6.html> (last accessed February 25, 2018).

9. For a description of this "minimal standard" of those who have a claim to asylum, see Javier Hidalgo, "Resistance to Unjust Immigration Restrictions," *The Journal of Political Philosophy* 23(4)(2015):450–70. Importantly, as noted in the previous chapters, both those supportive of more open borders, and those supportive of closed borders, tend to agree that forced return is unjust if those returning will be unable to ensure their right to life is protected. For a defense of this claim against objections, see Appendix A, and for authors supporting this claim, see Joseph Carens, "Aliens and Citizens: The Case for Open Borders," *Review of Politics* 49(1987):251–73; Matthew Gibney, *The Ethics and Politics of Asylum*, Cambridge: Cambridge University Press 2004; David Miller, "Immigration: The Case for Its Limits," in (eds) A. Cohen and C. Wellman, *Contemporary Debates in Applied Ethics*, Malden, MA: Blackwell Publishing 2005 at 193–206.

10. For the few discussions on payment schemes, see George Stoessinger, *The Refugee and the World Community*, Minneapolis: Minneapolis University Press 1963 at 68–71 and 202; Michael Barnett and Martha Finnemore, *Rules for the World: International Organizations in Global Politics*, Cornell: Cornell University Press 2004 at 106.

11. Agence France-Presse, "Somali Refugees Regret Returning Home from Kenya," World 24, June 27, 2017, accessed January 6, 2018 <https://m.news24.com/Africa/News/somali-refugees-regret-returning-home-from-kenya-20170627> (last accessed January 6, 2018).

12. IRIN News, "Will the UN Become Complicit in Pakistan's Illegal Return of Afghan Refugees?" November 10, 2016, <https://www.irinnews.org/analysis/2016/11/10/will-un-become-complicit-pakistan%E2%80%99s-illegal-return-afghan-refugees> (last accessed January 8, 2018).

13. Interview with Gatluak, Juba, March 15, 2012.

14. Fethi Mansouri and Sally Percival Wood, "Exploring the Australia-Middle East Connection," in (ed.) Fethi Mansouri, *Australia and the Middle East: A Front-Line Relationship*, London: Tauris Academic Studies 2011 at 9.

15. Ulrike von Lersner, Thomas Elbert, and Frank Neuner, "Mental Health of Refugees Following State-Sponsored Repatriation from Germany," *BMC Psychiatry* 8(88)(2008):1–16.

16. UNHCR, "Sweden, Afghanistan, UNHCR Sign Deal on Voluntary Return of Afghans," June 23, 2007, <http://www.unhcr.org/468bb4542.html> (last accessed February 26, 2018).

17. Katherine Haver, Felicien Hatungimana, and Vicky Tennant, "Money Matters: An Evaluation of the Use of Cash Grants in UNHCR's Voluntary

Repatriation and Reintegration Programme in Burundi," Policy Development and Evaluation Service 2009, <https://reliefweb.int/report/burundi/money-matters-evaluation-use-cash-grants-unhcrs-voluntary-repatriation-and> (last accessed February 26, 2018); Helen Morris and Machiel Salomons, "Difficult Decisions: A Review of UNHCR's Engagement with Assisted Voluntary Return Programmes," United Nations High Commissioner for Refugees Policy Development and Evaluation Service 2013, <http://www.unhcr.org/uk/research/evalreports/51f924209/difficult-decisions-review-unhcrs-engagement-assisted-voluntary-return.html> (last accessed February 26, 2018).

18. UNHCR, "Funding Proposal: Enhanced Voluntary Return and Reintegration for Afghan Refugees (EVRRP)," March 2015, <http://www.unhcr.org/562defe26.pdf> (last accessed February 26, 2018).

19. For an overview of key events and return rates, see Appendix B.

20. Ilan Lior, "Israel to Offer African Migrants $5,000 to Leave," *Haaretz*, October 10, 2013, <https://www.haaretz.com/.premium-israel-to-migrants-leave-and-get-5-000-1.5282114> (last accessed October 30, 2013).

21. Eric Davin, Viani Gonzalez, and Nassim Majidi, "UNHCR's Voluntary Repatriation Program: Evaluation of the Impact of the Cash Grant," Office of the United Nations High Commissioner for Refugees (UNHCR) in Kabul 2009, <http://www.unhcr.org/uk/research/evalreports/4fcf23349/unhcrs-voluntary-repatriation-program-evaluation-impact-cash-grant-altai.html> (last accessed February 26, 2018).

22. Katherine Haver, Felicien Hatungimana, and Vicky Tennant, "Money Matters: An Evaluation of the Use of Cash Grants in UNHCR's Voluntary Repatriation and Reintegration Programme in Burundi," Policy Development and Evaluation Service 2009 at 6, <http://www.unhcr.org/research/evalreports/4a5f436d9/money-matters-evaluation-use-cash-grants-unhcrs-voluntary-repatriation.html> (last accessed February 26, 2018).

23. Webber 2011 ibid.

24. Allen Wertheimer and Franklin Miller, "Payments for Research Participation: A Coercive Offer?" *Journal of Medical Ethics* 34(2008):389–92.

25. Katy Long, *The Point of No Return: Refugees, Rights, and Repatriation,* Oxford: Oxford University Press 2013 at 159–61; Mikhail Valdman, "A Theory of Wrongful Exploitation," *Philosophers' Imprint* 9(6)(2009):1–14; Jonathan Wolff and Avner DeShalit, *Disadvantage,* Oxford: Oxford University Press 2007 at 78.

26. Long 2013 ibid. at 161–3.

27. Long 2013 ibid. at 162–3.

28. Deborah Satz, *Why Some Things Should Not Be for Sale: The Moral Limits of Markets,* Oxford: Oxford University Press 2010; Anne Phillips, *Our Bodies, Whose Property?* Princeton: Princeton University Press 2013.

29. Seana Valentine Shiffrin, "Paternalism, Unconscionability Doctrine, and Accommodation," *Philosophy and Public Affairs* 29(3)(2000):205–50.
30. Interview with Assisted Voluntary Return official, Tel Aviv, August 7, 2013.
31. Richard Black, "Return and Reconstruction in Bosnia-Herzegovina: Missing Link or Mistaken Priority?" *SAIS Review* 21(2)(2001):177–99.
32. UNHCR, "Burundi: Repatriation from Tanzania – Numbers Remaining under 300,000," Briefing Notes, May 18, 2004, <http://www.unhcr.org/40a9e0a21.html> (last accessed September 19, 2015).
33. Haver, Hatungimana, and Tennant 2009 ibid.
34. Human Rights Watch, "Closed Door Policy: Afghan Refugees in Pakistan and Iran," 14(2)(2002), <https://www.hrw.org/reports/2002/pakistan/pakistan0202.pdf> (last accessed February 25, 2018).
35. UNHCR March 2015 ibid.
36. Human Rights Watch, "Pakistan Coercion, UN Complicity: The Mass Forced Return of Afghan Refugees,' February 13, 2017, <https://www.hrw.org/report/2017/02/13/pakistan-coercion-un-complicity/mass-forced-return-afghan-refugees> (last accessed February 26, 2018).
37. Human Rights Watch, "Kenya: Involuntary Refugee Returns to Somalia," September 14, 2016, <https://www.hrw.org/news/2016/09/14/kenya-involuntary-refugee-returns-somalia> (last accessed January 7, 2018).
38. Galia Sabar and Elizabeth Tsurkov, "Israel's Policies towards Asylum Seekers, 2002–2014," Istituto Affari Internazionali Working Paper, May 15, 2015.
39. See Appendix B.
40. Interview with Tigisti, Ethiopia, June 8, 2014; interview with Massawa, Addis Ababa, June 8, 2014.
41. UNHCR, "Israel: Subregional Operations Profile – Middle East," 2015, <http://www.unhcr.org/pages/49e4864b6.html> (last accessed February 26, 2018).
42. Interview with Tigisti, Ethiopia, June 9, 2014.
43. Interview with Daniel, Addis Ababa, June 10, 2014.
44. Megan Bradley, *Refugee Repatriation: Justice, Responsibility and Redress*, Cambridge: Cambridge University Press 2014 at 52.
45. Liz Fekete, "The Deportation Machine: Europe, Asylum, and Human Rights," *Race and Class* 47(1)(2005):64–78.
46. Michael Barnett and Martha Finnemore, *Rules for the World: International Organizations in Global Politics*, Cornell: Cornell University Press 2004 at 106.
47. Illan Lior, "Israel to Offer African Migrants $5,000 to Leave," *Haaretz*, January 10, 2013, <https://www.haaretz.com/.premium-israel-to-migrants-leave-and-get-5-000-1.5282114> (last accessed February 26, 2018).
48. Interview with Bol, Juba, December 21, 2013; interview with Nathaniel, Juba, December 14, 2013; interview with Vanessa, Juba, December 25, 2013.

49. Birgit Schwarz, "Nothing to Go Back to – From Kenya's Vast Refugee Camp," Human Rights Watch, May 26, 2016, <https://www.hrw.org/news/2016/05/26/nothing-go-back-kenyas-vast-refugee-camp> (last accessed January 7, 2018).
50. Interview with Bessie, Ethiopia, June 9, 2014.
51. Refugee Action, <http://www.choices-avr.org.uk> (last accessed March 12, 2015).
52. Gonzalez and Majidi 2009 ibid.
53. Haver, Hatungimana, and Tennant 2009 ibid.
54. Black 2001 ibid.

Chapter 6

CHILDREN

A child is very sick. Her parent refuses to bring her to a hospital, despite the risks of staying home. The child dies. We might blame the parent for being reckless. This is not because the parent neglected to save the child's life by acquiring medical skills to do so. Rather, the parent had a duty to be in a particular place, at a particular time, so others could save the child's life.

A hospital is a very narrow space. We might imagine a broader geographical location where children have a higher likelihood of being saved if they are in danger. It may be reckless for a parent to be in a particular neighborhood, region, or country if they are exposing their children to greater risks than parents are permitted to take. Should parents be able to live wherever they please? More specifically, should parents be able to migrate to any country they desire?

There are many reasons that parents may choose to live in an unsafe country, but perhaps the most common is that they wish to return to their countries of origin. In some such cases, refugees are returning to countries unsafe for children due to ongoing violence, insufficient food security, and a lack of public services. Such unsafe repatriation was common when parents returned from Australia to Afghanistan in the early 2000s,[1] from Norway to Iraq in the late 2000s,[2] and from Kenya to Somalia in the 2010s.[3] In these cases, parents left countries with relative security, education, and healthcare, traveling to countries without these basic necessities. Though some parents had savings, many did not. And of those who did, it was not clear how long their money lasted, nor if it helped.

As noted in previous chapters, when refugees repatriated from Israel to South Sudan, the country lacked basic safety and healthcare.[4] Despite the risks, parents returned with their children, wishing to raise them on their ancestral land, or feeling there were more opportunities in South Sudan compared to staying in Israel.

One returning family was comprised of Mary, Dak, their six-year-old son and their two newborn twins. They landed in Juba in the summer of 2012 and took a taxi to the neighborhood of Tong Peng, where friends awaited to host them until they found work. As weeks passed they failed to find jobs and were unable to pay for their children's schooling. In November, when their youngest son contracted malaria, they sent him to a hospital, using most of their $3,000 in emergency savings. As the treatment continued, their money ran out, and their son steadily lost the ability to walk or speak, dying in February 2013. He was one of seven children known to have died within the first three months of return.[5] At least two more were killed when civil war broke out in December 2013[6] and of the forty-eight children whose conditions I could confirm as of July 2014, five had died of malaria or were killed. This represented over 10 per cent of my sample. Importantly, I learned of these five children in relatively safe areas and from their guardians: had I confirmed the conditions of all of the children who returned, including those in unsafe areas and whose guardians had died, the percentage would likely be higher than 10 per cent.

It was not clear if these children's parents had a right to repatriate to South Sudan, or if others should have assisted with their repatriation.

The question of parental rights to repatriate has been largely overlooked in today's debates on immigration. Philosophers focus on whom states should not deport,[7] not whom states should allow to leave. The few discussions on the right to leave largely focus on adults, with most arguing that adults always have a right to leave.[8] Even if they do, it remains unclear if they have a right to bring their children with them.

In the following section I present a general theory of parental rights. I argue that parents must protect their children's welfare above a given threshold. When parents fail to protect their children's welfare, states have a right to intervene. In Section 6.2 I argue that states have a right to intervene to stop repatriation that undermines children's welfare. In Section 6.3 I address cases involving coercion, where the state forces parents and children to remain in detention or enclosed camps, and parents wish to repatriate as a result. I argue that humanitarian agencies should help parents repatriate if remaining is more dangerous than returning.

Before addressing the above arguments, a brief note on my focus and assumptions.

Throughout this chapter, I shall focus on families who leave a country and cannot easily re-enter this country. This is the case when families live without legal status in a host country and, once they repatriate, cannot re-enter the host country again. This is also the case when refugees repatriate and lack the means to re-enter their former host country.

Though I focus primarily on parents repatriating with their children, my conclusions may have broader implications. If parents have no right to repatriate when this places their children at risk, they may have no right to move to a new country that similarly places their children at risk. Moreover, if children should never be forced to live in an unsafe country, a state could justifiably deny entrance on the grounds that it is too dangerous for children within its territory. We might imagine, for example, that a state suffering from poverty, internal strife, or a natural disaster could refuse to grant visas to minors, or refuse to allow children to repatriate to its territory. Though I do not address these cases, it is possible that states ought to take such measures, based on the argumentation I put forth.

6.1 PARENTAL RIGHTS

Let us establish what rights parents have over their children. We can start with a consensus: Across cultures there is general consensus that parents have some rights to decide where their children live, what they eat, where they go to school, and what languages they speak. This is partly because, if parents have such authority, they can more easily care for their children, ensuring children have basic food and shelter, and various moral and inferential reasoning skills. Mary and Dak were able to speak to their children in Nuer while in Israel, and this allowed them to teach their children how to count to ten, tell their children to come inside when it grew dark, and encourage them to finish their homework on time. Parents also have rights over their children because parents' rights matter, and parental rights to share their culture and way of life ought to be respected.[9] When Mary and Dak spoke to their children in Nuer they were not only educating their children and keeping them safe, but choosing to share with them their tribal identity, a choice that ought to be respected regardless of educational benefits.

There is another consensus: parents have a right to raise their own biological children. Were the state to pry away children from competent parents, and give them to the very best adoptive parents, the psychological distress biological parents felt would be significant, and so such interference would be wrong, unless parents' care falls below a minimal threshold.[10]

Parents' care falls below a minimal threshold, I assume, if parents fail to help their children lead healthy lives and gain the skills to reason, form reciprocal relationships,[11] and function in the society they are residing in. For example, parents should try to teach their children to make friends, cooperate, and understand basic norms. While there are debates as to why parents should help their children gain these skills – some claim this protects children's happiness, others that it protects children's autonomy[12] – there is a consensus that parents do have duties to ensure children obtain these and other skills.

Perhaps one of the most central of these skills is the ability to function within an economy, allowing children to later access resources to survive, and the self-respect that comes with employment. For example, parents should bring their children to school to learn to read, as reading is essential for employment later in life. However, it is not clear whether parents must merely help children gain skills to function in the economy they live in, or to function in any economy they desire. Brighouse and Swift suggest the former, raising the example of nomadic tribespeople in sub-Saharan Africa who can function within their economy without a high level of literacy,[13] and so can respect children's rights without teaching them to read.

There is a problem with this reasoning. Children may be forced to live within a particular economy precisely because they only gained skills to function within this economy. If a young girl does not gain a high level of literacy because she is living in a rural area, then the reason she lives in her rural economy may be because she has not gained a level of literacy to function elsewhere. Indeed, if all children everywhere were illiterate and innumerate, and grew up into adults who formed verbal-based economies, they too may be able to function in their own economy without literacy. This tells us nothing about the sort of economy children ought to be able to function in as adults.

It seems that children ought to be able to function in an economy that can likely provide them a safe life, a long life, and a life they feel is worth living. Children accessing education can more easily obtain these goals, because they can access better employment with literacy and numeracy, essential for communicating across distances and keeping track of transactions. For this reason states aim to ensure that all children attend school. Even children who live a nomadic or subsistence lifestyle are normally required to gain a given level of education so that, once they become adults, they can access other jobs if their traditional economies fail.[14]

6.2 REPATRIATION

Though all states ought to provide education, healthcare, and security, many do not. When parents wish to repatriate to such states with their children, it is not clear if they have a right to do so. We might at first suppose that parents have no right to repatriate if this entails harms we do not allow parents to inflict on their children domestically. If parents act recklessly when failing to bring their children to hospitals and schools, they act recklessly when returning to a country without reliable hospitals and schools. But we might also suppose it would be wrong to stop parents from repatriating, as this would be a form of foreign interference. Just as it is wrong to send policemen to foreign countries to force parents to send their children to school, it would be wrong to prevent parents from returning to countries where their children will not attend school.

I shall accept that it is wrong to send policemen to foreign countries to improve safety and welfare for children, except in extreme cases. This would, indeed, entail intervening in the affairs of another state. But preventing a parent from repatriating would not entail intervening in the affairs of another state, because a parent who repatriates is engaging in a domestic act. His repatriation entails paying for transport and arranging travel documentation, arriving at the airport, sitting down in the departure lounge, boarding the flight, and sitting down in a seat. These actions all take place without leaving the state. Just as the act of theft involves not just placing money in a bag, but breaking, entering, and picking up the money, the act of repatriating involves not just arriving in a foreign country, but everything prior that is necessary to arrive in the foreign country. Even the moment a refugee's body passes over a border may be considered within the jurisdiction of the state, in the sense that borders are shared by states, and so within their jurisdiction. If a refugee is acting within the jurisdiction of the state when she repatriates, and she does not have a right to endanger her child within the jurisdiction of the state, then she does not have a right to endanger her child's life through repatriation.

More specifically, parents ought to be treated in the following manner: *When parents attempt to repatriate in a manner that entails risks for their children, states should prevent such repatriation when this entails risks parents are prevented from taking more generally.*

For example, if parents are required to bring their children to school until the age of eighteen, parents should be prevented from repatriating to a country without schooling for their seventeen-year-old child. In contrast, if parents are permitted to remove their children from school before the age of eighteen, they should be permitted to repatriate to a country without schooling for their seventeen year old.

Some may oppose to this rule of thumb, raising one of three objections.

The first relates to jurisdiction. If a parent is a foreign national, and wishes to repatriate to her home country, her home country should have jurisdiction over her children. The country she wishes to leave has a responsibility to protect its own nationals, rather than foreign nationals, and so ought to permit the repatriation of foreign national children. It would be wrong if the state of Israel had prevented refugees from repatriating to South Sudan, given that it is South Sudan that is responsible for the welfare of these children, rather than Israel.

I believe this objection is relatively weak. It is generally accepted that states can prevent risky illegal acts that take place within their jurisdiction, regardless of the citizenship of those who commit these acts. A parent who intentionally refuses to bring his child to the hospital may be tried for recklessness, regardless of his nationality. If repatriating is a domestic act that places a child at risk, and placing a child at risk is illegal, the state can legitimately prevent the parent from repatriating.

There is a second objection. Some claim states are generally permitted to deport foreign nationals, including children, unless they will almost certainly die from famine, violence, or persecution in their home countries.[15] Perhaps states are permitted to deport children who will merely lack reliable healthcare or education in their home countries. If states are permitted to deport such children, surely they are permitted to allow them to repatriate with their parents.

I believe, however, that states are not permitted to deport children who will lack reliable healthcare or education in their home countries. This is because children are owed greater protection than adults. Children have fewer mental capacities, and are less able to survive in an unsafe environment compared to adults. If a child is returning to a country without reliable healthcare, she will be more susceptible to various contagious diseases, partly because she has less immunity, but also because she may not take precautions that an adult would take against catching these diseases. If a child lacks education, she may also be unable to develop capacities to care for herself. Because of this, children should be protected from deportation even if the risks in the home countries are not substantial enough to warrant protection for adults.[16] If children should be protected from deportation to countries without reliable healthcare or education, they should be protected from repatriation to these same countries.

A third objection concerns cultural rights. Parents, we might suppose, have the right to deny their children some levels of education and general healthcare to promote their own culture. Different cultures have different conceptions of what is necessary in life, and so parents ought to have some discretion over what necessities their children obtain.[17] For this reason, parents are given the right to refuse to vaccinate their children as infants, and sometimes given the right to pull their children from school at an earlier age, as when Amish parents in the US withdraw their children from school at age fourteen.[18] If such policies are morally acceptable, then states ought not to prevent repatriation to countries with similar risks, such as repatriation to a country without vaccinations or reliable schooling. So long as children will not face immediate risks from repatriating – such as a child with diabetes returning to a country without insulin – repatriation should be permitted. Children will face some risks, but there are clear subjective benefits for the parents and, in these parents' minds, these benefits extend to their children.

These considerations ought to be taken seriously, but they are consistent with the general principle I put forth. The principle held that states should prevent repatriation when this entails risks parents are prevented from taking domestically. If a state prevents parents from removing children from school at fourteen, even if the parent believes this is necessary for their children, the state should not allow parents to repatriate with their children to a country without any secondary schooling. In contrast, if parents are permitted to remove their children from school at age fourteen, parents should be permitted to repatriate to a country without schooling at fourteen, assuming the risks are similar.

In establishing whether risks are similar, it is necessary to account for the irreversible nature of repatriation. When a child leaves school at fourteen within a state, but remains in the state, she can often return to school later as an adult, and leave her community behind. A fourteen year old repatriating to a country without schooling often cannot return to school and leave her community behind. Of course, even if a fourteen year old leaves school but stays in the country she will still suffer from some irreversible effects; missing school at an early age can mean challenges learning to read later on. But these challenges can be somewhat mitigated through adult education classes, classes often unavailable to those repatriating to low-income countries. Similar conclusions may be reached regarding some vaccinations and healthcare: A parent who refuses to vaccinate their children or bring them to a doctor within a state may be threatening their child's health in a way that is irreversible, but the threats can be somewhat mitigated through vaccinations obtained as an adult, in addition to the effects of herd immunity and general healthcare.[19] In contrast, a parent repatriating to a country without vaccinations or reliable healthcare prevents their child from accessing vaccinations and reliable healthcare in the future. As a general rule, irreversible repatriation requires greater safety than comparable acts within a state.

In current policies around the globe, the opposite is the case. States accept greater risks in repatriating compared to risks of remaining within a state. For example, the UK only bans parents from repatriating with their children if they are planning on marrying their child off or traveling to Islamic State-controlled territory.[20] In contrast, the UK permits families to repatriate to the Central African Republic or South Sudan, both of which lack universal schooling and reliable healthcare.[21] In other words, the UK gives parents no authority to remove children from school or a hospital domestically, but gives them authority to remove their children from a school or hospital through repatriation. But it is precisely repatriation that may be irreversible, requiring greater vigilance rather than less.

Now that I have established that parents have no right to repatriate when risking their children's safety and capacities, and states have a duty to prevent such repatriation, let us consider how the state should intervene. The state could consider the particular risks a child will face on a case-by-case basis. For example, the UK has a policy of preventing a parent from traveling to Pakistan with their child if there is evidence that the parent intends to marry their child off upon reaching Pakistan.[22] Such case-by-case determinations, however, may fail to protect most children, as risks often arise from the country the child is moving to, rather than the intentions or actions of the parents. A child can be at risk of malaria even if the parents have every intention to protect the child from malaria.

The state could instead ban parents from traveling to certain countries that are especially unsafe. This might involve, for example, banning travel to South Sudan, which has an 18 per cent school enrolment rate, an illiteracy rate above 50 per cent, and a child mortality rate of seventy-four deaths per 1,000 live births.[23] Under such a policy, the state would use physical force if a parent attempted to travel to South Sudan, either revoking their passports or imprisoning them as a last resort. Traveling would be permitted only if a parent proved that, due to their exceptional circumstances, they were able to provide security and education for their children. The burden of proof would be on parents to demonstrate that they could mitigate risks substantially.

Some may feel that this policy would be overly harsh. It would prevent even short trips to unsafe countries, as the state would be unable to differentiate between parents repatriating and those merely visiting. This would also conflict with the liberal assumption that states ought not to interfere with individuals' rights to leave the country they are residing in. Were the state to ban travel, this would prevent merely possible harm to children, while certainly undermining freedom for parents.

A less controversial policy would entail discouraging but not preventing parents from repatriating. This would entail informing parents of the risks of returning and the benefits of remaining, which would be particularly helpful for parents who know little about the country they intend to return to. Importantly, the goal of information should be to persuade parents to stay, rather than to simply inform parents of the various risks.[24] And for parents who are already aware of the risks, the goal should be to remind them that repatriating is unsafe, and that staying is preferable to protect the security and welfare of their children.

6.3 COERCION

The policy recommendations above would be rejected by governments actively encouraging refugees to repatriate, requiring any who remain to live in destitution, detention, and enclosed camps. In some such cases, the government does not itself provide funds for repatriation, and refugees lack the funds to repatriate on their own. Organizations step in to help by providing transport to parents and their children.

In earlier chapters, I argued that organizations should help with return if there is little else they can do, if the return does not encourage further detention, and if refugees are informed and unlikely to feel regret. Even if these conditions are met, perhaps organizations should not help parents return with children, given the risks children will face.

This question is particularly relevant in Kenya, where in 2016 the government announced the intended closure of the Dadaab refugee complex, where over 260,000 refugees reside. It later closed the Department of Refugee Affairs, refusing to register new babies as refugees,[25] and parents and their children began lining up at the UNHCR Return Help Desks, hoping to return to Somalia. Close to 70,000 refugees returned by the end of 2017, the majority children, and they struggled to access food, security, and education once there.[26] Given the difficulty children faced in both remaining and returning, it was not clear whether UNHCR ought to have helped them repatriate.

In Pakistan and Iran this issue has been relevant for several years, as the Pakistani government threatens to detain or deport many who remain, and the Iranian government restricts internal movement for refugees, conscripting thousands into the Syrian Army. Many wish to repatriate as a result, with over two million returning home since 2015, 81 per cent of which are children. Children face considerable risks after returning, with mortality rates amongst them increasing, and access to schooling low.[27] Despite these risks, UNHCR continues assisting with their return. It is not clear it should.

In Israel this question was relevant from 2012, when two immigration officials in Israel sat in their offices and printed out white Excel sheets, listing the names and addresses of several hundred South Sudanese children and their parents. They handed these sheets to dozens of policemen who traveled the country, visiting each family on the list, and using metal batons to bang on their doors. One door belonged to the family of Nyandeng, the fifteen-year-old girl described in this book's introduction. She had arrived in Israel six years earlier with her

mother, eventually settling in the northern town of Naharia. As policemen arrived, Nyandeng and her younger brother were both wearing
their backpacks, about to walk to school:

> My little brother left the house and saw big men come and enter.
> They said to us, "Sit. You are not going to school." They were
> very scary looking and huge. My mother wanted to call friends
> for help, and the three men said, "No you cannot call anyone."
> The immigration police told my mother to just sign some papers
> and that's all. She signed that paper that says she wants to go
> back. Everyone signs it. She needed to sign, otherwise we would
> go to prison.[28]

Nyandeng's mother agreed to return, and describes how she felt before
boarding the flight:

> I was crying and crying. I did not want to go to prison, but I have
> nothing to do in South Sudan. I was not born in South Sudan and
> I have nothing here. Even my mother and father had spent most
> of their lives outside of South Sudan, and died in Port Sudan.[29]

When Nyandeng and her family returned they did not receive assistance from OBI, as OBI had discontinued its program by the time they
returned. But other families did, and returned under nearly identical
conditions as Nyandeng.

There are two reasons we might suppose organizations like OBI
should help with repatriation in such cases.

6.3.1 Freedom

The first relates to freedom. Children have a right to freedom, and
children cannot be free in detention. If children cannot be free from
detention, and repatriation assistance does not contribute to detention,
perhaps helping with repatriation is better than doing nothing at all.
Even if repatriation will risk children's health and safety, basic freedom
is often more important than health and safety.

This reasoning is relatively weak. Even if children's basic freedom is
more important than health and safety, health and safety is more important than general freedom, such as the freedom to leave a detention

center. If children will be able to run, play, and attend school in detention, their freedom is not sufficiently undermined to justify repatriation to a country without education, security, or medical care. Repatriation is only justified if children will face serious insecurity in detention, such that remaining is as dangerous as repatriating.

In many cases, remaining really is as dangerous as repatriating, to the best of our knowledge. Such is often the case for Somali children in Dadaab and Kakuma refugee camps in Kenya, who will face similar risks in remaining and returning, as noted by single mother Sacdiya Noor. Noor repatriated with her children in 2015 and then crossed back into Kenya because, as she explains:

> There was no security in [Mogadishu], no free services and nothing special [to help] returnees. I left [Somalia] for the safety of my children ... I am stuck [in Kenya] with no rights. It is like they are saying, "You either die of gunshot in Somalia or come back to starve in Dadaab."[30]

In cases like that of Noor, organizations are morally permitted to help with repatriation if they have established that returning and remaining are equally as dangerous. This is because helping with return protects the rights of parents, without undermining the children's welfare compared to remaining. It is also because parents may have information about their children that organizations do not have, and so may be best placed to decide what is best when neither outcome is acceptable. In other words, while organizations should not help return when returning will clearly undermine the rights of the child compared to remaining, organizations should help with return if both options seem equally unsafe, but parents insist returning is safer.

6.3.2 Burdens

Even when remaining is safer than returning, there is a second reason facilitators might help with return. They might feel no parent should be forced to accept certain burdens. No parent, for example, should be forced to work in a dangerous and demeaning job to feed their children, such as working in prostitution to pay for dinner. Similarly, no parent should be forced to stay in detention or an enclosed camp to protect their children. Parents have certain rights as distinct from those of their children, and the right to be free is one such right.

This is one reason to help parents repatriate, even if this places their children at risk.

Though there are burdens parents should not be forced to accept for their children, there are burdens children should not be forced to accept for their parents. Were children forced to repatriate, because parents did not wish to remain in detention or a camp, children would be losing their own welfare for their parent's freedom. Children's welfare should be prioritized, given that children are more vulnerable than adults, and so deserving of special protection. Children should therefore not be provided repatriation by organizations, even if this is what parents desire.

There are cases, however, where children will repatriate regardless of whether organizations help. As noted in Chapter 2, organizations often exist alongside government-funded repatriation programs, and refugees can utilize these programs, or pay for their own flights home. When a given organization knows that parents will repatriate with children regardless, the organization is not making unsafe repatriation possible, and so helping with repatriation seems acceptable.

The problem with this logic is that an organization can never be certain a given refugee will leave if the organization refuses to help, because it can never be certain a refugee will have other means of leaving. There is always a possibility that, had the organization not helped, refugees would remain and their children would be safe. They should therefore avoid assisting with return, even if there is a likelihood refugees would return regardless. An exception should only be made when organizations can ensure a much safer return than would otherwise take place. This might be the case if a parent will almost certainly return regardless and, if she does not receive help to return, she will use clandestine means to return home, placing herself and her child at risk. If an organization can provide a very safe passage home, then helping with return may be justified.

The above cases involve parents returning to avoid insecurity, hunger, and life in a camp or detention center. In reality, many refugees return because they are misinformed about what to expect, as noted in Chapter 3. Such was the case when Somali refugees in Kenya were told by UNHCR that return was safe, and when refugees in Israel were never told that education was of poor quality in South Sudan.

Sometimes parents are told misinformation not about conditions if they return, but about their rights if they remain. Of the 128 individuals I interviewed after return to South Sudan, fourteen believed their children would have been homeless and hungry had they remained in Israel. These parents told me that, in South Sudan, they could at least ask relatives and friends for help. Importantly, of the fourteen who believed their children would have no food in Israel, four left for this reason alone. Had these parents stayed, their children would have likely been placed in foster care, or detained with their parents, but still able to access food, shelter, and education. These parents told me that, had they known their children would have basic necessities if they remained, they would never have returned. To ensure parents are fully informed about what will happen to children who remain, organizations should inform parents of children's rights, encouraging better decisions under coercive conditions.

6.4 CONCLUSION

Children often lack the capacity of adults, and so lack the right to decide where they will live. Parents decide on their behalf, taking into account children's interests. To protect these interests, parents should avoid repatriating to a country that fails to provide sufficient security or welfare. States should discourage such repatriation if it places children under risk that would be unacceptable for those remaining within the state. When states insist on encouraging unsafe repatriation, organizations should only assist if returning is safer for children than remaining, or much safer than returning via other means.

The analysis I raise may have implications beyond repatriation. As noted in the introduction to this chapter, states may have a duty to discourage all forms of migration unsafe for children, and not merely repatriation unsafe for children. Moreover, states suffering from internal strife should possibly deny visas to minors attempting to enter their territory, and perhaps have a duty to help evacuate children from their territory, or from unsafe regions within their territory. We might imagine a government helping relocate families from high-crime cities to low-crime cities, or a government helping families relocate from combat zones to areas at peace. Such policies may be the best option when children's lives and education are at immediate risk, and change will not come in the near future.

The policies I have proposed address repatriation alone, but still have broad implications. Some of these implications are slightly disturbing, such as states refusing to honor the choices of refugees, and organizations refusing to help with return, even as minors and their parents are forced to live inside the barbed-wire borders of detention and camps. These policies, though disturbing, are still preferable to the alternatives. We may no longer see a child once she returns home, but she may be suffering nonetheless. We must account for such suffering in protecting children's rights. Just as parents should protect children within a state, they should protect them when traveling between states, providing them the safety, education, and healthcare they need.

NOTES

1. A similar issue arose with repatriation from Sweden to Afghanistan. See Fethi Mansouri and Sally Percival Wood, "Exploring the Australia-Middle East Connection," in (ed.) Fethi Mansouri, *Australia and the Middle East: A Front-Line Relationship*, London: Tauris Academic Studies 2011 at 9; UNHCR, "Sweden, Afghanistan, UNHCR Sign Deal on Voluntary Return of Afghans," June 23, 2007, <http://www.unhcr.org/468bb4542.html> (last accessed February 26, 2018).

2. A similar issue arose with repatriation from Denmark to Iraq. See Helen Carr, "Returning 'Home': Experiences of Reintegration for Asylum Seekers and Refugees," *British Journal of Social Work* 44(1)(2014):1–17; Arne Strand, "Review of Two Societies: Review of the Information, Return and Reintegration of Iraqi Nationals to Iraq (IRRINI) Program," Chr. Michelson Institute, 2011, <http://www.cmi.no/publications/publication/?4155=between-two-societies-review-of-the-information> (last accessed February 25, 2018).

3. Moulid Hujale and Karen McVeigh, "'I feel betrayed': The Somali Refugees Sent from Safety into a War Zone," *The Guardian*, June 22, 2017, <https://www.theguardian.com/global-development/2017/jun/22/betrayed-somali-refugees-kenya-dadaab-camp-sent-from-safety-into-war-zone> (last accessed February 16, 2018).

4. Jared Ferrie, "More Than 200 Die in South Sudan Tribal Feud, Official Says," CNN, March 12, 2012, <http://edition.cnn.com/2012/03/12/world/africa/south-sudan-violence/> (last accessed February 26, 2018); D. Maxwell, K. Gelsdorf, and M. Santschi, "Livelihoods, Basic Services, and Social Protection in South Sudan," Working Paper 1, Secure Livelihoods Research Consortium, Feinstein International Center, 2012, <https://www.odi.org/sites/odi.org.uk/files/odi-assets/publications-opinion-files/7716.pdf> (last accessed February 26, 2018); Al Jazeera, "'Hundreds Dead' in South Sudan Cattle Raids," August 22, 2011, <http://www.aljazeera.com/news/africa/2011/08/201182220946583842.html>

(last accessed February 26, 2018); Una McCauley, "Separated Children in South Sudan," *Forced Migration Review* 24(2005):52–5; MSF, "Patients and Families Killed Outside of MSF Compound," November 29, 2007, <http://www.msf.org/article/patients-and-family-members-killed-inside-msf-compound> (last accessed February 26, 2018); MSF, "Patients and Families Killed Outside of MSF Compound," November 29, 2007, <http://www.msf.org/article/patients-and-family-members-killed-inside-msf-compound> (last accessed March 15, 2012); MSF, "South Sudan: Violence against Healthcare," July 1, 2014, <http://www.msf.fr/actualite/publications/south-sudan-conflict-violence-against-health-care> (last accessed February 26, 2018); R. K. Rai, A. A. Ramadhan, and T. H. Tulchinsky, "Prioritizing Maternal and Child Health in Independent South Sudan," *Maternal and Child Health Journal* 16(6)(2012):1139–42; Small Arms Survey, "Fighting for Spoils: Armed Insurgencies in Greater Upper Nile," November 2011, <http://www.smallarmssurveysudan.org/fileadmin/docs/issue-briefs/HSBA-IB-18-Armed-insurgencies-Greater-Upper-Nile.pdf> (last accessed February 26, 2018); UNICEF in South Sudan, "Summary Finding of Sudan Health Household Survey (SHHS) 2010 and Multiple Indicator Cluster Survey," 2010, <http://southsudan-embassyfrance.org/files/helth.pdf> (last accessed February 16, 2018).

5. Yuval Goren (Hebrew), "Aid Organizations: Over 22 Refugees Expelled to South Sudan Die within the First Year," June 5, 2012, <http://www.nrg.co.il/online/1/ART2/477/197.html> (last accessed February 25, 2018) and Dimi Reider, "Israeli Children Deported to South Sudan Succumb to Malaria," October 8, 2012, <https://972mag.com/israeli-children-deported-to-south-sudan-succumb-to-malaria/57287/> (last accessed September 26, 2018).

6. Interview with Matthew, Juba, January 4, 2014.

7. Matthew Gibney, *The Ethics and Politics of Asylum: Liberal Democracy and the Response to Refugees*, Cambridge: Cambridge University Press 2004; Matthew Lister, "Who Are Refugees?" *Law and Philosophy* 32(5) (2013):645–71; David Miller, "Immigration: The Case for Its Limits," in (eds) A. Cohen and C. Wellman, *Contemporary Debates in Applied Ethics*, Malden, MA: Blackwell Publishing 2005 at 193–206.

8. Anna Stilz, "Is There an Unqualified Right to Leave?" in (eds) Sarah Fine and Lea Ypi, *Migration in Political Theory: The Ethics of Movement and Membership*, Oxford: Oxford University Press 2016.

9. David Archard, *Children: Rights and Childhood*, 2nd ed., London and New York: Routledge 2004; Ferdinand Schoeman, "Rights of Children, Rights of Parents, and the Moral Basis of the Family," *Ethics* 91(1980):6–19 at 14.

10. Matthew Clayton, *Justice and Legitimacy in Upbringing*, Oxford: Oxford University Press 2006; Joseph Millum, "How Do We Acquire Parental Rights?" *Social Theory and Practice* 36(1)(2010):112–32; Norvin Richards,

The Ethics of Parenthood, Oxford: Oxford University Press 2010; Edgar Page, "Parental Rights," *Journal of Applied Philosophy* 1(2)(1984):187–203. Such a principle may also better protect children. Historically, when states have denied parents authority over their children, prying them from their arms and giving them to supposedly better parents, the results have at times been detrimental, with children experiencing greater incarceration, drug addiction, and anti-social behavior. See Australian Human Rights Commission, "Bringing Them Home: Report of the National Inquiry into the Separation of Aboriginal and Torres Strait Islander Children from Their Families," Human Rights and Equal Opportunity Commission Report, April 1997.

11. Amy Guttman, *Democratic Education,* Princeton: Princeton University Press 1999; Martha Nussbaum, *Liberty and Conscience: In Defence of America's Tradition of Religious Equality,* New York: Basic Books 2008.

12. Samantha Brennan, "Children's Choices or Children's Interests: Which do their Rights Protect?" in (eds) David Archard and Colin M. MacLeod, *The Moral and Political Status of Children,* Oxford: Oxford University Press 2002; Shelley Burtt, "What Children Really Need: Toward a Critical Theory of Family Structure," in (eds) David Archard and Colin M. MacLeod, *The Moral and Political Status of Children,* Oxford: Oxford University Press 2002 at 231–52; Eamonn Callan, "Autonomy, Child Rearing, and Good Lives," in (eds) David Archard and Colin M. MacLeod, *The Moral and Political Status of Children,* Oxford: Oxford University Press 2002 at 118–40; Matthew Clayton, "Anti-Perfectionist Childrearing," in (eds) Alexander Begattini and Colin Macleod, *The Nature of Children's Wellbeing,* Dordrecht, Heidelberg, New York and London: Springer 2015.

13. Harry Brighouse and Adam Swift, *Family Values: The Ethics of Parent-Child Relationships,* Princeton: Princeton University Press 2014 at 60.

14. John Aluko Orodho, Peter Ndirangu Waweru, Kennedy Nyambeche Getange, and Justus Mbae Miriti, "Progress towards Attainment of Education for All (EFA) among Nomadic Pastoralist: Do Home-Based Variables Make a Difference in Kenya?" *Research on Humanities and Social Sciences* 5(18)(2013):54–68.

15. Matthew Gibney, *The Ethics and Politics of Asylum: Liberal Democracy and the Response to Refugees,* Cambridge: Cambridge University Press 2004; David Miller, "Immigration: The Case for Its Limits," in (eds) A. Cohen and C. Wellman. *Contemporary Debates in Applied Ethics,* Malden, MA: Blackwell Publishing 2005 at 193–206.

16. Indeed, this general approach is taken on an ad hoc basis in some states which may protect a family from deportation because of the harms towards children, even though adults could generally survive. A recent case in the UK involved a woman and her son, both from Nigeria, who avoided

deportation largely because of the effects on the son of returning to Nigeria. See *RA v. The Secretary of State for the Home Department*, JR/2277/2015, <https://www.judiciary.gov.uk/wp-content/uploads/2015/04/ra-and-bf-v-sshd-21.pdf> (last accessed February 26, 2018).

17. William A. Galston, "Two Concepts of Liberalism," *Ethics* 105(3)(1995): 516–34 at 529; Chandran Kukathas, "Are There Any Cultural Rights?" *Political Theory* 20(1)(1992):105–39 at 117.

18. David Archard and Colin MacLeod, "Religious Parents, Secular Schools: A Liberal Defense of an Illiberal Education," *Review of Politics* 56(1) (1994):51–70; Shelley Burtt, "In Defense of Yoder: Parental Authority and the Public Schools," in (eds) Ian Shapiro and Russell Hardin, *Political Order*, New York and London: New York University Press 1998 at 412–37.

19. When vaccinations cannot be obtained as an adult, and there is no herd immunity or reliable treatment, we might argue states really do have a duty to require vaccinations.

20. 2015 EWHC 869 (Fam) Case No: FD15P00125, FD15P00126, FD15P00127, FD15P00128, FD15P00129; Court 46, The Royal Courts of Justice, Strand, London, WC2A 2LL, March 27, 2015. Before: Mr. Justice Hayden, Between The London Borough of Tower Hamlets, Claimant, and M and Ors, Defendants.

21. Clár Ní Chonghaile, "Central African Republic Facing Chronic Healthcare Crisis as Scars of Conflict Abide," *The Guardian* May 3, 2015, <https://www.theguardian.com/global-development/2015/may/03/central-african-republic-chronic-healthcare-crisis-malaria-msf> (last accessed April 27, 2018); UNICEF in South Sudan, "Summary finding of Sudan Health Household Survey (SHHS) 2010 and Multiple Indicator Cluster Survey," 2010, <http://southsudan-embassyfrance.org/files/helth.pdf> (last accessed February 16, 2018); World Health Organization, "South Sudan: Country Profile," <http://www.who.int/gho/countries/ssd/country_profiles/en/> (last accessed April 27, 2018).

22. Forced Marriage (Civil Protection) Act 2007, <http://www.legislation.gov.uk/ukpga/2007/20/contents> (last accessed February 16, 2018).

23. World Health Organization, South Sudan, Global Health Observatory 2014, <http://apps.who.int/gho/data/node.cco> (last accessed August 26, 2016).

24. In the UK, the NGO Refugee Action provided limited information to refugees considering return, but the goal was to ensure choices were informed, rather than to persuade parents to avoid repatriating. See Refugee Action, <http://www.choices-avr.org.uk/countries_of_return> (last accessed October 19, 2015).

25. BBC News, "Kenya Closure of Dadaab Refugee Camp Blocked by High Court," February 9, 2017, <http://www.bbc.co.uk/news/world-africa-38917681> (last accessed February 17, 2017).

26. UNHCR, "Weekly Update: Voluntary Repatriation of Somali Refugees from Kenya," December 15, 2017, <http://www.unhcr.org/ke/wp-content/uploads/sites/2/2017/12/Voluntary-Repatriation-Analysis-15-December-2017.pdf> (last accessed February 17, 2018).

27. Assessment Capacities Project, "Afghanistan: Undocumented Returnees," Briefing Note, April 7, 2017, <https://www.acaps.org/special-report/afghanistan-undocumented-returnees-pakistan-and-iran> (last accessed February 21, 2018).

28. Interview with Nyandeng, Entebbe, May 9, 2013.

29. Interview with Nicole, Entebbe, May 9, 2013.

30. Hujale and McVeigh 2017 ibid.

Chapter 7

DISCRIMINATION

In 1972 a severe famine broke out in Ethiopia, leading to the deaths of roughly 60,000 individuals. Amidst unrest, the Marxist Derg assassinated the Emperor Haile Selassie, leading to the start of civil war in 1974.[1] Three years later the war reached the town of Axum in northern Ethiopia, where a toddler named Milka lived with her mother. Together, Milka and her mother walked into Sudanese territory where, she explains, she grew up learning:

> English, Arabic, and Tigrinya in school ... We would also get money every month from UNESCO, where we also studied. But [people] in Sudan ... would swear at us, and they wanted us to dress like them. They would collect us some time and force us over the border.[2]

In 2003, frustrated by the xenophobia she had experienced her whole life, she paid smugglers to take her by bus to Wadi Halfa, and then by boat to Egypt, and then by Jeep to the Sinai Desert, eventually reaching the border fence with Israel. She climbed the fence, dropped onto a mound of sand on the other side, and brushed herself off, hailing a cab to Tel Aviv an hour later. Once there, she worked on the black market for over a decade, cleaning rooms in hotels, and then selling fresh Ethiopian *injera* bread to locals in the surrounding neighborhoods. She married, had two children, and divorced in 2011, the same year her *injera* business began floundering. She struggled to pay rent or purchase food for herself or her children, and considered returning to Ethiopia. She felt it would be safe, and had extensive knowledge about her hometown, her sister having moved back several years earlier.[3]

As Milka considered whether to repatriate, an Israeli Member of Knesset stepped onto a podium in South Tel Aviv. Standing before thousands of anti-immigration protesters, she declared that Africans were "a cancer to the body," an opinion shared by most in Israel.[4] Shortly after her speech citizens smashed windows of African-owned shops, a protester threw a grenade at a nursery with African children, and three Eritreans were stabbed to death walking home from work.[5] The prime minister condemned the attacks, but promised to decrease the number of Africans in the country. Three months later, he worked with the Ministry of Interior to offer free flights and money to almost all non-citizen Africans agreeing to repatriate or resettle to a third country in Africa.[6] Non-Africans of comparable legal status, such as those from Myanmar or Ukraine, were never offered such assistance to repatriate. As a result, Milka was told she could receive a free flight and $14,000 if she left, money that would help sustain herself and her children in Ethiopia. "My dream," she explained,

> is to open a restaurant in Ethiopia . . . where I hope to live a good life, an easy life, next to the church if possible, so I can pray every Sunday with my children, and so my children will be well.[7]

She accepted the government's offer of $14,000, and returned in 2014.

When Milka decided to return home, she was clearly wronged in many ways. Like other migrants, she faced violence and inflammatory speeches, and would likely be deported without the right to apply for refugee status. But imagine she faced no violent attacks or inflammatory speeches, nor likely deportation. Instead, she received a quiet letter from the Ministry of Interior offering her assistance to repatriate, part of a policy to encourage Africans to leave using no coercion or incitement, making return possible for some but not others.

This chapter considers whether such a policy would be wrong. More generally, it considers whether it is wrong to assist unwanted minorities to leave. In addressing these questions, I move beyond discussing refugees, and address migrants not at serious risk from returning, but who are assisted in returning because of their race. Such migrants are not victims of coercion, but may be victims of discrimination.

If they are, it is not clear why. When we think of discrimination, we often imagine victims harmed, or at least not benefiting. Victims are denied visas, jobs, apartments, places in universities, and equal rights before the law.[8] Rarely do we imagine victims treated differently in a way that is beneficial for them precisely because they are not wanted.

Such beneficial discrimination is not limited to immigration control in Israel. Over fifty years ago in New Orleans, white segregationists assisted African-American families agreeing to move to New York City.[9] In a recent case in New York, a landlord offered black tenants $12,000 to leave their apartments, increasing the value of his property as only white tenants remained.[10] In 2009 Japan paid thousands of dollars to Latino migrant workers agreeing to repatriate, never paying other migrants to leave.[11] A year later the British National Party promised to pay $78,000 to asylum seekers voluntarily leaving the country, making clear that only those not "White British" would qualify.[12] Five years later British Prime Minister David Cameron discussed the refugee influx, and his only mention of African refugees was in the context of a "return path," implying that African refugees would receive assistance to repatriate, never mentioning similar return assistance for Syrian refugees.[13] When Milka was paid to leave, her case was not exceptional. Like similar cases, it has simply been overlooked.

In the next section I will describe cases outside the sphere of immigration, including cases where individuals pay minorities to leave towns, businesses, and apartment buildings. I address such cases outside immigration to determine whether, more generally, it is permissible to pay minorities to leave. I will demonstrate that such payments are wrong in one sense: they demean recipients of the payments, who understand how much they are not wanted. In Section 7.2 I argue that paying minorities to leave is not merely wrong, but can be morally impermissible if certain conditions are met. In Section 7.3 I apply my arguments to cases of repatriation.

Before proceeding, let me clarify my focus and assumptions.

I assume that an act – such as paying minorities to leave – can be wrong but still permissible. When I write "wrong" I mean there are wrong-making features of the act, even if there are also right-making features of the act. When the right-making features outweigh the wrong-making features, the act can be permissible and others have reason to permit and legalize the act. I assume that others have reason to permit an act that provides major benefits for victims.

Here is an example. Imagine an individual believes women are mentally inferior to men and so helps women in need by providing donations to women's shelters. This man's actions have wrong-making features: he has sexist motivations and his donations are perhaps demeaning. His actions also have right-making features: he is helping women in need. These right-making features could render his actions permissible because of the benefits for women he assists. At the very least, it is worth considering when actions are permissible despite their wrong-making features. This is not to claim that actions are permissible based solely on consequences or that, if an individual acts permissibly, they are not worthy of moral criticism from others. I assume this man is worthy of criticism for his sexism. Nor do I assume that, if an individual benefits from a permissible act, they must be grateful: the women assisted by this man needn't be grateful given his attitudes. Rather, my assumption is merely that benefits can create countervailing reasons for establishing permissibility.[14]

I shall demonstrate in Section 7.1 that paying minorities to leave is wrong in some ways, but potentially permissible because of the benefits for recipients like Milka. Only in Section 7.2 do I set out the conditions under which payments are impermissible despite the benefits accrued.

In addressing payments for minorities, I shall not distinguish between payments which make it possible to leave – as when a state pays for transport home – and payments which incentivize a person to leave – as when a state provides money to encourage repatriation. I refer to both cases as "paying minorities to leave." I make no distinction primarily for simplicity, to focus on puzzles of discrimination that cut across both types of cases.

There are other forms of assistance, besides payments, which similarly encourage minorities to leave. Minorities may be offered free housing far away, or food aid in a distant refugee camp. Though I focus on money to leave, the conclusions I reach are applicable for other cases involving benefits for the discriminated.

In describing minority members, I shall mostly focus on ethnic and gender groups, all of whom I shall call "minorities." I will not significantly address discrimination against other groups, such as poor, disabled, or elderly individuals paid to leave institutions, companies, or states. This is for simplicity. If you believe that discrimination against other groups is similar, this is consistent with the argumentation I put forth. Finally, I put aside cases of structural injustice, where no agent has an explicit intent to exclude.[15] In all of the cases I present, the discriminator pays minorities with the intent of encouraging them to leave precisely because the discriminator thinks they are less valuable. The politician who paid Milka to leave had openly racist preferences, but was giving Milka an opportunity she otherwise would not have.

Given the opportunity for Milka, it is not clear if she was treated in an impermissible manner.

7.1 A THEORY OF WRONGFUL DISCRIMINATION

Current theories of discrimination cannot establish whether paying minorities to leave is impermissible. To demonstrate this point, consider what different theories might say about an organization established in 1954 called the White Citizens' Council.

The White Citizens' Council had one primary goal: to keep segregation legal in the American South. It spent a decade boycotting black-owned businesses, lobbying congressmen to keep segregation legal, and producing a children's book that taught heaven was segregated.[16] By 1962 it failed to keep segregation legal, and so changed its tactics, offering thousands of African Americans transport and money to leave southern states and move north. The first family to accept this offer was Louis and Dorothy Boyde and their eight children, all living in New Orleans. Louis had recently lost his job after falling ill, and Dorothy was expecting another child. They quickly packed their bags and accepted the Council's $50, food, and bus tickets out of town, boarding a bus for New York City, elated to start a life with more stability and employment.[17] The Council had many goals in sponsoring their migration, but one was simple: to reduce the number of African Americans in New Orleans.[18]

There are four theories we might raise to establish whether the Council's offer was permissible. The first three theories struggle to establish if the Council's offer was wrong at all, let alone impermissible. I take this as a point against such theories, given the intuitive feeling that something was wrong with the Council's offer. The fourth theory establishes the wrongness of the Council's offer, but does not establish if it was permissible, given the benefits for the Boydes.

7.1.1 Other Features

The first theory is not quite a theory, but a claim: The Boydes were not wronged by the payments themselves, but by general inequality in New Orleans and the Council's other racist actions. Because of general inequality and racism, they were essentially compelled to accept the free transport and cash.[19] If ethnic minorities are compelled to leave town, they are victims of forced discrimination, rather than voluntary offers. It is forced discrimination that disturbs us, rather than the payments themselves.

I do not believe racism and inequality in New Orleans fully explains the intuition that something was wrong with the payments. Imagine the Council consisted of only one white supremacist in a very tolerant city, and she spent her days approaching ethnic minorities, offering them money to leave, and recipients accepted the money without facing any coercion or other form of racism. Many may feel uneasy about such payments even though they entail no other forms of racism. Something seems wrong with the payments themselves, and a good theory will explain why.

7.1.2 Harm and Beliefs-Based Theories

Two common theories of discrimination struggle to explain why the Council's actions were wrong, let alone if they were impermissible.

According to the harm-based theory, discrimination is wrong when it harms minority members, either by excluding them, denying them opportunities, or widening the gap between them and more advantaged groups.[20] It is wrong, for example, if white business owners are biased against black job applicants, because this excludes many potential black employees from employment, denying them equal opportunities for employment, and widening the likely income gap between black and white job applicants.

This theory seems to imply that the Boydes were not wronged when paid to leave. Though they left New Orleans, they were not excluded in the traditional sense. They were never forced to leave, and the money helped them escape a society full of exclusion, and join one with less segregation and far more job opportunities. While it is true that leaving New Orleans was likely a difficult experience, prying them away from the home they knew, it also helped them obtain opportunities they preferred having. Nor did they just happen to benefit from the Council's discriminatory payment scheme, as when a person is denied a job opportunity, moves to another city, and happens to find greater opportunities and advantages in this new city.[21] The White Citizens' Council specifically intended for African Americans to benefit from migrating, to persuade them to leave and never come back.

The Boydes, as members of a disadvantaged group, were also never made worse off by the payments, and the payments did not widen the gap between their position and the position of white residents of New Orleans. Precisely the opposite: As they boarded the bus, cash in hand, they were given an extra opportunity whites did not have, including poor white residents who wished to have funds to leave.

These harm-based theories also cannot explain why other forms of payments are wrong. Today, some attorneys claim women can receive higher severance pay if they prove they were discriminated against, including in the termination of their contracts.[22] If this is true, some companies may essentially pay women to leave, offering generous severance to women who agree to quietly accept termination. We might imagine a woman paid to leave and made economically better off than if no discrimination had taken place at all, receiving more money than the men received in their salary. If there is something wrong with such severance pay, a good theory will explain why.

A second theory of discrimination is more promising. It holds that discrimination is wrong when the result of racist or sexist beliefs, regardless of whether victims are harmed.[23] The Council paid the Boydes to leave because of racist beliefs, and companies may pay women to leave because of sexist beliefs.

This theory, however, is still limited, as sometimes it seems wrong to pay minorities to leave despite the payer holding no racist or sexist beliefs. In 2015, for example, a Brooklyn landlord paid $12,000 to black residents agreeing to vacate his apartments, never offering white residents this money. He did not act because of racist beliefs, but because of financial interest: An all-white building increased the market value of his property, allowing him to charge more rent.[24] His actions seem disturbing even if motivated by financial gain alone.

Some may claim the landlord was acting on racist beliefs, as he was responding to the demands of white renters willing to pay more to live in an all-white building. These white renters had racist beliefs, or at least objectionable biases. It is wrong to discriminate in response to the racist beliefs or biases of others. For example, it is wrong for an employer to only hire white salespeople to successfully sell to white racist costumers. This would be wrong even if the employer herself held financial motives alone.[25]

But even if racist beliefs can explain why the landlord acted wrongly, they struggle to explain the wrongness of payments in some fictional cases. Consider a case by Deborah Hellman, in which a principal asks black and white children to sit on opposite sides of a classroom for aesthetic reasons alone, completely unaware of the history of segregation. His actions seem wrong even if he holds no objectionable beliefs, and is not intending to fulfill the objectionable preferences of others.[26] We might similarly imagine a principal paying black students to leave the room, similarly for purely aesthetic reasons. His actions would seem wrong, even if his beliefs were not.

7.1.3 Expressivist Theory

"Expressivist" theories of discrimination best explain the wrongness of the payments, but do not establish whether they are permissible.

These theories hold that discrimination is wrong because it expresses the demeaning message that minority groups are "not fully human or . . . of equal moral worth."[27] One can express a demeaning message without holding racist or sexist intentions, and without being aware one is offending and demeaning others.[28] For example, if I use a racist slur I can demean the recipient of the slur even if I am not aware of the meaning of my utterance. One can even demean someone who is not aware they are being demeaned.[29] A girl with cognitive disabilities may be demeaned if taunted on the playground, even if her impairment means she is not aware she is being taunted. Importantly, one can demean another even if they benefit from an offer. It would be demeaning to go up to a stranger on the street and ask if she would be willing to take part in violent sexual acts in return for money, even if the woman accepted the offer and benefited from the money.

There are a number of reasons why offers can be demeaning, even if recipients benefit. One reason is that offers objectify recipients, as in the case of the woman above, or because they are combined with an endorsement of racism or sexism, such as offering women extra severance pay to leave. Offers can also be demeaning because they imply a certain meaning due to historical practice. When the principal offers black students money to leave the classroom, he is engaging in the practice of segregation. Because segregation had a certain meaning in the past – in the past, it was used to dehumanize minorities – the meaning still lingers today, explaining why the principal's actions seem offensive.

Discriminatory offers can also be demeaning because they treat minorities as members of a group, rather than as individuals with their own autonomous decisions, preferences, and talents. This is wrong even if the recipients of the offers benefit. In an example demonstrating this idea, Benjamin Eidelson asks us to imagine an orchestra director selecting an East-Asian violinist despite her poor performance, because he is influenced by the stereotype that women of East-Asian descent are better at playing the violin. The director disrespects her because he treats her as a member of a group, rather than an individual with her own unique character and skills. He demeans her even if she is happy to pass the audition.[30]

This general theory of discrimination explains why the White Citizens' Council's actions were wrong. The Council treated the Boydes as members of a group, rather than as individuals to be judged according to their skills, character, and unique attributes. Because the Council was also openly racist, the payments also implied a particularly demeaning message: "We do not want you so much, that we are willing to give you money to leave." Indeed, the more money a discriminator is willing to pay, the more strongly he expresses how much he is willing to sacrifice personal resources to meet his racist preferences. In this sense, payments are distinct from merely requesting that another person leave, without offering any money at all. The money is constitutive of the message, and so constitutive of the wrong.[31]

The idea that payments can be demeaning may be consistent with some harm-based accounts. If payments are demeaning, they often socially exclude, in the sense that individuals are told how little they are valued in society. If payments are demeaning, they also undermine equality of opportunity, in that individuals no longer have the opportunity to be free from the demeaning message implied by the payments. Similarly, if payments demean the worst off in society, and harming the worst off is what makes discrimination wrong, then we can view demeaning payments as wrong in this sense. In other words, some harm-based theories, like the expressivist theory, can view demeaning others as wrong even when they benefit. It remains the case that the expressivist theory is useful for establishing why certain types of discrimination are wrong despite no reduction in wellbeing, resources, or preference-fulfillment.

Though the expressivist theory establishes when discrimination is wrong, it does not establish when it is permissible. As Hellman herself notes, her theory does not "say when the wrongfulness of [discrimination] may be overridden by other considerations."[32] Other considerations may include the benefits minorities gain, and their acquiescence in light of these benefits. Were payments to cease, minorities would be denied access to money they could otherwise obtain, and which some feel is beneficial.

Some might argue that benefits for victims – even significant ones – are not competing moral considerations, and so ought not to make wrongful discrimination permissible. Hellman and Yuracko separately discuss a case evoking this intuition, involving a casino that forced female workers to wear makeup, forbidding male employees from doing so. For different reasons, Hellman and Yuracko both conclude that the casino wrongfully discriminated against the women.[33] This case is interesting, I believe, partly because the employees gained a salary, were not forced to work at the casino, and possibly benefited compared to alternative forms of employment. I still feel the women were treated impermissibly for the reasons raised by Hellman and Yuracko. The benefits they received seem irrelevant.

Even if this is true, the women were not benefiting from the discrimination itself; they would still gain a salary in a world where employers stopped requiring women to wear makeup, assuming the casino retained its customers when the women stopped wearing makeup. If the government banned sexist dress codes in casinos, women would not lose money. This is not the case with payments to leave: Minorities would lose money if this type of discrimination ceased, because the payments are precisely what the discrimination entails.

Some might argue that, even if minorities prefer the payments, preferences are not strong reasons to permit otherwise wrongful discrimination. This is because, more generally, preferences hold little weight in establishing permissible discrimination. If most women in a country prefer banning the vote for women, their preferences are less important than ensuring all women have freedom to vote. But there is an important distinction between preferences for forced exclusion and preferences for voluntary incentives. When individuals support forced discrimination, they are denying opportunities to others. When women support banning voting they deny other women the opportunity to vote, potentially harming them in the process. The same cannot necessarily be said about the Boydes. When they boarded the bus, cash in hand, nobody else was forced onto the bus. It was their private choice alone, and one to which they consented.

Of course, perhaps it was not their private choice alone, and perhaps they never really consented. These are possibilities I shall now address.

7.2 A THEORY OF IMPERMISSIBLE DISCRIMINATION

If payments are only permissible because recipients consented and no one else is harmed, payments are impermissible if recipients have not consented or third parties are harmed.

7.2.1 Consent

There are, broadly speaking, three groups of individuals who may fail to consent to the payments to leave, and so have been impermissibly wronged. One group is comprised of those offered money to leave who reject the offer. We might imagine women rejecting the offer of severance pay to leave, and black families rejecting funds to relocate. Such women and families have been exposed to a demeaning offer without benefiting, given that they turned the money down. If they have been demeaned without benefiting, they have been wronged without benefiting, and so have been impermissibly wronged.

Even when individuals do accept money to leave, they may still fail to give their consent. Some individuals accept money offered, but would rather money not be offered at all.[34] Imagine a tenant in Brooklyn receives a call from her landlord offering her $12,000 to leave the apartment. She realizes that all black tenants received the same phone call, while white tenants did not, and decides it would be preferable to leave her apartment than remain in the building of a racist landlord. She accepts his offer, despite wishing he had never posed it at all. Such a woman has not consented to being given the offer, even if she consented to the offer itself. More generally, individuals may accept money because they feel that, once the demeaning offer is on the table, the expressive meaning has already been conveyed, and so they may as well accept the money and leave. Individuals may also accept an offer to be polite, or to avoid creating tension, while still wishing the offer was never posed.[35] When individuals prefer not to be offered money, they do not feel they are benefiting compared to no offer. If they are not benefiting while being demeaned, they are not benefiting while being wronged, and so are being impermissibly wronged.

Some may claim that, even if most minority members do not want the offer to leave, the offers should still be permitted. If offers are not made, no one will be able to accept them, including those who want them. Importantly, we cannot know if someone would have consented to being given the offer unless they are asked, "Do you want me to offer you money to leave?" and this question would be tantamount to an offer. To address this concern, we may wish to distinguish between the ways in which offers are posed. Very public advertisements may be more intrusive compared to private ones, and more likely to offend those who would rather not receive these offers at all. If payments should ever be permitted, offers should be limited to discretely advertised offers alone.

7.2.2 Third Party Harm

There is a third category of individuals who have not consented to payments. They are comprised of third parties never offered payments, but harmed by their provision.

In general, third parties harmed by a transaction have a complaint against parties to the transaction. For example, if an individual suffers from health conditions because others are buying and selling polluting cars, she has a complaint against those buying and selling polluting cars. If third parties are negatively impacted by payments for minorities to leave, they too have a complaint: they have been forced to endure harm against their will, without having consented to this harm.

This raises the question of how much weight we place on the harms these third parties face. While it is difficult to establish a precise rule, it seems the more disadvantaged the third parties are, and the more significant the harms they face, the greater weight their interests hold. If paying minorities to leave creates significant harm against those already disadvantaged, we have a weightier reason to view the payments as all-things-considered impermissible, rather than just wrong in one way.

There are a number of ways paying minorities to leave can impact third parties.

One way is by increasing implicit bias, harming all members of a given group, including members never offered money to leave. If the public is unaware there is an exchange of payments, they may assume minorities are less willing to stay, reinforcing the stereotype that members of this group are less committed to staying.[36] Imagine, for example, a sexist chief executive officer offering women generous severance payments to retire, leading more women to retire early. Others may assume women choose to retire early because they are less committed to their jobs when, in fact, they choose to retire early because they are paid to leave their jobs. If this stereotype about women sets back the interests of other women, including those never offered money to leave, then others are harmed without the corresponding benefit.

Even if payments do not have these impacts, they may still demean all members of a minority group. The discriminator is sending a general message: "I am willing to pay money to encourage members of this group to leave." Other members of the group understand that, in a close possible world – a world where they lived in a particular building, or held a different position in a company – they, too, would be unwanted.

Indeed, payments can even demean individuals who are not of the group paid to leave, but of other disadvantaged groups, including other ethnicities, religions, genders or sexualities. These groups may understand that, in a close possible world in which their group was targeted, they too would be unwanted. Being exposed to this possibility may be unsettling, and possibly offensive, without the financial benefit obtained by the parties paid to leave. Payments may even offend members of the majority who oppose the racist and sexist ideals being promoted by the payment schemes. If my employer paid minority workers to leave, this would be offensive towards the ideals I hold of creating a society where all are valued regardless of their race, ethnicity, sexuality, or gender. A small part of my interests would be set back as a result of the payments, without any corresponding benefits.

Payments do not necessarily harm or demean others in the manner described. They needn't enhance biases if they occur sparingly, and needn't be offensive if they occur privately. If the landlord in Brooklyn only offered these payments once, and if he never advertised his actions, perhaps only those directly paid were demeaned and, if they benefited and consented, were not treated impermissibly. Moreover, even in cases where third parties are clearly harmed, we might still think payments should be permissible if the benefits for the recipients are substantial enough. The White Citizens' Council provided the Boydes access to basic goods, including an income and schooling for their children, and perhaps these goods could outweigh the harms third parties faced, assuming these harms were limited. Harms might be limited when few know about the payments, and others feel no psychological offence by their provision. It remains the case that harms towards third parties can outweigh the benefits for recipients of payments, making the payments impermissible, rather than just wrong in one way.

7.3 MIGRANT RETURN

Let us return to Milka, and consider whether she was treated impermissibly when paid to leave Israel. As with domestic cases, we can consider whether she consented and whether third parties were harmed.

7.3.1 Consent

In domestic cases, individuals not consenting to payments are demeaned
without benefiting, and so impermissibly demeaned. We might suppose this consideration is less relevant for cases involving immigration.
In cases of immigration, perhaps states can permissibly deport ethnic
minorities. If states can permissibly deport such minorities, paying
them to leave seems permissible as well. In the private cases of the
last section, we needn't have delved into this issue; it seems obviously
impermissible for a landlord to accept white tenants alone, and for an
organization to force individuals to leave a city, so the question was only
whether payments were also impermissible. But if states are permitted
to deny visas based on race, even without migrants' consent, perhaps
they can offer payments based on race, even without migrants' consent.

There are reasons to believe states are not permitted to deny visas
based on race. Consider two common justifications for immigration
control. One is that citizens have freedom of association.[37] Citizens
are members of states, and states are similar to private associations
like clubs. If clubs can exclude, states can as well. Another justification
is that, if states have no control over who enters and stays, this can
overwhelm welfare institutions, harming residents within the state.
If these are the justifications of immigration control, it seems they do
not permit racist exclusion. This is because, in general, freedom of
association and welfare do not permit racist exclusion. Private clubs,
though they have a right to exclude, do not generally have a right to
ban members of a given ethnic group.[38] Local municipalities, though
they have a right to force some to sell homes for overall welfare, do
not have a right to force only some ethnicities to sell their homes
for overall welfare. For example, a municipality wishing to build a
train line cannot build the line on the homes of unwanted ethnic
groups, forcing only them to sell their homes to advance racist goals.
If excluding unwanted ethnicities is wrong regardless of association
and welfare on the domestic level, then such exclusion is wrong in
immigration control.

Why make this leap? One reason is that consistency is important in determining how states ought to act. If the justification for immigration control is it upholds freedom of association, and we feel freedom of association does not justify discrimination, then freedom of association does not justify discrimination in immigration control. Similarly, if the justification of immigration control is that it protects welfare for citizens, and if we feel welfare ought not to be protected with discrimination, then protecting welfare does not justify discrimination in immigration control. At the very least, freedom of association and welfare are not particularly good reasons for states to discriminate against visa applicants based on their race. This conclusion is consistent with a range of theories on immigration ethics. Even David Miller, a strong proponent of states' right to exclude, agrees that racist immigration control is generally wrong.[39] It is wrong, presumably, because it demeans migrants, treating them as members of a group who have lesser worth.

If denying visas to ethnic minorities is wrong because it is demeaning, then offering payments is similarly wrong when it is demeaning. If it is wrong, then a question arises as to whether the payments are still permissible if migrants consent to their provision. As with domestic cases, migrants have not consented if they would rather the offer never be given at all. If Milka would rather she was never offered money to leave, then she was treated impermissibly. There is some evidence this was the case. Milka felt that the government's offer indicated how much she was not welcome in Israel, and felt she may as well repatriate rather than remain in a country where she was not welcome. She preferred a world where she was welcome in Israel, and so may have preferred never being offered money to leave.

7.3.2 Third Party Harm

Some might disagree with my argumentation above. My argumentation assumed racist selection methods in private clubs are wrong, despite freedom of association, and so racist visa denials are wrong, despite freedom of association. Some might hold that private clubs do have a right to select membership based on race,[40] and so states have a right to provide visas based on race. By extension, states have a right to pay migrants to leave based on race.

Even if states have a right to deny visas based on race some of the time, it seems unlikely they have a right to deny visas based on race when this harms their own citizens. Were a state to deny visas to black applicants, this would harm black citizens, communicating to them that their race indicates their lesser worth in the eyes of the government.[41] At the very least, it communicates that if they were not citizens, they would be unwanted because of their race.

Paying minorities to leave harms citizens in the same manner. When Milka was paid to leave, she was essentially told, "You are not wanted." "You" referred to individuals of African descent. This demeaned citizens of African descent, who were communicated the following message: "If you were not a citizen, you would be unwanted because of your race." The more race is used as an indicator of who receives money to leave, the more citizens of the same race understand that, in a close possible world, they too would be unwanted. This message additionally demeans members of other disadvantaged minorities who understand that, in a world where they were targeted, they too would be unwanted. And it demeans members of the majority who feel offended by the racist ideals promulgated by the payments offered.

As with domestic cases, payments may also reinforce stereotypes and biases, and so further harm citizens of the state. If the government pays minorities to leave because of their race, then race may be viewed as indicative of who is an outsider, causing the public to view citizens of the same race as outsiders. In some instances, this may place these citizens' lives at risk. In Israel, shortly after the government began paying Eritrean and Ethiopian migrants to leave, assailants attacked two Jewish citizens of Ethiopian descent, mistaking them for non-Jewish non-citizens from Eritrea or Ethiopia.[42] This not only harmed the men who were attacked, but members of the public who opposed discrimination against Ethiopian Jewish citizens. The more governments use race as a criterion for who should be encouraged to leave, the more citizens may view race as an indicator of who should be attacked or, at the very least, viewed as different, suspected as not belonging.

Of course, harms towards citizens could be avoided entirely if the government offered payments to all migrants, regardless of their race. Such payments would not be discriminatory, and so citizens not harmed in the manner I just described, and migrants would still access the benefits of being paid to leave. But if the government is unwilling to provide payments in a non-discriminatory manner – it insists on only paying unwanted minorities to leave – then payments may be impermissible if the harms towards citizens are substantial.

The above general rule is not absolute. In some cases migrants may have very strong interests in accessing payments to leave so they can acquire more food, shelter, mobility, and freedom from violence. Their interests in accessing basic necessities may trump others' interests in avoiding the harms of payments. Milka's interests in accessing assistance for repatriation perhaps trumped the interests of citizens of Ethiopian descent to avoid harms arising from the prevalence of payments. At least, this is a possibility if the harms for citizens fell below a given threshold. It remains the case that, if the harms against citizens are significant enough, the benefits for migrants may be insufficient to deem the payments permissible. Moreover, the benefits for migrants are not relevant if migrants would prefer to not be offered payments at all. If payments that harm citizens are only permissible when migrants' interests trump those of citizens, and migrants feel their interests would be better met if never offered money to leave, the money is impermissible.

7.4 CONCLUSION

Milka was paid to leave partly because she was from Africa. She was a victim of wrongful discrimination, demeaned by the government that provided her assistance. But like other migrants, she preferred to accept assistance to repatriate than to face violence on the streets, incitement by politicians, and continued unemployment. Other migrants wished to repatriate not because they faced violence, incitement, or unemployment, but because they hoped to find better opportunities elsewhere, only possible when handed a large amount of cash to board a flight home. While such payments may seem intolerable, they help minorities escape intolerance, making it easier to resettle, start a business, and integrate into a new city or country. And while such payments are demeaning, they give resources to the demeaned, helping ensure their exit is smoother than it otherwise would be, at times enriching them more than if no discrimination took place at all.

Given the benefits for migrants, it is unclear if they are morally permissible. To establish if they are, we must appeal to two considerations, the first relating to consent. Payments may be impermissible when they are given to migrants who have not consented to their provision, and wish they had never been available at all. Even if one holds that the consent of migrants is not relevant, payments may be still impermissible when they harm citizens of the same minority, signaling to them that their race is indicative of their lesser worth.

Accounting for these considerations is essential for establishing a more complete theory of repatriation. It is true that Milka felt $14,000 provided more opportunities then staying in Israel. But we ought to shift our gaze away from her and onto other migrants and citizens. In doing so, we can consider a broader array of people and outcomes, better determining when discrimination is permissible and when repatriation is wrong.

NOTES

1. Cormac Ó Gráda, *Famine: A Short History*, Princeton: Princeton University Press 2009; Benjamin A. Valentino, *Final Solutions: Mass Killing and Genocide in the Twentieth Century*, Ithaca: Cornell University Press 2004.
2. Interview with Milka, Tel Aviv, July 29, 2014.
3. Ibid.
4. A study conducted in 2012 asked a random sample of respondents, "To what extent do you agree with the statement that 'Africans are a cancer to the body'?" 52 per cent stated that they agreed with this statement. See Ephraim Yaar and Tamar Hermann, "Peace Index – May 2012," <http://en.idi.org.il/media/602071/Peace%20Index-May%202012(1).pdf> (last accessed October 3, 2014).
5. Haggai Matar, "Community Shaken after Night of Arson Attacks on African Refugees," 972 Magazine, April 27, 2012, accessed February 26, 2012 <https://972mag.com/community-shaken-after-coordinated-attacks-on-african-refugees/43727/> (last accessed February 26, 2013); Haggai Matar, "Three Eritreans Stabbed in South Tel Aviv Internet Cafe," 972 Magazine, July 31, 2012, <https://972mag.com/three-eritreans-stabbed-in-south-tel-aviv-internet-cafe/52142> (last accessed February 26, 2018).
6. *Haaretz*, "Israeli MK: I Didn't Mean to Shame Holocaust by Calling African Migrants a 'Cancer,'" May 27, 2012, <http://www.haaretz.com/israel-news/israeli-mk-i-didn-t-mean-to-shame-holocaust-by-calling-african-migrants-a-Cancer-1.432809> (last accessed July 19, 2017); Ilan Lior, "Israel to Offer African Migrants $5,000 to Leave," *Haaretz*, October 30, 2013, <https://www.haaretz.com/.premium-israel-to-migrants-leave-and-get-5-000-1.5282114> (last accessed February 26, 2018).
7. Interview with Milka, Tel Aviv, July 29, 2014.
8. Deborah Hellman, *When Is Discrimination Wrong?* Cambridge, MA: Harvard University Press 2008; Kasper Lippert-Rasmussen, *Born Free and Equal? A Philosophical Inquiry into the Nature of Discrimination*, Oxford:

Oxford University Press 2014; Shlomi Segall, "What's so Bad about Discrimination?" *Utilitas* 24(1)(2012):82–100.

9. Clive Webb,"'A Cheap Trafficking in Human Misery': The Reverse Freedom Rides of 1962," *Journal of American Studies* 38(2)(2004):249–71.

10. D. W. Gibson, '"I Put in White Tenants': The Grim, Racist (and Likely Illegal) Methods of One Brooklyn Landlord," *New York Magazine*, March 12, 2015, <http://nymag.com/daily/intelligencer/2015/05/grim-racist-methods-of-one-brooklyn-landlord.html> (last accessed September 20, 2016).

11. Hiroko Tabuchi, "Japan Pays Foreign Workers to Go Home," *The New York Times*, April 22, 2009, <http://www.nytimes.com/2009/04/23/business/global/23immigrant.html> (last accessed June 14, 2017).

12. Jon Smith,"BNP Would Offer £50,000 to Leave the Country," *The Independent*, April 29, 2010, <http://www.independent.co.uk/news/uk/politics/bnp-would-offer-pound50000-to-leave-the-country-1957668.html> (last accessed November 17, 2014).

13. Emma Dabiri, Leah Green, and Bruno Rinvolucri, "Africans Being Left Behind by a Two-Tiered Refugee System," *The Guardian*, September 30, 2015, <https://www.theguardian.com/commentisfree/video/2015/sep/30/africans-left-behind-two-tier-refugee-system-video> (last accessed November 11, 2015).

14. We might call such acts "wrongful permissible acts," or "suberogatory" acts but, for simplicity, I shall use the word"permissible"on its own. Some deny the existence of wrongful permissible acts, arguing that there are only right and permissible acts, or wrongful impermissible acts, or neutral acts that are neither right nor wrong. If one holds this, then when I write "permissible" I merely mean that others should not interfere and attempt to stop the act. See Julia Driver,"The Suberogatory," *Australasian Journal of Philosophy* 70(1992):286–95; and Hallie Rose Liberto,"Denying the Suberogatory," *Philosophia* 40(2)(2012):395–402.

15. Fred Pincus,"From Individual to Structural Discrimination," in (eds) Fred L. Pincus and Howard J. Ehrlich, *Race and Ethnic Conflict*, Boulder, CO: Westview 1994: 82–7 at 84.

16. Timothy B. Tyson, *Blood Done Sign My Name: A True Story*, New York: Crown 2004 at 182.

17. Webb 2004 ibid. at 249.

18. Webb 2004 ibid. at 253.

19. Webb 2004 ibid. at 249.

20. See Hugh Collins,"Discrimination, Equality, and Social Inclusion,"*Modern Law Review* 66(1)(2003):16–43.; Tarunabh Khaitan, *A Theory of Discrimination Law*, Oxford: Oxford University Press 2015; Lippert-Rasmussen 2014 ibid. at 175; and Segall ibid. 2012 at 82–100.

21. Lippert-Rasmussen 2014 ibid. at 157.

22. Andrew S. Bosin, LLC. "Discrimination and Harassment Claims Could Increase Amount of Severance Offered," <http://www.njbusiness-attorney.com/articles/discrimination-harassment-claims-increase-severance.html> (last accessed July 20, 2015).

23. Richard Arneson, "What is Wrongful Discrimination?" *San Diego Law Review* 43(4)(2005):775–807; Larry Alexander, "What Makes Wrongful Discrimination Wrong?" *University of Pennsylvania Law Review* 14(1) (1992):149–219.

24. Importantly, he did not discriminate in his choice of tenants; he merely encouraged black tenants to leave, while white tenants remained. He could then raise the rent of the vacated apartments, as white residents were willing to pay more money to live in an all-white apartment building. See Gibson 2015 ibid.

25. This is similar to an argument raised by Benatar to defend the view that discrimination is wrong when it involves differential treatment for characteristics that are irrelevant. For example, it is wrong to not hire a black salesperson if being black is irrelevant to the position. If an employer does not hire black salespeople because customers are racist, this is still wrongful discrimination because, though the salesperson's race really is relevant to the position, it is only relevant because of customers who are discriminating based on characteristics irrelevant to the position. See David Benatar, *The Second Sexism: Discrimination against Men and Boys*, Sussex: Wiley-Blackwell 2012 at 7.

26. Hellman 2008 ibid. at 26.

27. Hellman 2008 ibid. at 35.

28. Hellman 2008 ibid. at 26.

29. Hellman 2008 ibid. at 27.

30. Benjamin Eidelson, "Treating People as Individuals," in (eds) Deborah Hellman and Sophia Moreau, *Philosophical Foundations of Discrimination Law*, Oxford: Oxford University Press 2013. Sometimes, such treatment is not demeaning, or seems less demeaning. If a white man is elected because of his gender and ethnicity, despite poor performance, it does not seem he is demeaned, despite being treated as a member of a group, rather than an individual. It may only be demeaning if the minority group is in some ways disadvantaged, or has been historically disadvantaged. See Tarunabh Khaitan, "Prelude to a Theory of Discrimination Law," in (eds) Deborah Hellman and Sophia Moreau, *Philosophical Foundations of Discrimination Law*, Oxford: Oxford University Press 2013 at 145.

31. This is not to claim that, whenever an agent pays minorities to leave, they are necessarily demeaning these minorities. We might imagine an anti-racist NGO that provides funds to rescue minority members from a racist society. Its actions may not be demeaning if it provides money alongside

lobbying for the end of racism, and makes clear the payments are to help individuals achieve equal opportunity, rather than to reinforce racial separatism. But when payments are provided as an endorsement for racism or sexism, or in a way that evokes an offensive meaning due to historical injustice (as with the principal), then the payments do imply a demeaning message.

32. Hellman 2008 ibid. at 31.
33. Hellman 2008 ibid. at 46; and Kimberly Yuracko, "Sameness, Subordination, and Perfectionism: Towards a More Complete Theory of Employment Discrimination Law," *San Diego Law Review* 43(2006):857–97.
34. As David Velleman puts it: "Preferring to accept an invitation is consistent with wishing you had never received it." See J. David Velleman, "Against the Right to Die," *Journal of Medicine and Philosophy* 17(6)(1992):665–81 at 672. More generally, it can be rational to consent to an offer, but also rational to prefer the offer never be available at all.
35. More generally, we often would be better off without an offer even if we would consent to an offer once it was given. For example, in a country where dueling is legal, individuals may consent to duel to save their honor; but many would prefer to never have the option to duel, to avoid being in a position where they need to accept a duel to save their honor. Velleman 1992 ibid. at 676.
36. A related argument has been raised by Deborah Satz with regards to some market transactions. In her example, a reason to ban surrogacy services is that it reinforces stereotypes of women as baby-making machines, and this may harm other women. See Deborah Satz, *Why Some Things Should Not Be for Sale: The Moral Limits of Markets*, Oxford: Oxford University Press 2010 at 130.
37. Christopher Heath Wellman, "Immigration and Freedom of Association," *Ethics* 119(2008):109–41.
38. Of course, there is some private freedom of association where discrimination is permissible. If a person is less attracted to members of other ethnic groups, they are not acting impermissibly when marrying a member of their own ethnicity. For it is generally accepted that we cannot quite control who we love, or who we are attracted to, and even who we become friends with. But such ethnic and gender-based exclusion is unacceptable in more public establishments, where members have no intimate attachments to each other, such as golf clubs, schools, and apartment buildings. See Sarah Fine, "Freedom of Association is Not the Answer," *Ethics* 120(2010):338–56 at 351.
39. See David Miller, "Immigration: The Case for Its Limits," in (eds) A. Cohen and C. Wellman, *Contemporary Debates in Applied Ethics*, Malden, MA: Blackwell Publishing 2005 at 204.

40. Thomson holds the view that private companies are permitted to discrimi-
     nate in hiring. Matt Zwolinski compellingly argues that, if we accept that
     private discrimination is permissible – we accept that it is permissible for
     an individual to discriminate in selecting their friends or lovers – then a
     case can be made for permitting discrimination in less-private spheres,
     such as in firms and clubs. See Judith Jarvis Thomson, "Preferential Hiring,"
     in (ed.) William Parent, *Rights, Restitution, and Risk*, Cambridge: Harvard
     University Press 1986; and Matt Zwolinski, "Why Not Regulate Private
     Discrimination?" *San Diego Law Review* 43(2006):1043–62.

41. Michael Blake, "Discretionary Immigration," *Philosophical Topics* 30(2)
     (2002):273–89 at 284; Wellman 2008 ibid. at 139.

42. Vered Lee, Tomer Zarchin, and Yaniv Kubovich, "Protesters Attack Israeli
     of Ethiopian Origin in Rally against African Migrants," *Haaretz*, June 20,
     2012, <https://www.haaretz.com/anti-migrant-protesters-mistakenly-
     attack-ethiopia-originated-israeli-1.5165737> (last accessed August 9,
     2016); Arin Hillel Mizrahi (Hebrew), "Police Officer Hits Border Patrol
     Soldier: Thought He Was Foreign National," Ynet, January 1, 2015, accessed
     February 5, 2015 <http://www.mynet.co.il/articles/0,7340,L-4631012,00.
     html> (last accessed February 5, 2015).

Chapter 8

RESTITUTION

In 1992 Kiden was a young Bari woman living in Juba when she was forced to move with her family to Khartoum. Once there she sold tea by the side of the road, later boarding a train to Wadi Halfa, a boat to Egypt, and a Jeep to Israel. In Israel she found work, managed to save over $10,000, and flew back home to Juba in 2012, investing her money in small businesses, making more money still. In 2013 she traveled to a land registry office where she obtained the deeds to the land she had once owned, submitting them to a judge shortly after, and successfully winning her land back.[1]

Abdalla returned to South Sudan in 2010 and achieved similar success. Like Kiden he accessed the property he fled as a young boy, located near the Jebel Lado mountain north of Juba. He was largely successful because of his brother:

> My older brother was here the whole war. He did not go to any place. He said, "this is my land" and protected it for us . . . Agriculture is important. I see they bring all of the vegetables from other countries. It's important, more than offices. Offices are maybe something to think about after I succeed.[2]

He is based in Juba, where he established a bar near his home, and travels Friday to Saturday to his land, growing tomato, cucumber, and cabbage to support his wife and daughter.

Other returnees were less successful in re-obtaining their land. Daniel, as noted in Chapter 5, failed to obtain his parents' land in Addis Ababa. Some returnees, such as Emmanuel, re-obtained their land but have little control over this land in practice:

I started working as a farmer when I came [to South Sudan]. You work and in the night people come and steal your things. The JIU – Joint Integrated Unit – is the integrated army. They were there stealing my things. This was my ancestor's land. It was very big and near the river. Around 25 dumas.[3]

Kiden and Abdalla were more successful in their repatriation than Daniel and Emmanuel. They returned to the particular home they fled, and to the property they lost, experiencing what many consider a more just return.[4]

Though returning to property seems just, it benefits some refugees more than others. Kiden is settled comfortably on her land, and Abdalla is farming his, but their fellow returnees are living without basic shelter and food, having held relatively little property before their displacement. Such was the case for Peter and Nyanuer:

We were here a year and there was no school for the kids. There was malaria and no money. The school was too expensive here. It was $1,000. So I sent the children to Kakuma refugee camp [in Kenya] . . . To eat I come to this shop, have tea with milk, and then go home.[5]

No milk, no gas, nothing. If you don't have money for something for cooking, like coal and dishes, then there's nothing you can cook with. Just this nylon sheet we sit on, on the ground. There are just so many problems. I can deal with them, a little, but my kids just can't.[6]

If most returnees are living without basic necessities, it is not clear if property ought to be returned to its original owners, rather than redistributed to those most in need.

This issue is not merely academic. In the history of restitution, some governments have limited full restitution, instead redistributing property to those in greater need. Such was the case in Guatemala, where the government redistributed land based on need, rather than returning land to the original owners.[7] In Hungary, following the end of the Cold War, the government sold refugees' former property to the highest bidder, redistributing profits to social programs.[8] In Rwanda, following the 1994 genocide, the government limited restitution to those who had left in the last ten years, redistributing land in a manner deemed helpful for improving food security.[9] The question of restitution is not merely whether refugees once owned the property they left; it is whether they ought to own this property today.

This chapter addresses this question. In doing so, I focus on property restitution alone, putting aside other forms of reparations. For example, I do not address whether returnees have a right to financial compensation for the human rights violations they experienced. It may be that Kiden had a right not only to her family's property in the suburb of Juba, but to reparations for being forced from her home as a small girl, and experiencing the trauma of being torn away from her family. I focus on restitution not because it is more important, but because it is more common,[10] and clearly conflicts with the values of distributive justice.

When I write "values of distributive justice," I refer to the value of bringing about a just distribution of goods. There may be value in the South Sudanese government redistributing Kiden's land to Peter and Nyanuer. Of course, there is disagreement over what a just distribution entails. Some argue that this entails all having equal resources,[11] while others hold this entails all having equal opportunity to resources or happiness.[12] Still others hold that a just distribution entails prioritizing the welfare of the worst off, rather than equality itself. This might involve the government investing more in the educational opportunities of those from more disadvantaged families, or investing more money in ensuring those who have short life expectancies can live a few extra years, even if this comes at the expense of health amongst the general population. Others hold that a just distribution entails all having a minimally decent standard of living, regardless of whether there is gross inequality.[13] For example, the government could give some of Kiden's land to Peter and Nyanuer, so that they can grow crops for their children, but needn't ensure that Kiden, Peter and Nyanuer have exactly the same amount of land.

While there is disagreement over what a just distribution entails, there is broad agreement that redistribution from the very wealthiest to the very poorest is justified, if this ensures the very poorest have enough to survive, while making the wealthiest only slightly worse off. My aim is to consider whether, if one supports such redistribution, one ought to support restitution that conflicts with this redistribution.

The chapter is organized as follows. Section 8.1 presents common justifications for restitution which, I argue, cannot fully explain why restitution is justified when it conflicts with the value of distributive justice. In Section 8.2 I present a new and more promising justification: property restitution avoids wrongful discrimination, which can express a demeaning message to both the wealthy and the poor. To avoid discrimination, governments ought to return to refugees their former property, or also redistribute non-refugees' property at the same rate. In Section 8.3 I respond to objections against this claim.

8.1 FOUR COMMON JUSTIFICATIONS FOR RESTITUTION

There are, broadly speaking, four common justifications raised for restitution. All four, I argue, fail to fully explain why restitution is justified for wealthy refugees whose property could easily be provided to those in far greater need.

8.1.1 Harm

One common argument raised in favor of restitution is related to harm. It begins with the premise that those who are harmed from wrongdoing ought to be given reparations for this harm. If a wealthy individual is violently punched in the stomach, and as a result is forced to give up her money, she loses wealth in a manner that is wrong. She is therefore owed reparations for this wrong in the form of the assets she lost.[14] When refugees are displaced and lose their property as a result, they are wronged and harmed as a result. They are therefore owed reparations to counteract this harm.[15]

This argument is relevant not only for refugees re-obtaining moderate amounts of wealth, like Kiden, but for refugees re-obtaining large amounts of wealth, like Maria Altmann. Maria Altmann was a young Jewish girl living in 1930s Austria when her uncle's paintings were confiscated by the Nazis. They both fled the country, the paintings remained in the hands of the Austrian government, and sixty-four years later Altmann won a restitution case against the Austrian government, receiving her uncle's paintings back. Shortly after she sold them for $150 million. Like Kiden, she was harmed in multiple ways when she fled, and so harmed multiple ways from a wrong. One way she was harmed was through the loss of property she would have inherited. Like Kiden, the restitution she received countered this harm.

There are two objections commonly raised to this harm-based argument. One is that we cannot give someone reparations for what they would have had were they not wronged, because we cannot know what someone would have had were they not wronged.[16] But this objection is not relevant if we can guess what they likely would have were they not wronged. If Kiden and Altmann would have likely had certain assets had they not been displaced, we can claim they were owed restitution for these likely losses.

The second potential objection is that this harm-based account will have absurd implications. Imagine an individual is wrongly displaced but, had they not been displaced, they would have died in a natural disaster, such that being displaced saved their life. This individual is not harmed from the displacement, given that she is alive as a result of the displacement, and would otherwise be dead.[17] A harm-based theory of reparations seems to imply she is not owed reparations. If this seems odd, and we feel she is owed reparations, another theory of reparations must explain why.

This objection can be avoided if we expand the scope of harm to include non-counterfactual harms. As noted in Chapter 2, non-counterfactual harms occur when an agent's actions cause harm, and this harm would have occurred in the absence of the agent's actions.[18] If I steal your laptop, you experience harm even if someone else would have stolen your laptop had I not stolen it first. If I also wronged you in stealing your laptop, I ought to return the laptop even though you are not counterfactually worse off from my actions. Similarly, if a woman is displaced because of her ethnicity, and loses property as a result, she is harmed even if she would have died had she not been displaced. She is therefore owed reparations for the harm she experienced.

There is a third and more promising objection to the harm-based account. Even if a person has been wronged, and is harmed as a result, it does not follow she is owed reparations for this harm. This is because, in general, we cannot claim a person is owed reparations for the harm of losing assets they had no right to own, even if they experienced a wrong when losing these assets. Imagine I steal your laptop, and someone violently assaults me, taking the laptop from my possession. Though I have been wronged and harmed, given that I have one less laptop in my possession, this particular harm is not the sort that ought to be rectified, because I had no right to the laptop. Instead, the laptop should be returned to you, assuming you are the rightful owner.

A similar claim could be raised regarding Kiden and Altmann. If we think that Kiden and Altmann had no right to all of the assets they lost from displacement, then even if they were harmed from losing these assets, they had no right to having all of these assets back. One reason we might think Kiden and Altmann had no right to all of the assets is because nobody has a right to large amounts of wealth in a world where others lack basic necessities. Kiden had no right to all of her land when others were in desperate need, and Altmann had no right to paintings worth tens of millions of dollars, dollars she could easily give away to those in desperate need. If they had no right to all assets lost from displacement, they had no right to reparations for all assets lost from displacement.

Similar concerns arise with other cases of restitution. In the 1940s Czech royalty were displaced with the rise of communism, some forced into slave labor, others forced to flee the country to avoid death. With the fall of communism sixty years later, some began re-obtaining their castles, including the count Joseph Kinsky and the former prince William Lobkowicz. Though their restitution countered some of the harms from wrongful displacement, it is not clear they had a right to re-obtain castles if they had no right to their castles prior to communism. Indeed, after obtaining their castles some political actors protested, feeling the castles should have been sold to the highest bidder, and profits distributed to social programs.[19]

Some might object to the above claims. Even if a person has no right to the property they lost, because others are in far greater need, they still have a right to not lose this property through persecution. This is because, more generally, even if a person has no right to property they lost, they have a right to not lose this property through wrongful means. Imagine, for example, that a prosecutor barges into my home with no evidence I had committed any crime, and begins using physical violence against me, forcing me to reveal a laptop I had stolen from you, and the evidence that I had stolen this laptop. She then bags the laptop, brings it to the police station, and stands before a judge several months later, using the evidence she had obtained through violent means. If the prosecutor's only evidence was obtained through violence, the evidence would likely be inadmissible, and she would fail to obtain a conviction.[20] After the trial, she would be forced to return to me the laptop I had stolen. This is true even though everyone knows, including the judge, that the laptop is rightfully yours.

Just as a prosecutor should return me the laptop, perhaps the state should return refugees their assets, even if they had no right to these assets. The state ought to return assets taken through persecution, or another form of wrongful violence, because persecution and violence are wrongful means of obtaining property. For this reason, both Kiden and Altmann had a right to obtain restitution, regardless of whether they had a right to the assets they lost.

The above argument has sway in cases where the agent taking property through wrongful means is the same agent returning the property. When the prosecutor returns the laptop she obtained through violence, she is returning goods she herself obtained through violence. Similarly, if a state takes property by persecuting a minority, it ought to return this property at a later point in time, because it is the agent that took the property wrongfully at an earlier point in time. This argument has less sway, however, when the agent who took property is different than the agent returning property. In the case of Kiden, it was the former Sudanese government that had taken her land, rather than the newly established state of South Sudan. If the new state is a separate agent from the one who wrongfully took her land, then the state is not utilizing violence or persecution when refusing to return her land.

To see the force of this claim, imagine that Svetlana barges into my home, using violence to obtain the laptop I had stolen from you. Svetlana is later arrested by the prosecutor who opens the laptop, and realizes it belongs to you. It seems the prosecutor does no wrong if she returns you your laptop, rather than giving it to me, because the prosecutor has done no wrong herself; it is Svetlana who has committed the wrong. If Sudanese militias took Kiden's property in the 1980s, it does not follow that the new South Sudanese government must return this property to Kiden; it did no wrong itself, and so does no wrong in redistributing her property to those in greater need.

8.1.2 Right-Libertarianism

There is a second justification for restitution. Refugees, some may claim, have a right to the property they fled if, prior to the atrocity, they justly acquired this property. One can justly acquire property, according to right-libertarians, by acquiring un-owned natural resources in a manner that makes others no worse off compared to a world where these natural resources remained un-owned.[21] If one accepts this claim, then

Kiden's ancestors would have acted permissibly in acquiring their land if it was un-owned prior to the acquisition, and acquiring this land made others no worse off than had the land remained un-owned. Had her ancestors then provided this land to their children as gifts, and their children provided this land to their children as gifts, and Kiden's parents bequeathed her this land as a gift, then Kiden would have obtained this land through just means, and her ownership would be just. She therefore would have a right to re-obtain this land upon repatriation.

The above theory of property rights, however, is controversial. If Kiden's ancestors happened to find land before others, it is not clear they had a right to this land simply because others are not made worse off. In arriving first, they not only grew wealthy compared to others in their generation, they helped their children grow wealthy compared to others in their children's generation. If they did not have a right to create such inequality, the theory of property rights should be revised: Rather than claiming one has a right to acquire un-owned resources whenever others are no worse off, one has a right to acquire un-owned resources only when others have an equal or better ability to improve their welfare,[22] or at least live a minimally decent life. If Kiden's ancestors left future generations without a chance of living a minimally decent life, Kiden had no right to this land. At the very least, she would have no right to keep all her land if some land could be redistributed to those who cannot currently live an even minimally decent life.

8.1.3 *Plans*

The third theory of restitution begins with the premise that humans often plan their lives around the assumption that a given state of affairs will persist. For example, a farmer toiling her land will often presume the land she toils will remain in her possession, because she is living in a system of property that allows her to keep land in her possession. She would have difficulty planning for the harvest if she did not know whether the land she toiled now would be hers tomorrow. There is something morally desirable in individuals being able to plan their lives and follow through on these plans. Planning enables autonomy, giving individuals control over their lives, and planning creates certain utilitarian benefits, such as helping economies function.[23] Planning can also contribute to the development of a routine, which can make various tasks easier to fulfill. It is often easier for a farmer to harvest her crops if she plans to wake up every day at 5 am, prepare breakfast at 5:15, rev up the reaper engine at 6, take a break at 12, and so forth. If her surroundings remain the same, this regular routine is easier to follow, becoming a habit with time, and requiring far less willpower to pursue.[24]

If the ability to plan has value, and a person cannot continue plans because their lives have been altered, something morally undesirable has occurred.[25] This person ought to receive compensation to return to the status quo ante, allowing them to continue their plans. Or, at the very least, they ought to receive compensation to continue plans that were based on a reasonable expectation that the status quo would continue, or a reasonable expectation that the status quo ought to continue.[26] If a farmer had a reasonable expectation that land would remain in her possession, or had a moral reason to believe it ought not to be taken through racism and violence, the farmer is owed restitution if her land is unexpectedly taken from her through violent racism.

When Kiden made her life plans in the early 1990s, she made these plans based on the reasonable expectation that her land would remain in her possession, and had a moral reason to believe it ought not to be taken through violent discrimination. When she suddenly lost her land, she could not continue plans she had created based on these reasonable expectations, and so she had a right to get her land back to continue her plans. When Maria Altmann was living in Vienna, she had a reasonable expectation that she would not be forcibly displaced because she was Jewish. Even if she had no reasonable expectation that this would be the case – and she suspected she would be displaced – she had a moral reason to believe displacement should be prevented, and so made life plans with this expectation in mind. Given that these expectations were dashed, she had a right to restitution to continue her plans once again.

There are a number of problems with the above argument. For one, it is only relevant when victims are given swift restitution for the property taken, allowing them to realize the plans they created prior to displacement.[27] Such swift restitution is rare.[28] In Kiden's case, swift restitution was not possible, because the Second Sudanese Civil War lasted for over a decade. When she finally received her land back, she could not continue the plans she had begun when last occupying her land. In Altmann's case, she could not continue her life plans as a young girl in Vienna, nor would she likely wish to, given the trauma she experienced. If neither Kiden nor Altmann would be able or willing to continue the plans they started prior to displacement, neither woman's restitution could be justified by appealing to the plans they started prior to displacement.

Moreover, even when refugees can continue their previous plans through restitution, restitution can come at the expense of other individuals' life plans. In many cases, secondary occupants have moved into refugees' property, and begun forming life plans around the property they now inhabit. Those living in Juba without property titles were often forced to find empty lots and build homes on them. They hoped to obtain squatters' rights as secondary occupants, but in 2009 thousands of these squatters were left homeless when the government destroyed their homes, considered illegally built on the land of previous refugees.[29] These squatters – many of them returning refugees themselves – could not continue their plans because of restitution. If their plans were cut short, we cannot claim protecting life plans is sufficient to justify restitution.

A similar issue arose in Burundi when, in 1972, 120,000 Hutu civilians were killed, and tens of thousands fled, their land left to Tutsi citizens. These Tutsi citizens used this land for agriculture, grazing, and building homes for themselves and their children. Thirty years later, over half a million Hutu refugees demanded their land back, hoping to continue growing crops on the land they had left behind, continuing the plans they had begun prior to the atrocity. The new government faced a dilemma: it could return land to original owners, or allow secondary occupants to remain.[30] Given that secondary occupants had developed life plans dependent on this land, we cannot claim that former refugees' plans provide decisive reasons to support restitution.

More importantly, even when there are no secondary occupants, the claim that life plans matter conflicts, once again, with certain principles of distributive justice. It seems unfair if wealthy individuals are able to create plans dependent on vast amounts of wealth, while the poor are not. This is especially true if the poor have unequal access to assets that can ensure a minimally decent life. If this is unjust, then we can correct for this injustice by redistributing assets to the poor, rather than returning assets to the wealthy. Even if this interrupts wealthy individuals' life plans, it is not clear they had a right to plans dependent on assets to which they had no right, given the needs of others.

To see the force of this claim, return again to the stolen laptop. Imagine that I steal your laptop and pursue life plans around the laptop I stole. One day I am suddenly attacked by Svetlana who steals the laptop. It does not seem that I have a right to obtain this laptop back, even though re-obtaining the laptop would help me realize my life plans. I have no right to realize life plans that were dependent on a laptop I stole, as this was not an asset to which I had a right. If we take seriously the idea that the wealthy often have no right to all of the assets they lost, in the same way I have no right to the laptop I lost, then protecting plans seems like a poor reason to provide restitution.[31]

We could stop here, concluding that many victims of displacement have no right to all of the assets they lost. Some philosophers have reached versions of this conclusion. Jeremy Waldron argues that, even if a population faced an injustice when displaced, they no longer have a claim to their former property if others have become dependent on this property to live a minimally decent life, and those displaced have more than enough to live a minimally decent life.[32] Anna Stilz argues that individuals do not have rights to occupancy over territory if they are not dependent on this territory for subsistence or wellbeing, while others are.[33] This suggests that former refugees do not have a right to return to their former property simply because it was once legally theirs; they have no such right if others require this territory for subsistence and wellbeing. Christopher Kutz, Pablo Kalmanovitz, and others have reached similar conclusions: dispossessed individuals like Kiden do not necessarily have a right to all of the assets they lost, assuming they can maintain a minimally decent life, while others cannot.[34] Even if Kiden was wronged, and perhaps owed funds to compensate for the psychological harm she felt from displacement, she was not owed the assets she would have likely had were she never wronged at all.

8.1.4 Ties

Perhaps restitution is not justified to protect plans, but to protect ties. Many refugees feel ties to their lost property, feeling it has personal cultural resonance, or evokes memories of their lives prior to displacement.[35] Such was the case when South Sudanese farmers re-obtained land they worked prior to the war, and when Czech princes re-obtained castles they lived in prior to fleeing. This was also the case when Bosnians re-obtained their homes in the 2000s, a decade after being expelled by Serb forces.[36] More recently, Greek Cypriots requested restitution from the Turkish government for property they left during the violence of the 1960s and 70s, feeling a personal connection to this property.[37]

Such personal connections are important. Just as our connections to friends and family are important to us, and essential for our identity, so are the homes we live in and the objects we possess. If this is true, then refugees ought to re-own homes they once occupied and the objects they once possessed.[38]

One potential criticism of the above argument is that, in reality, refugees rarely view their property as essential to their identity; if they did, they would not quickly sell it once re-obtained. Bosnians repatriating often sold their homes quickly after repatriating, and Maria Altmann sold her favorite painting for $135 million after it was returned. Indeed, some humanitarian workers discourage refugees from selling their restituted property, feeling this undermines the justification of restitution.[39]

I do not believe this criticism is valid. Humans can feel strong ties to that which they sell, as when painters sell their paintings and authors their books. Indeed, humans sometimes sell their property because of their ties; they want others to feel a similar tie, and benefit from its value. More often, individuals prefer money to continuing ownership despite their strong ties, as when an artist sells her artwork to pay rent. Refugees are no different. They can feel ties to former property, even if they feel it is preferable to sell this property than keep these ties.

There is a more serious objection to the claim that ties justify restitution. It seems unfair that individuals with ties to greater wealth are given this wealth back, especially when this wealth is substantial and non-essential. When Bosnians repatriated, some used their restituted homes for weekend purposes while others – including displaced Roma – remained homeless.[40] It seems unfair that their ties provided them an extra home for the weekend while others were provided no homes at all. When Greek Cypriots requested restitution from the Turkish government, one claimant asked for twenty-six properties.[41] It seems unfair that this claimant's ties gave him a legal right to far more homes than others, while others were left with no homes at all. Ties seem a problem, rather than a justification: a world where individuals feel their identities are tied to their property is a world of special inequality, where individuals have a hard time envisioning themselves with less, and so are reluctant to let go of the properties they own when others are in need. There may be value in a world where individuals learn to have identities that are not tied to this wealth. Such a world would not encourage property restitution in its current form.

If restitution cannot be defended by appealing to harm, libertarianism, plans, or ties, we might suppose restitution is unjust when refugees hold considerable wealth and others are in far greater need. This is the conclusion reached by some governments. Following the collapse of the Soviet Union, Hungary provided refugees no more than an upper threshold of the value of their lost property, limiting their claims to small personal homes, rather than the castles and corporations they fled.[42] Guatemala in the 1990s did not provide refugees full access to the land they fled, instead redistributing land partly based on need.[43] Perhaps Hungary and Guatemala acted more justly than Austria and South Sudan.

There remains nonetheless something appealing about restitution. After fleeing her home Kiden spent decades abroad, traveling from country to country until she finally returned to the land she remembered as a young girl. Maria Altmann fled the Holocaust, never caring about the materials she left behind, but felt an injustice arose when her family's paintings remained in the hands of the Austrian government. There is something inspiring about a South Sudanese refugee obtaining her childhood home, and a Holocaust survivor obtaining the artwork she remembers as a child.

Indeed, some refugees garner their strongest support for restitution from those most supportive of redistribution. Holocaust survivors seeking restitution in the 1950s received their strongest support from the Socialist party in Germany,[44] and subjects I interviewed in South Sudan received their strongest support from those identifying themselves as communists. The socialists in Germany and the communists in South Sudan felt restitution for the wealthy was important despite valuing redistribution from the wealthy.

Maria Altmann recalled similar support for restitution while visiting Austria shortly after receiving her paintings:

> I thought people were going to say, "It's disgusting what you are doing," but out in the streets, people said: "Are you Mrs. Altmann? We are so happy that justice prevailed and you got the pictures back."[45]

8.2 EXPRESSIVE HARMS

Here is one reason justice prevailed when Mrs. Altmann got her pictures back. The reason begins with a premise regarding discrimination from the last chapter: Discrimination against a member of a minority can be wrong because it demeans others of the same minority. For example, if an elite members' club rejects dark-skinned members, this sends a demeaning message not only to dark-skinned individuals hoping to join the club, but to dark-skinned individuals with no interest in joining the club. The latter understand that their skin color is viewed as indicative of their worth, even if they never seek membership.

If discrimination against one minority member can demean other members of the same minority, discrimination against one wealthy minority member can demean other members of the same minority. Consider the following case:

> Racist Robin Hood steals from wealthy individuals of a histori-
> cally-disadvantaged ethnic minority blamed for the ills of soci-
> ety, and redistributes this to all poor individuals. She never steals
> from the ethnic majority.

Racist Robin is giving an advantage to the preferred ethnic majority, allowing them to keep their wealth intact. In doing so, she demeans all members of the minority, including those not wealthy enough to lose property themselves. Those not wealthy understand that a characteristic they hold – their ethnicity – is indicative of their lesser worth.[46] To counteract this harm, the government would have good reason to institute the following rule: If Racist Robin steals from wealthy minority members, the government will force wealthy majority members to give up wealth at the same rate. If this is not possible, the government has a weighty reason to return the property back to the wealthy minority members. Were the government to not return the property back, it would be allowing Robin to demean not only the wealthy, but poor minority members as well. Regardless of whether the wealthy have a right to the wealth they lost, all have a right to be free from the demeaning message implied by Robin's actions.

This has implications for cases involving refugees. Just as Racist Robin demeans all members of a minority when taking the property of the wealthy and redistributing it to the poor, a government or militia demeans all members of a minority when taking the property of the wealthy and redistributing it to the poor. And just as we have reason to adopt a rule with Robin that avoids this demeaning message, we have reason to adopt a rule for refugees that avoids this demeaning message. I call this the Restitution Rule: *if a government or militia confiscates the property of wealthy minority members, then future governments have a weighty reason to either (a) confiscate the property of majority members at the same rate, or (b) return property to the original members.*

Option (a) in the above rule does not involve restitution, but instead confiscation of property owned by majority members. If the Nazi government confiscated the property of Jews, blacks, and Roma in the 1930s and 40s, then future governments could confiscate the property of non-refugees at the same rate. For example, if the Austrian government established Maria Altmann's wealth at $1 million without her uncle's paintings, and the paintings were worth $150 million, it could refuse to return her paintings and then tax all non-refugee Austrians worth $151 million at $150 million. Similarly, if the South Sudanese government established Kiden's wealth at $15,000 without her land, and the land was worth $10,000, it could refuse to return her land and tax all non-refugees worth $25,000 at $10,000. This policy would ensure that the demeaning message of discrimination was avoided, as ethnic minorities would not lose property at a greater rate than ethnic majorities.

In reality, it is often easier for a government to redistribute what it already controls compared to taxing what it does not. When the government controls refugees' former property, it can more easily redistribute this property compared to taxing non-refugees' property at the same rate. The South Sudanese government had control over Kiden's land, and the Austrian government had control over Maria Altmann's painting, so redistributing their assets was easier than taxing wealthy individuals at similar rates.

In such cases, the government has a weighty reason to return property to those returning, even if those returning have no right to the property they seek. Providing restitution is justified to mitigate the demeaning messages arising from discrimination, a message effecting not only the wealthy, but poor individuals of the same minority.

Though the government has a weighty reason to return property, this reason is not absolute. If the number of lives saved by refusing restitution is considerable enough, this may provide a decisive reason to not return property. If the South Sudanese government refused to facilitate restitution, and instead allowed secondary occupants to remain, the benefits of helping the worst off may trump the benefits of avoiding discrimination. It remains the case that, if the benefits for the worst off fall below a given threshold, there is good reason to return property to the original owners even if these owners have no right to the property they lost. In other words, there is some amount of property that the wealthy have no right to own, and which therefore usually ought to be given the poor, but which ought not to be given to the poor if this expresses a demeaning message of discrimination. In such cases, the value of avoiding the expressive harm of discrimination outweighs the value of ensuring a more just distribution of property.

This leaves open the question of how governments weigh the value of avoiding the expressive harm of discrimination against the value of helping those in need. I shall not attempt to provide a set of precise rules, but there are some useful rules of thumb. The first is that, if taking property through discrimination is preferable to no redistribution, then redistributing property taken via past discrimination is preferable to no redistribution. Imagine, for example, that a government took the property of ten members of an ethnic minority, saving hundreds of lives in the process. Though the confiscation was impermissible, given that the discrimination demeaned all members of the minority, perhaps it was preferable to no taxation at all, given the lives saved. If this is true, then when a government inherits property confiscated from ten individuals, and can save hundreds of lives by redistributing the property, redistribution may be preferable to returning the property to its original owners.

The opposite may not be true: If a government in the past confiscated property, and no confiscation would have been preferable, it may still be preferable to redistribute this property today. The earlier government's wrong of confiscating property through discrimination was worse than a current government's wrong of distributing property taken via discrimination. The Nazis confiscating Altmann's paintings and Sudanese militias confiscating Kiden's land were worse than the Austrian government keeping Altmann's paintings and the South Sudanese government keeping Kiden's property. This is because the first two governments acted through intentional racism, while the latter two governments do not. Assuming racist confiscation of property sends a more demeaning message than inheriting property confiscated by others, current governments should adopt a discount rate: If a government confiscates property from 100 ethnic minority members to provide necessities to fifty individuals, it may be acting wrongly, but if a current government inherits the property of 100 ethnic minorities members, it may be acting rightly in redistributing this to fifty individuals. At least, this is a possibility I leave open.

There is an additional consideration we ought to account for when weighing the value of avoiding discrimination against the benefits of redistribution. We ought to account for the rights of secondary occupants. It may be that secondary occupants have greater rights than the rights of other poor individuals. When secondary occupants are both dependent on property for basic needs and also have strong ties to this property, their ties may matter. This is because, while having ties is not a sufficient condition to justify ownership – princes do not have a right to return to their castles simply because of their ties to these castles – ties combined with great need can perhaps jointly create sufficient conditions for ownership. If so, we can adopt a type of discount rate here, as well. For example, if a government refuses to provide restitution to 100 ethnic minority members, instead letting fifty secondary occupants remain, it may be acting rightly, but if it refuses to provide restitution to 100 ethnic minority members, instead redistributing this to fifty individuals who never occupied this land, it may be acting wrongly.

Regardless of how we weigh various values, the conclusion remains: Avoiding the expressive harm of discrimination can provide a decisive reason to support restitution to refugees, even when the refugees have no right to the property they seek.

This conclusion is predicated on the assumption that refugees lost their earlier property because they fled ethnic, religious, social, or political-based persecution. Such refugees were victims of discrimination, creating the need for the Restitution Rule I described. But many refugees were not victims of discrimination when they fled, but of general violence, or an environmental or economic disaster. If such refugees leave behind property because they fled, and this property is given to others, there seems to be no expressive harm towards other members of a given ethnic, religious, social, or political group. Unlike in the case of Kiden, where other Bari members might have suffered an expressive harm when she lost her property, or Altmann, where other Jews may have suffered an expressive harm when she lost her paintings, there are no other members of a group harmed when refugees lose property fleeing general violence or disasters. If so, perhaps there is no need for the Restitution Rule.

Even when refugees flee general violence or disasters, rather than persecution, they can still be members of a defined group. If they are members of a defined group, the group might include poorer members who are offended if their wealthy co-members cannot obtain their property back. Consider, for example, economic refugees born into poverty who are forced to leave to find employment abroad, their property used by secondary occupants the moment they leave. Were the government to refuse to return them their property upon return, on the grounds that they were wealthy upon return, the government would be disadvantaging them compared to those never forced to leave because they were born into wealth. The government would therefore be disadvantaging individuals born into poverty compared to those born into wealth. This can be demeaning towards all individuals born into poverty, signaling to them that their poverty at birth indicates their access to property rights.

It might be comparable to a state that only taxed those who grew up poor and were now wealthy, while not taxing those who had been born into wealth. This would send a message to those who were born poor and remain poor: "If you ever become wealthy we will disadvantage you compared to your peers born into wealth." The state ought to change the tax code so that all of equal wealth are taxed at the same rate, regardless of their economic status at birth. The same holds true for restitution: the government has good reason to provide restitution to the former poor who are now wealthy as a result of migration, assuming it is unable or unwilling to confiscate the property of the wealthy never forced to migrate.

This leaves open the possibility that a state refusing to provide restitution sometimes expresses no demeaning message. It expresses no demeaning message if there is no clear group that is more susceptible to disaster. Imagine everyone is born into life-threatening poverty, some leave in search of basic necessities abroad, and some who leave grow wealthy. If these wealthy individuals cannot access the property they left behind, the government would not be sending a demeaning message to any group, as all individuals in society were born into the same poverty. The government would merely be sending the message that, if one chooses to leave the state, and grows wealthy abroad, one will lose property to those in greater need.

Moreover, the government would not be sending a demeaning message if it refused to return property that was owned by those who were members of particularly privileged social groups. The princes who fled Czechoslovakia may have been disadvantaged compared to other princes around the world, but they were advantaged compared to most others in Czechoslovakia. If such refugees are not truly members of a disadvantaged group, it is unlikely that their inability to access restitution will create an expressive harm towards other group members. In such cases, restitution is less important than in the cases of Kiden and Altmann.

8.3 OBJECTIONS

Some might reject my conclusion that restitution is justified to counter the demeaning messages arising from discrimination. They might raise one of three objections.

8.3.1 No Expressive Harm

Some object to my claim that, if wealthy refugees are not given restitution, this will create an expressive harm towards others. They might claim that, so long as refugees are only given that to which they have a right, no expressive harm will arise.

> To see the appeal of this claim, consider the following fictional case: Bob is a racist prosecutor who dislikes Russians. He therefore assumes that Svetlana is guilty of stealing Jamal's laptop and pursues her as a suspect. By chance, the laptop is found in Svetlana's home, along with evidence that proves Svetlana stole Jamal's laptop.

Bob acted wrongly when pursuing Svetlana, but the state should not right this wrong by letting Svetlana keep the laptop, as she is not the rightful owner. Instead, Bob should himself be fired, due to his racist intentions, or perhaps he owes Svetlana an apology or compensation for the discrimination she faced. If he refuses to let her keep the laptop, this does not communicate an expressive harm toward other Russians, because Svetlana is not denied that to which she has a right.

The same can be said about refugees. A government ought not to return property for which refugees have no right. The government, if it wishes to right the wrong refugees experienced, should provide reparations for the wrong of discrimination or displacement, distributed equally amongst all refugees. If it refuses to provide restitution, this does not communicate an expressive harm, any more than Bob refusing to let Svetlana keep the laptop communicates an expressive harm towards others.

The above objection holds in a world where the state redistributed all wealth for which individuals had no right. In such a world, refugees would not receive their property back, and non-refugees would be taxed at the same rate, such that refugees would no longer be disadvantaged. However, if such a scheme is not implemented – if the government refuses to return property to refugees but also allows non-refugees to keep their property intact – then the government is allowing discrimination to occur. When the discrimination negatively effects the wealthy of a given group, this can express the idea that being a member of this group is indicative of one's rights, offending the poor members of this group.

It would be comparable to Bob pursuing suspects who are Russian, while avoiding the pursuit of suspects who are non-Russian. If neither group of suspects is entitled to stolen goods, it seems wrong to give Russian suspects only what they are entitled to – goods they did not steal – while allowing other suspects to keep what they are not entitled to – goods they stole. When Bob lets non-Russian suspects off the hook, he is communicating an expressive harm towards all Russian individuals: that their nationality indicates their lesser rights. If the state must decide how to respond, it has good reason to begin pursuing non-Russian suspects to a greater degree, or Russian suspects to a lesser degree, avoiding the discrimination that arose, and the expressive harm arising from this discrimination.

Similarly, if a government refuses to return wealth to the refugees who fled, allowing those who remained to keep their wealth intact, the government would be giving refugees what they deserve – no more than an upper threshold of wealth – while giving non-refugees that which they do not deserve – wealth above this threshold. Doing so demeans members of the minority forced to flee, including poor members of this same minority. This provides one reason for the government either to take the wealth of non-refugees at the same rate, or to provide restitution to refugees returning.

8.3.2 *The Discrimination is Indirect*

Some might claim that, when a government refuses to provide restitution, it is merely engaging in permissible indirect discrimination. Permissible indirect discrimination occurs when an agent disadvantages a given minority, but does not explicitly target this minority, nor intends to disadvantage this minority. Doing so creates no expressive harms against other members of this minority. Consider the following case:

Firm I: A firm selects applicants for promotion based on their
score on a test. Members of ethnic minorities tend to score less
well because they are also new immigrants without the relevant
educational background. As a result, they are disadvantaged.

According to some, the above is not a case of wrongful discrimination,
as the firm does not directly target minorities, nor intends to disadvantage minorities. Minorities just happen to hold characteristics disqualify-
ing them for promotion. Similarly, when the government redistributes
refugees' former property, it does not target refugees or the group which
refugees are members of. It intends to merely redistribute the property of
those who left the country and, by chance, refugees have left the country.

Even if indirect discrimination is not wrong, there is reason to believe
refugees are victims of direct discrimination, rather than indirect discrimination. Or, more specifically, they are victims of what I call Direct
Indirect Discrimination (DID).

DID occurs when a policy disadvantages a minority with characteristics obtained from direct discrimination by a third party.

Here is an example based on an actual case:

Firm II: Throughout the 1950s the Duke Power Company, based
in North Carolina, required that employees pass an aptitude test
and have a high school diploma. This disadvantaged African-
Americans, more likely to fail the test, having been banned from
attending adequate schools under North Carolina's policy of
forced segregation.[47]

The Duke Power Company did not (ostensibly) intend to prevent
African Americans from being promoted. It intended to prevent all
individuals from being promoted if they failed the test or had no high
school diploma. But the reason African Americans failed the test or
had no high school diploma was because of direct discrimination by
the state.

If direct discrimination is wrong, there is reason to avoid DID, which
enhances the negative effects of direct discrimination. The Duke Power
Company enhanced the negative effects of direct segregation by creating yet another barrier to those who faced direct segregation as children. Even if a given African American employee managed to pass the
test and obtain a diploma despite the negative effects of segregation,

the company would be requiring him to do what white employees need not: pass an exam despite a childhood of segregation. For this reason Firm II has a stronger moral reason to avoid the test compared to Firm I. The same holds for cases involving refugees. When states refuse to return refugees their property, they institute a policy indirectly impacting victims of persecution, a form of direct discrimination. In doing so, they reinforce disadvantages that members of the persecuted group face, potentially offending other victims of this persecuted group.

Some refugees, of course, are not victims of direct discrimination, having fled natural or economic disasters. They are therefore victims of indirect discrimination alone. But even indirect discrimination can send a demeaning message to members of the group discriminated against. For example, imagine that a state required lower taxes for private homes, on the grounds that one's home is a necessity, and necessities ought not to be taxed at the same rate. Imagine, also, that those born into wealth tended to have more of their assets placed into homes, such that those lucky enough to be born wealthy were taxed at a lower rate than those born poor. Even if such a tax code is only indirect discrimination, it could still send a demeaning message towards those born poor: "Your wealth at birth determines how much taxes you will pay." Similarly, there is something demeaning about a tax code that disadvantages individuals who were unlucky enough to have had to flee because of a natural or economic disaster. Refusing to return refugees their property back would be such a tax code. It would be better, all else being equal, for the government to take the property of all individuals at the same rate, regardless of whether they were victims of bad luck in the past. When this is impossible, the government has one reason to implement restitution.

8.3.3 Refugees Redistributing Property

There is a final objection. We might suppose there is no demeaning message when the bodies redistributing property are run by refugees themselves. Such was the case in 1950s Germany, when charities run partly by refugees were in charge of administering property confiscated during the Holocaust, and in 1990s Rwanda when the refugee-led government took charge of property restitution.[48] If refugees are in control of property that wealthy refugees lost, and choose to redistribute wealthy refugees' former property to those in greater need, they are engaging in collective decision-making. Such collective decision-making ought to be respected, rather than viewed as a form of demeaning discrimination.

In some cases, the above is true. If refugees redistributing property receive the consent of the previous owners, they are not engaging in wrongful discrimination against these previous owners, but are engaging in collective decision-making. But if refugees redistribute property without the consent of the previous owners, they are disadvantaging a minority against their will, and so reinforcing a demeaning message against members of this minority. It does not matter if the refugees disadvantaging the minority are also members of this minority.

This is because, more generally, it does not matter if agents disadvantaging a minority are members of the same group discriminated against. Imagine Racist Robin was also sexist, and steals from women alone. Her actions are demeaning towards women even if she is a woman herself. Even if the government was headed by a woman, it would also have good reason to return the property she stole, or tax men at the same rate to ensure women are not disadvantaged. In taking either approach, the government avoids expressing the idea that one's gender indicates one's rights.

Refugee-headed governments similarly have good reason to return property or tax non-refugees at the same rate, avoiding similar expressive harms. While this reason is not always decisive – the need to help the poor may triumph in some cases – it is a reason nonetheless, and decisive in a range of cases.

8.4 CONCLUSION

When states provide restitution to refugees, they help princes access castles, collectors their artwork, and the wealthy their land. It is not clear if such restitution is justified, when others are in far greater need. I considered four common reasons to believe such restitution is justified. The first was related to wrongdoing: we might suppose that if a person is wronged and loses property as a result, they are owed restitution for this harm. I rejected this claim: if a person has no right to the property they lost, they are not owed restitution for this property, even if their loss was the result of a wrong. I then considered the claim that refugees have a right to property that their ancestors obtained, rejecting this as well: just because one's ancestors obtained property, it does not follow that one has a right to this property, especially when others are destitute. The third justification for restitution was related to plans: refugees have a right to property they once possessed to continue the life plans they began. This justification, however, is rarely relevant for refugees, who often cannot continue the plans they began because they fled their property decades prior. The final justification was related to ties: individuals have a right to property to which they feel strong ties. I rejected this justification, arguing that ties seem like a poor justification when others are in great need.

There is a more promising justification for restitution: Restitution prevents the expressive harms arising from discrimination. If a government refuses to give victims of persecution their property back, it disadvantages the persecuted compared to those who never fled, as those who never fled can keep their property intact. This sends a demeaning message not only to the persecuted seeking to obtain their property back, but to poor individuals of the same group persecuted against. These poor individuals understand that a characteristic they hold – their ethnicity, religion, or social or political group – grants them fewer rights. To avoid this demeaning message, the government has a weighty reason to either tax the property of non-refugees at the same rate, or return property to refugees returning home.

NOTES

1. Interview with Kiden, Juba, December 15, 2013.
2. Interview with Abdalla, Juba, March 19, 2012.
3. Interview with Emmanuel, Juba, March 20, 2012.
4. Megan Bradley, *Refugee Repatriation: Justice, Responsibility and Redress*, Cambridge: Cambridge University Press 2013 at 48; "Housing and Property Restitution in the Context of Return of Refugees and Internally Displaced Persons – Preliminary Report of the Special Rapporteur, Paolo Sergio Pinheiro," 2003. Text available at Scott Leckie (ed.), *Housing, Land, and Property Restitution Rights of Refugees and Displaced Persons*, Cambridge: Cambridge University Press 2007.
5. Interview with Peter, Juba, December 20, 2013.
6. Interview with Nyanuer, Juba, December 23, 2013.
7. Leckie 2007 ibid. at 140.
8. Michael Heller and Christopher Serkin, "Revaluing Restitution: From the Talmud to Postsocialism," *Michigan Law Review* (97)(6)(1999):1385–1412 at 1402.

9. The government's goal is to consolidate land holdings, based on the assumption that consolidation creates more efficient land use, which will help improve the economy for all. In reality, such redistribution programs may harm the poorest in society, as Pottier has pointed out. See Johan Pottier, "Land Reform for Peace? Rwanda's 2005 Land Law in Context," *Journal of Agrarian Change* 6(4)(2006):509–37.

10. Though it is more common than other forms of reparations, it is still uncommon in absolute terms. The vast majority of refugees around the world cannot obtain the property they left behind. See Kate Clarke, "War Reparations and Litigation: The Case of Bosnia," Report of an international meeting held at the Law Faculty of the University of Amsterdam, April 17–18, 2014, <http://www.nuhanovicfoundation.org/user/file/bosniareport-digi.pdf> (last accessed February 27, 2018); Rhodri C. Williams, "The Significance of Property Restitution to Sustainable Return in Bosnia and Herzegovina," *International Migration* 44(3)(2006):39–61. For analysis on reparations in Burundi, see Immigration and Refugee Board of Canada, "Burundi: Status of Land Disputes and Process for Recovering Property Seized by People in Power during the Genocides," <http://www.refworld.org/docid/4b20f0322b.html> (last accessed April 23, 2017); and Jennifer Moore, *Humanitarian Law in Action within Africa*, Oxford: Oxford University Press 2012 at 141. For a general discussion on the lack of reparations for human right violations, see Rama Mani, "Reparations as a Component of Transitional Justice: Pursuing 'Reparative Justice' in the Aftermath of Violent Conflict," in (eds) Koen De Feyter, Stephan Parmentier, Marc Bossuyt, and Paul Lemmens, *Out of the Ashes: Reparations for Victims of Gross and Systematic Human Rights Violations*, Antwerp and Oxford: Intersentia 2005: see, in particular, 62–5.

11. Ronald Dworkin, "What is Equality? Part 2: Equality of Resources," *Philosophy and Public Affairs* 10(4)(1981):283–345.

12. Richard J. Arneson, "Equality and Equal Opportunity for Welfare," *Philosophical Studies* 56(1)(1989):77–93; G. A. Cohen, "On the Currency of Egalitarian Justice," *Ethics* 99(4)(1989):906–44; Shlomi Segall, *Equality and Opportunity*, Oxford: Oxford University Press 2013.

13. Harry Frankfurt, "The Moral Irrelevance of Equality," *Public Affairs Quarterly* 14(2000):87–103; Liam Shields, *Just Enough: Sufficiency as a Demand of Justice*, Edinburgh University Press 2016; Martha Nussbaum, "Aristotelian Social Democracy," in (eds) R. B. Douglas, Gerald M. Mara, and Henry Richardson, *Liberalism and the Good*, New York: Routledge 1990.

14. Gerald F. Gaus, "Compensation and Equality," in (ed) John Chapman, *Nomos XXXIII*, New York University Press 1991; Dennis Klimchuk, "On the Autonomy of Corrective Justice," *Oxford Journal of Legal Studies* 23(1)(2003):49–64 at 50; Christopher Kutz, "Justice in Reparations: The Cost

of Memory and the Value of Talk," *Philosophy and Public Affairs* 32(3) (2004):277–312 at 300; Robert Nozick, *Anarchy, State and Utopia*, Oxford: Blackwell 1974 at 152–3; Stephen Perry, "On the Relationship Between Corrective and Distributive Justice," in (ed.) Jeremy Horder, *Oxford Essays in Jurisprudence*, Oxford: Oxford University Press 2000 at 269; Judith Jarvis Thomson, "Preferential Hiring," in (ed.) William Parent, *Rights, Restitution, and Risk*, Cambridge: Harvard University Press 1986 at 149.

15. UN Commission on Human Rights, "The Right to Restitution, Compensation and Rehabilitation for Victims of Gross Violations of Human Rights and Fundamental Freedoms," Final Report of the Special Rapporteur, Mr. M. Cherif Bassiouni, submitted in accordance with Commission Resolution 1999/33, E/CN.4/2000/62 (2000); Hanoch Dagan, *Unjust Enrichment: A Study of Private Law and Public Values*, Cambridge: Cambridge University Press 1997.

16. Rodney C. Robert, "The Counterfactual Conception of Compensation," *Metaphilosophy* 37(3–4)(2006):414–28 at 416; and Jeremy Waldron, "Superseding Historical Injustice," *Ethics* 103(1)(1992):4–28, at 8–14.

17. Robert ibid.

18. There are different formulations of causation that allow for an agent to cause an outcome in this way. See Frank Jackson, "What Effects?" in (ed.) Jonathan Dancy, *Reading Parfit*, Oxford and Malden, MA: Blackwell Wiley 1997; David Lewis, "Causation as Influence," *The Journal of Philosophy* 97(4)(2000):182–97; Michael McDermott, "Influence vs. Sufficiency," *The Journal of Philosophy* 99(2)(2002):84–101. For the discussion from Chapter 2, see pages 38–41.

19. Heller and Serkin 1999 ibid. at 1401; Marjorie Miller, "Noble Try to Reclaim Heritage: Czech Republic is Reviving Aristocrats' Old Dreams by Returning Castles, Land Seized by Communists," *LA Times*, June 28, 1994, <http://articles.latimes.com/1994-06-28/news/mn-9588_1_czech-republic> (last accessed April 13, 2017).

20. More generally, even if evidence is relevant for determining if an individual likely committed a crime, there are cases where we still ought not to use this evidence. See H. L. Ho, *A Philosophy of Evidence Law: Justice in the Search for Truth*, Oxford: Oxford University Press 2008 at ch. 5 and 6.

21. Nozick 1974 ibid. at 150–78.

22. Michael Otsuka, *Libertarianism without Inequality*, Oxford: Oxford University Press 2003 at 27 and 35–7.

23. Robert Goodin, "Compensation and Redistribution," *Nomos, Compensatory Justice*, 33(1991):143–77 at 153–7.

24. Cara Nine, "The Wrong of Displacement: The Home as Extended Mind," *The Journal of Political Philosophy*, 26(2)2018:240–57.

25. Anna Stilz, "Nations, States, and Territory," *Ethics* 121(2011):572–601 at 582–7; Anna Stilz, "Occupancy Rights and the Wrong of Removal," *Philosophy and Public Affairs* 41(4)(2013):324–56 at 336–41; Nine, 2018, ibid.

26. It is not enough, as many note, to claim that an individual has a right to reparations to continue plans formed with reasonable expectations, because one can reasonably expect to be wronged. If a farmer expects to have her land taken because of her ethnicity, we cannot claim the theft disrupted her reasonable expectations, as she expected her land to be taken. In such cases the farmer was still wronged because she had reason to believe her land ought not to be taken due to discrimination. See Goodin, 1991 ibid. at 153–7; Waldron 1992 ibid. at 18; Perry 2000 ibid.

27. Goodin 1991 ibid. at 153; Waldron 1992 ibid. at 18–19; Kutz 2004 ibid. at 295.

28. For example, requests for reparations to Holocaust survivors, and to sex slaves of the Japanese wartime army, took decades to reach the courts. See Michael J. Bazyler, "The Holocaust Restitution Movement in Comparative Perspective," *Berkeley International Law Journal* 20(1)(2002):11–44.

29. Naseem Badiey, *The State of Post-Conflict Reconstruction: Land, Urban Development, and State Building in Juba, Southern Sudan*, Woodbridge: James Currey 2014 at 169.

30. IRIN News, "Burundi's Land Conundrum," November 14, 2013, <http://www.irinnews.org/report/99126/burundis-land-conundrum> (last accessed May 11, 2017).

31. I am not claiming here that poor individuals' rights to redistribution takes priority over wealthy individuals' rights to reparations. I am claiming that the wealthy have no rights to reparations if they lost wealth to which they have no right. For claims similar to the former, see Kutz 2004 ibid. at 295–6 and Klimchuk 2003 ibid. at 63.

32. Waldron 1992 ibid. at 24–8.

33. Stilz 2013 ibid. at 342 and 351–5.

34. Kutz 2004 ibid. at 301–2; Jon Elster, "On Doing What We Can: An Argument against Post-Communist Restitution and Retribution," *East European Constitutional Review* 1(2)(1992):15; Kutz 2004 ibid. at 301–2; Section 4 in Pablo Kalmanovitz, "Corrective Justice vs. Social Justice in the aftermath of War," in (eds) Morten Bergsmo, César Rodríguez Garavito, Pablo Kalmanovitz, and Maria Paula Saffon, *Distributive Justice in Transitions*, Oslo: Torkel Opsahl Publisher, International Peace Research Institute 2010. Some have argued not that individuals have no right to reparations, but that states that have committed a wrong in the past needn't be required to provide reparations if they cannot then provide for populations in need. See, for example, Catherine Lu, *Justice and Reconciliation in World Politics*, Cambridge: Cambridge University Press 2017 at 229–30.

35. Scott Leckie, "Introduction," in *The Pinheiro Principles: United Nations Principles on Housing and Property Restitution for Refugees and Displaced Persons*, Geneva, Switzerland: Center on Housing Rights and Evictions 2005; Janna Thompson, "Cultural Property, Restitution and Value," *Journal of Applied Philosophy* 20(3)(2003):251–62; United Nations General Assembly Resolution 217A, "Universal Declaration of Human Rights," 1948; United Nations Resolution 61/295, "Declaration on the Rights of Indigenous Peoples," 2007.

36. US Department of State, "Bosnia and Herzegovina," Bureau of Democracy, Human Rights, and Labor, March 11, 2008, <https://2009-2017.state.gov/j/drl/rls/hrrpt/2007/100551.htm> (last accessed April 26, 2017).

37. European Court of Human Rights (ECtHR). 2010. *Demopoulos and Others v. Turkey* (Admissibility) § 19–31, <http://hudoc.echr.coe.int/app/conversion/pdf/?library=ECHR&id=001-97649&filename=001-97649.pdf> (last accessed May 4, 2018).

38. Some have claimed that all property rights can be defended by appealing to the way property is essential for our sense of self. We needn't accept this more radical claim, however, to accept that property can be essential for our sense of identity, and reparations to refugees can be defended by appealing to this sense of identity. See Stephen Buckle, *Natural Law and the Theory of Property*, Oxford: Clarendon Press 1991; Charles Fried, *Contract as Promise: A Theory of Contractual Obligations*, Cambridge: Harvard University Press 1981 at 99–101; Will Kymlicka, *Multicultural Citizenship: A Liberal Theory of Minority Rights*, Oxford: Oxford University Press 1995 at 220.

39. Megan J. Ballard, "Post-Property Restitution: Flawed Legal and Theoretical Foundations," *Berkeley Journal of International Law* 28(2)(2010):462–96 at 476; Sandra F. Joireman and Jason Brown, "Property: Human Right or Commodity?" *Journal of Human Rights* 12(2)(2013):165–79; Jon Unruh, "Humanitarian Approaches to Conflict and Post-Conflict Legal Pluralism in Land Tenure," in (ed.) Sara Pantuliano, *Uncharted Territory: Land, Conflict and Humanitarian Action*, Bourton on Dunsmore, UK: Practical Action Publishing Ltd. 2009 at 65.

40. Stef Jansen, "Refuchess: Locating Bosnian Repatriates after the War in Bosnia-Herzegovina," *Population, Space and Place* 17(2011):140–52 at 148; Tatjana Perić, "Displaced Roma in Bosnia and Herzegovina," European Human Rights Center, July 11, 2000, <http://www.errc.org/article/displaced-roma-in-bosnia-and-herzegovina/877> (last accessed January 9, 2018).

41. ECtHR. 2010. *Demopoulos and Others v. Turkey* (Admissibility) § 19–31.

42. Heller and Serkin 1999 ibid. at 1402–3.

43. Housing and Property Restitution ibid. 2003 at 140.

44. Hal Lehrman, "The New Germany and Her Remaining Jews: Reporter's Notebook," *Commentary Magazine*, December 1, 1953, <https://www.commentarymagazine.com/articles/the-new-germany-and-her-remaining-jewsa-reporters-notebook/> (last accessed April 18, 2017).

45. Isabel Wilkinson, "Remembering Maria Altmann, Holocaust Hero Who Won Back Klimt Paintings," The Daily Beast, February 8, 2011, <http://www.thedailybeast.com/articles/2011/02/08/remembering-maria-Altmannn-holocaust-hero-who-won-back-klimt-paintings.html> (last accessed April 17, 2017).

46. Some may feel that Racist Robin acts wrongly only because she steals, and not because of her discrimination. But imagine Racist Robin did not steal, and merely donated her own money to members of the historically advantaged majority, refusing to donate to the disliked ethnic minority. She would be acting wrongly due to her racism, even though she was involved in no theft at all, and even if she was creating a more just distribution of resources. For a similar case and argument, see Adam Slavny and Tom Parr, "Harmless Discrimination," *Legal Theory* 21(2) (2015):100–14 at 109.

47. *Griggs v. Duke Power Co,* 401 US 424 (1971).

48. Lehrman 1953 ibid.; Aline Mutabazi, "Redistribution Land Reform in Rwanda: The Impact on Household Food Security," *Rwanda Journal* 22(B) (2011):129–57.

Chapter 9

CONCLUSION

At 1:35pm on January 15, 2013, Nhial boarded Ethiopian Airlines flight 491 from Juba to Addis Ababa. He wore a hat to cover his Nuer tribal scars, settled into his seat, and landed two hours later in Ethiopia. He took off his hat, strode into the sunlight, and asked a Nuer stranger for help. Together, they drove into town.

When Nhial was a small boy, Northern Sudanese militias entered his village, grabbed his leg, and pulled him into a truck. They took him to their home in the north of the country, where he worked as a slave into adulthood, eventually escaping to Khartoum, and then Egypt, arriving in Israel in 2007. Once there he worked in a hotel in Jerusalem, saved money, and read extensively about the risks of living in modern-day South Sudan. In June 2011 he bought a ticket for Juba, arriving on July 2, 2011, a week before South Sudan became an independent country. He rested for a day, and then sought employment in the oil industry, but his applications were ignored, even as his Dinka friends were hired. Instead, he opened a small stall in a market, selling sweets, making just enough to live.[1]

In 2013, a day after the outbreak of the civil war, Dinka soldiers arrived at his market stall, grabbed his sweets and money, and demanded that he leave. He did, jogging to the IDP camp, where we ran into each other a week later, recognizing each other from Jerusalem. He told me he did not regret his choice to return, despite being forced to flee to the camp. We met again on January 16, by chance on the same flight to Addis, him fleeing the country, me returning home. He still did not regret his choice and, half a year later, joined the opposition military in South Sudan. In 2014 I visited him in Gambella in Ethiopia, where he was still satisfied with his choice to repatriate.

OBI never assisted Nhial in returning, but if they had, they would have done no wrong. He was never coerced into leaving nor paid to leave, saving up money himself. He researched the risks of living in South Sudan before he returned, thought about his decision extensively, and endangered himself alone when boarding the flight. Nor was he likely to regret his choice. The year he returned, past returnees in Juba were happy with their decisions, and it was likely he would be happy as well.

Unlike Nhial, most refugees leaving Israel were coerced into their decisions, either threatened with deportation or living in destitution. Such coercion is common around the globe, with governments insisting that refugees live in enclosed camps, often threatening to deny aid to those who stay. In such cases, humanitarian organizations should refuse to help with return unless they also lobby for the end of these coercive practices, and unless their assistance does not causally contribute to more coercion. Organizations should avoid being necessary for repatriation when repatriation contributes to coercion, and they should avoid increasing the probability of repatriation occurring, when doing so increases the probability of coercion occurring. Humanitarian organizations should only help with return that increases the probability of coercion if they can ensure a much safer return than would otherwise take place, and can warn refugees of the risks of returning.

In providing information on risks, organizations should disclose what they already know, but they should also strive to know more, conducting their own post-return evaluations when no such evaluations exist. Such organizations have a duty to find information because they have a duty of care, given that they were created to assist vulnerable populations. Governments may have no duty of care, but they have a duty to conduct research on repatriation if this is necessary to fulfill duties unrelated to repatriation. If, for example, governments have duties to help prevent atrocities abroad, they have a duty to research data on atrocities abroad. If they do not, they are culpable for failing to inform refugees of the risks of atrocities abroad.

Even if repatriation facilitators do warn refugees of risks, they still have reason to discontinue return if most who return regret their decision, while those who remain do not. More specifically, facilitators should discontinue return if returnees could not comprehend what returning would be like prior to their choice, and now feel that the best life they can live is worse than the worst life they could have lived had they remained. Even when such regret is not widespread, and so assisting with return justified, facilitators should not encourage return through payments, assuming payments motivate refugees to return unsafely.

The above conclusions suggest that some repatriation assistance is morally permissible even if return is unsafe. It is permissible if facilitators do not encourage return, fully inform refugees of risks, ensure refugees will be unlikely to feel regret, and do everything possible to end coercion. Such return may involve risks, but adults have a right to take such risks.

Children, in contrast, do not have a right to take such risks. Of the over 500 children who returned from Israel, at least seven died within the first three months, and in my own sample of forty-eighty children, five died within the first two years. Regardless of how informed and voluntary return is, children should not be assisted in repatriation that places their lives at considerable risk compared to remaining.

Even when return is completely safe, or when only adults are returning, governments and organizations should avoid only assisting a given racial group to return. When the goal of this assistance is to decrease the number of members of racial minorities in a country, the assistance is demeaning towards citizens of the same racial group who understand that, in a close possible world, they too would be unwanted.

After refugees have repatriated, their newly adopted governments will face their own set of dilemmas. I lacked the space to list them all, but one concerns restitution: governments must decide whether to return to refugees their former property, or distribute this property to those most in need. I argued that, were a government to redistribute refugees' former property, it would be disadvantaging refugees compared to non-refugees who never fled. This disadvantage is a form of discrimination, which can be demeaning towards all refugees of the same persecuted minority forced to leave. Governments can avoid this form of discrimination by either providing restitution, or taxing non-refugees' property at the same rate, ensuring refugees are not disadvantaged.

In light of these conclusions, repatriation facilitators should introduce a number of policy changes. One is related to coercion: when governments coerce refugees to repatriate, humanitarian organizations should invest resources in lobbying for the end of such coercion, meeting with policymakers to explain the risks that refugees will face if they return, and raising court petitions to free refugees from detention. Such efforts will often mean organizations have fewer resources for repatriation itself, but the repatriation that does take place is more likely to be voluntary, rather than forced. Organizations should also invest resources in evaluating the outcome of repatriation, finding information on the mortality rate, rate of displacement, rate of education, and access to healthcare amongst those who returned. This requires traveling to IDP camps and to surrounding countries, interviewing returnees who have migrated or fled, and interviewing relatives to find out if returnees have died after returning. The findings from such interviews must be clearly communicated to refugees who have yet to return. If the findings include evidence that past returnees have severely regretted their decisions to return, there are strong reasons to discontinue repatriation until conditions in countries of origin improve.

In addition to gathering and disclosing more information, facilitators should discontinue providing payments that encourage unsafe repatriation. To determine if payments encourage repatriation, facilitators should determine if there are strong correlations between return rates and payments, even while detention rates and conditions in home countries remain the same. If they determine that payments do encourage unsafe return, payments should be discontinued. They may still provide aid to those who have already returned, if there is no evidence that such post-return aid encourages future unsafe returns.

When parents wish to return with their children, or when unaccompanied minors are returning on their own, facilitators should only assist if return is safe or as safe as remaining. To determine safety, facilitators should consider the mortality, literacy, and numeracy rates amongst children in the country of origin. If facilitators determine that the country is insufficiently safe, they should deny repatriation assistance, and states should possibly block families from attempting to pay for their own flights, stopping them at the airport and revoking their passports. At the very least, governments and organizations should implement campaigns to discourage such returns. When possible, NGOs and social workers should meet with parents, try to persuade them to not repatriate, and provide them detailed information on the lack of clinics, schools, and safe locations in the country of origin. Facilitators should also communicate to parents their rights in the host country, explaining what will happen to their children if they are detained or forced into enclosed camps. In cases where children will not have access to basic services if they remain, and will likely go without sufficient food, shelter, and security, organizations should ultimately help with repatriation, but only if remaining is no safer than returning.

When return is perfectly safe, facilitators should avoid supporting programs aimed at reducing the number of unwanted minorities in the country. When programs entail paying unwanted minorities to leave – as when Israel paid East African refugees and migrants to leave – the payments are wrongfully discriminatory, and are only morally permissible if recipients prefer to have been offered the payments than not, and no third parties are demeaned or harmed. To avoid discriminatory payments, governments should provide equal payments to all, rather than to unwanted minorities alone.

In addition to the policy conclusions above, there are three broad theoretical conclusions, relevant beyond the scope of repatriation. The first regards consent.

We should not assume that coerced consent is invalid. We must first consider whether agents obtaining consent have a duty to stop the coercion. To do so, we must consider whether they have the ability to stop the coercion, and whether they have great enough resources to do so.

We should similarly not assume that individuals must be fully informed to give their valid consent. We must consider whether agents obtaining consent have a duty to provide information. I provided one novel reason why they do: because they have other unrelated duties giving them a duty to know. If I have a duty to not collide with anyone in my car, I have a duty to know if my brakes are faulty. If I do not know they are faulty, and sell you my car without informing you of the faulty brakes, I am culpable for your uninformed consent. Importantly, culpability for uninformed consent can arise even if the recipient of a service would have consented had they been more informed. Even if Yasmin would have consented to repatriate to South Sudan had she known about widespread poverty, she still lacked control over her consent at the time she returned, for she did not know what she was consenting to. To ensure that individuals have control over their decisions, providing information is essential.

There is a final general conclusion regarding consent: sometimes it is not enough. When an individual consents to a service they will likely regret, there are good reasons to deny them this service. This is especially true for services that are "epistemically transformative," where individuals cannot know the nature of the risks they are accepting. This is relevant not only for refugees returning home, but for other life-altering services, most notably medical interventions. If a hospital learns that most patients regret accepting a given medical intervention, this can provide a reason to discontinue providing this intervention.

In addition to general conclusions regarding consent, I have attempted to contribute to the broader discussion of children's rights. It is widely accepted that children have a right to education that provides them the capacity to function within an economy. I argue, more specifically, that children have a right to education necessary for upholding an economy that protects basic welfare. This would entail a right to fluent literacy and numeracy, in addition to the more basic rights of immediate security, shelter, and healthcare. Parents have a correlative duty to avoid moving to a country without these necessities, and should be dissuaded from doing so.

The final major conclusion concerned discrimination. While harmful discrimination is often wrong, it is less clear whether beneficial discrimination is right. If a landlord, organization, or government pays a minority to leave a building, city, or country, perhaps this is acceptable if the minority members benefit. I argued that such payments can be unacceptable because they imply an offensive message to recipients: "We do not want you so much, that we are willing to pay you a large amount of money for your exit." This demeans not only minority members who reject the payments, but minority members who accept payments they wish had never been offered at all. The latter are demeaned by the money's implied message without actually benefiting, and so are impermissibly wronged.

In reaching the above theoretical conclusions, I have attempted to draw upon a diverse array of examples, reaching a methodology conclusion: Fieldwork is essential for making us realize what we overlook, rather than just applying what we already know. If we wish to make robust and specific rules in ethics, we must consider a broader range of cases. This is only possible if we learn of cases we might otherwise not consider, which is easier when speaking to individuals we might otherwise not meet. This is especially true in studying the ethics of immigration, an area involving millions of individuals crossing borders annually, and hundreds of organizations that hinder or help.

In exploring these agents, qualitative fieldwork is particular helpful. Through in-depth interviews, refugees described the coercion they experienced, their reasons for their actions, and their current judgments about their past decisions. Organizations similarly explained to me the dilemmas they faced, and the choices they made. Such interviews included details often missing in aggregate data on immigration, helping better formulate informed, relevant, and ethical policies for refugees.

NOTES

1. Interview with Nhial, Juba, January 4, 2014.

APPENDICES

APPENDIX A: DEFINING REFUGEES

This book assumes what I call the Life Claim: an individual is a refugee if their right to life is threatened in their home countries, regardless of whether it is threatened from persecution, violence, poverty or other life-threatening conditions.[1] All such refugees have a right to asylum, assuming they have no other mechanism for accessing protection, and assuming states have the capacity to accept such individuals.

The Life Claim is limited in scope, establishing a sufficient but not necessary condition: it is sufficient that a refugee's right to life is undermined, but not necessary. It is not necessary because those suffering other harms, such as life-long detention, are likely refugees as well.[2] The Life Claim is also neutral as to when, precisely, states no longer have the capacity to accept refugees, and so can ethically turn them away. It may be that a state lacks capacity if the costs of accepting more refugees are very high,[3] or if accepting refugees endangers citizens' access to basic rights and liberal institutions.[4] My aim here is merely to demonstrate that, however we measure capacity, states ought not to differentiate between those fleeing persecution, those fleeing general violence, and those fleeing other life-threatening conditions.

Importantly, I do not claim that all individuals fleeing life-threatening conditions are refugees. A ninety year old without access to very costly cancer treatment does not necessarily have a right to asylum abroad to obtain treatment, because the right to life needn't entail the right to access costly life-saving treatment at age ninety. In contrast, an individual who cannot access basic medical care does have a right to asylum, assuming an individual's right to life is violated if they lack access to basic medical care. Determining who precisely has their right to life violated would require a broader discussion of rights, but this is not necessary for my purposes: I merely wish to demonstrate that those fleeing persecution do not have a special right to asylum as compared to those fleeing other equally life-threatening rights violations.

There are two common claims that are inconsistent with the Life Claim. I describe them below, along with my objections.

1. The Aid Claim

According to the Aid Claim, states have a duty to protect the right to life of individuals outside of their borders, assuming such protection does not rise above a given cost. States can often protect the right to life by sending aid, as when states send food aid to individuals suffering from severe malnutrition. For such individuals, states can fulfill their duties without granting asylum. States must only grant asylum to those who cannot be saved any other way. In general, those who are fleeing persecution and general violence cannot be saved any other way.[5] Sometimes individuals suffering from hunger also cannot be saved any other way, because their home government is blocking the provision of international aid, and such refugees simply must obtain asylum to obtain food.[6] Regardless, most individuals who find their right to life threatened can be helped with aid, and so states needn't grant them asylum.

The problem with the Aid Claim is that it confuses what states can do with what they will do. States can send aid, but they often do not – at least, they do not send nearly as much aid as they have a duty to send. In 2016 wealthy states' total aid was $142.6 billion, averaging only 0.32 per cent of gross national income, far less than states can afford to send, and far less than the minimum necessary to secure poor individuals' right to life.[7] If states are not sending sufficient aid, then those living in poverty can only save themselves through asylum. They therefore have a right to asylum.

Importantly, even if states do fulfill their duties to provide aid, in that they are sending as much aid as they can before the costs become too high, they may still have a duty to provide asylum. This is because asylum does not necessarily incur costs. If asylum does not incur costs, states cannot claim they have no duty to provide asylum because they have already incurred costs in sending aid. It would be comparable to a philanthropist donating most of her life savings to charity, and then failing to save a drowning child whom she can save at no cost. If the philanthropist can save the child at no cost, she has a duty to do so, even if she has donated money already.

There are a number of instances where asylum involves no costs, as when refugees arrive with savings which they pay as a tax to the government, receiving services equivalent in value to what they pay. We might also imagine refugees paying into a type of insurance scheme upon arrival, with each refugee paying a given sum, and only some refugees receiving services more than this sum, such that the group as a whole is given asylum without costs. Just as well-run health insurance involves no net costs, a well-run refugee scheme – with refugees paying into the scheme – needn't involve net costs. Similarly, if a group of highly-skilled refugees is given asylum, the predicted cost of each refugee may be less or equal to the predicted sum they will pay in taxes while given asylum. If such refugees will contribute more than they gain in services, states cannot claim that costs justify no asylum. Therefore, even if states have already accepted their fair share of costs in sending aid oversees, they still have a duty to provide asylum to these no-cost refugees. This is consistent with the Life Claim, which holds that all individuals are refugees if their right to life is threatened, and states have an obligation to accept refugees if the costs fall below a given threshold.

2. The Membership Claim

There is a second claim inconsistent with the Life Claim, which I call the Membership Claim. It holds that refugees are those who are no longer members in their home countries, and so holding a right to membership elsewhere. True membership entails eventual citizenship, and so true refugees have a right to eventually obtain citizenship. Some individuals fleeing life-threatening conditions are still members of their home state, and so have no right to citizenship in another state. They merely have a right to temporary protection until returning home is safe.

The Membership Claim is similar to the Life Claim, because it accepts that all those fleeing life-threatening conditions have a right to asylum. It simply does not call individuals "refugees" if they will eventually be required to return home. If one accepts the Membership Claim, then replace my use of the word "refugees" with "those who cannot currently return to their home country because their lives will be at risk."

However, I still believe the Membership Claim is wrong, and that all those whose right to life are at risk at home ought to be called refugees, and that we ought not to prioritize those fleeing persecution in granting citizenship. Let me briefly present the Membership Claim, and why it is faulty.

The Membership Claim begins with the premise that all individuals have a right to be members of a state. An individual is no longer a member if her membership has been repudiated by the state. Her membership can be repudiated when a core feature of her identity is rejected, and this can occur if she is persecuted because of her religion, race, politics, or social membership. She therefore has right to membership in a new state, rather than mere temporary asylum. In contrast to those who are persecuted, those fleeing purely natural disasters or general violence are not living in states that have rejected a core feature of their identity. Their membership has therefore not been repudiated by their government, and so they are not in need of new membership elsewhere. They have a right to merely temporary protection in another state until returning home is safe.[8]

Below is a summary of this general argument:

1. All have a right to membership in a state.
2. Those who are persecuted are targeted for a core feature of their identity.
3. Therefore, their membership has been repudiated by their government.
4. Therefore, they have a right to obtain membership in another state.
5. Those who suffer from famine or general violence never had their membership repudiated by their government.
6. They therefore do not have a right to membership in another state.

One problem with the above is the second premise. It is not true that those persecuted because of their race, religion, social membership, or political opinion are necessarily targeted because of a core feature of their identity. Many individuals do not feel that their race is a core feature of their identity, and some do not feel that their religion is a core feature of their identity. An agnostic may not strongly identify with her agnosticism, but she is still persecuted if the government threatens to kill her unless she stops being agnostic. More generally, a person may be targeted for being of a given race, religion, or social group they do not identify with, as when individuals with one Jewish grandparent were targeted during the Holocaust, because it was presumed they were Jewish, and individuals with glasses were targeted during the Cambodian genocide, because it was presumed they were part of the suspect class of intellectuals.[9] If being persecuted does not indicate that a core feature of a person's identity is rejected, there is no reason to believe persecution indicates a special severing of membership compared to other forms of life-threatening treatment.

There is another problem with the Membership Claim. A person can be persecuted but remain a member of the state, so long as they are persecuted by independent militias who do not represent the state. Such a person's bond with their government can remain intact if their government is doing everything to stop the militias' actions. Once the government succeeds, they can return home. If this is true, there is no reason to distinguish all those fleeing persecution from all those fleeing general disasters: both could be in need of only temporary protection.

Lister, a proponent of the Membership Claim, addresses this objection. He argues that when militias target individuals, the militias usurp the state's authority, essentially becoming the state. The state is therefore repudiating victims' membership, because the state has become the militias engaging in persecution.[10] For example, when Hutu militias targeted Tutsi citizens, the power of the original Rwandan government became usurped, and the true state was represented by the Hutu militias. The state – represented by the Hutu militias – repudiated the membership of Tutsi residents, and these residents therefore had a right to citizenship elsewhere.

Such an explanation, however, rests on a view of the state rejected by many refuges themselves. When a refugee flees a militia that has usurped the government, the government may remain in exile. When refugees feel a strong bond to such governments-in-exile, and feel this government is the true representative of the state, they may plan to return to their homelands when these governments-in-exile gain power. From the refugees' own perspective, their bond with their state remains strong. Just as those fleeing famine or natural disasters still maintain a bond with their state, even if the government is powerless to stop the famine and natural disaster, refugees fleeing persecution from militias can maintain a bond with their state, even if the government is powerless in preventing these militias from functioning.

Importantly, when one's bond remains intact, one might still have a right to citizenship in another state. This is because, even when one's bond remains intact, one cannot always experience one's citizenship in practice. All those who cannot live in their home countries, because their lives will be at risk from hunger or ill health, cannot vote in their home countries, engage in public debate in their home countries, work in their home countries, or enter and exit their home countries safely. Assuming such a circumstance will continue for a prolonged period of time, their access to citizenship is severed in practice, providing a compelling reason to access citizenship elsewhere.

We might claim, as Lister does, that those who are directly targeted by their government are more likely to require protection for an extended period of time, in contrast to those fleeing natural disasters and general violence, who can safely return home after a shorter period of time.[11] But that is not necessarily true: those fleeing life-threatening poverty may find that their home country cannot ensure their food security for decades, while those once targeted for their ethnicity may be able to return safely to their home states soon after. The relevant criteria for new citizenship, then, should not be based on whether one was targeted, but on how long one is required to remain abroad. If this is true, then those fleeing persecution, and those fleeing non-man-made disasters, ought to obtain similar conditions for asylum: all individuals have a right to initial protection, and then eventually obtain the right to citizenship if they have been unable to return home for a significant number of years.

There is a final objection to the Membership Claim. It is not true that one can only have one's membership repudiated by being persecuted. A person can have their membership repudiated if they are no longer benefiting from the state, even if they are not targeted by this state. This is because, more generally, a person can lose membership when no longer receiving a benefit constitutive of membership. For example, if a member of an insurance plan receives a letter informing her that no pay-outs would ever be provided, due to insufficient funds in the plan, she would no longer be a member of the insurance plan in any relevant sense. The same can be said about those leaving states unable to protect their rights to life. Assuming that being a member of a state is constitutive of receiving minimal protection from the state, these individuals are no longer members of the state. They therefore have a right to membership elsewhere.

To account for some of the objections above, we might adopt another version of the Membership Argument. Shacknove's Membership Argument, one of the earlier versions, begins with the empirical premise that individuals experience insecurity from other humans when living outside the confines of society. They experience theft, murder, and rape in the absence of protection from clans, tribes, and states. The purpose of the state today, he argues, is to mitigate these insecurities, ensuring that citizens are not harmed by outsiders, nor harmed by each other. When the state fails to protect citizens in this manner, it no longer has a special bond with its citizens, and those harmed are no longer true citizens. Because all individuals have a right to citizenship, such individuals have a right to citizenship abroad as refugees.

Shacknove emphasizes that only those fleeing man-made harms are refugees, because the function of the state is to protect humans from other humans. He notes, however, that many natural disasters are caused by humans: humans are responsible for the failure to build infrastructure to counteract floods, responsible for a failure to reduce carbon dioxide emissions to counter climate change, and responsible for a failure to create an economy that can withstand droughts. Nearly all those fleeing economic and natural catastrophes, then, are refugees.[12]

Shacknove's account nonetheless implies that, if an individual is fleeing a disaster caused by no other human, they are not refugees. An individual suffering from a flood, virus, or drought for which nobody is responsible, and which nobody could prevent, keeps their bond with their home government according to Shacknove's account. They therefore have no right to citizenship in a new state.

Shacknove's account suffers from weaknesses similar to those plaguing the first Membership Claim. Even if one is fleeing harms from other humans, it does not follow that one's membership has been repudiated; one can retain membership if one is attacked by a militia, and one's own government remains committed to protection. Just as those fleeing a virus can retain their bond with the government, even if the government is temporarily powerless in the face of the virus, those fleeing a militia can retain their bond with the government, even if the government is powerless in the face of the militia.

More importantly, one can cease to be a member of a state that is unable to prevent entirely non-man-made disasters. Perhaps the best example of this is an individual on a sinking island. Assuming the island is sinking for reasons unrelated to human actions, and assuming there is no way to prevent the island from sinking, and assuming there are no other territories where the state can be reconstituted, the island's residents will soon no longer have citizenship in a state. If all individuals have a right to citizenship in a state, then such individuals have a right to citizenship in another state, rather than being forced to drown as the island sinks, or living the rest of their lives as stateless people in other countries.[13]

In short, the Life Claim remains more compelling than alternative claims, which is why I adopt this claim throughout the book. And, as noted above, one can still accept the arguments throughout the book while rejecting the Life Claim. The arguments simply become narrower in scope, limited to a narrower range of individuals.

NOTES

1. As noted, this stance is widely accepted. See Michael Dummett, *On Immigration and Refugees*, London and New York: Routledge 2001 at 37; Matthew Gibney, *The Ethics and Politics of Asylum*, Cambridge: Cambridge University Press 2004 at 84; David Miller, "Immigration: The Case for Its Limits," in (eds) A. Cohen and C. Wellman, *Contemporary Debates in Applied Ethics*, Malden, MA: Blackwell Publishing 2005 at 202.
2. Luara Ferracioli, "The Appeal and Danger of a New Refugee Convention," *Social Theory and Practice* 40(1)(2014):123–44 at 125.
3. Gibney 2004 ibid. at 84; Kyrie Kowalik, "Defining Refugees in Terms of Justice," *Peace Review* 29(1)(2017):68–75 at 71; Miller 2005 ibid. at 85–93.
4. Arash Abizadeh, "The Special-Obligations Challenge to More Open Borders," in (eds) Sarah Fine and Lea Ypi, *Migration in Political Theory*, Oxford: Oxford University Press 2016; Joseph Carens, "Aliens and Citizens: The Case for Open Borders," *Review of Politics* 49(2)(1987): 251–73 at 259; Ferracioli 2014 ibid. at 132; and Dummett 2001 ibid. at 14 and 50–2.
5. Max Cherem, "Refugee Rights: Against Expanding the Definition of 'Refugees' and Unilateral Protection Elsewhere," *Journal of Political Philosophy* 24(2)(2016):183–205 at 190; Matthew Lister, "Who Are Refugees?" *Law and Philosophy* 32(5)(2013):645–71 at 660; David Miller, *Strangers in Our Midst: The Political Philosophy of Immigration*, Cambridge: Harvard University Press 2016 at 83.
6. Gibney 2004 ibid. at 84; Julian F. Müller, "The Ethics of Commercial Human Smuggling," *European Journal of Political Theory*, (forthcoming)

at 12, <http://journals.sagepub.com/doi/full/10.1177/1474885118754468> (last accessed May 4, 2018).

7. OECD, "Development Aid Rises Again in 2016 but Flows to the Poorest Countries Dip," March 11, 2017, <http://www.oecd.org/dac/development-aid-rises-again-in-2016-but-flows-to-poorest-countries-dip.htm> (last accessed February 22, 2018).

8. Lister 2013 ibid. at 662 and 669–70; Cherem 2016 ibid. at 191–2; Michael Walzer, *Spheres of Justice: A Defence of Pluralism and Equality*, New York: Basic Book 1983 at 48.

9. William A. Schabas, "Problems of International Codification: Were the Atrocities in Cambodia and Kosovo Genocide?" *New England Law Review* 35(2)(2011):287–302 at 290.

10. Lister 2013 ibid. at 662.

11. Lister 2013 ibid. at 669.

12. Andrew E. Shacknove, "Who is a Refugee?" *Ethics* 95(2)(1985):274–84 at 278–80.

13. Cherem argues that such individuals are distinct from refugees, because their membership has not been repudiated; it has simply been lost. In such cases, solutions other than asylum may be more appropriate, such as ceding territory to such individuals. However, if no state is willing to cede territory – the current reality – then such individuals lack membership and require asylum. In other words, in determining who has a right to citizenship abroad, there is no principled reason to distinguish between one whose membership is repudiated and one whose membership is lost, assuming both groups cannot re-obtain the membership they no longer possess. See Cherem 2016 ibid. at 192.

APPENDIX B: TOTAL RETURNING, MONEY,
AND DETENTION IN ISRAEL

Month	Total returning to South Sudan, Sudan, and Eritrea	Money paid to South Sudanese, Sudanese, and Eritreans	Significant events
May–June 2012	1,200–3,000 to South Sudan	$1,500[1]	South Sudanese told they will be detained indefinitely or deported if they do not repatriate.
July–August	Unknown	0–100	
September	Unknown	0–100	On September 16, 2013, the High Court of Justice invalidates provisions of Anti-Infiltration Law which allows for prolonged detention.[2] The government then issues a new procedure allowing the state to arrest anyone suspected of criminal acts, without trial.[3]
October	Unknown	0–100	Human rights organizations submit petition against procedure above.[4]
November 2012 – February 2013	Unknown	0–100	

March 2013	53	$1,500[5]	UNHCR submits a request to file a friend of the court brief with the High Court of Justice on March 7, 2013.[6] In an initial hearing at the High Court of Justice on March 12, an order is issued for the government to explain why the amendment to the Anti-Infiltration Law should remain intact.[7]
April	59	$1,500	
May	70	$1,500	
June	75	$1,500	State prosecutor announces that the state is unlikely to accept any claims of Eritrean nationals for refugee status.[8]
July	164	$1,500	
August	170	$1,500	Hotline for Migrant Workers reports slight improvements in living conditions in detention facilities.[9]
September	89	$1,500	Nullification of Anti-Infiltration amendment which allows detention of asylum seekers.[10]

October	180	$1,500	Interior Minister Gideon Saar proposes plan to Prime Minister Netanyahu to raise grant from $1,500 to $5,000. No final decision reached and no asylum seekers released, despite High Court order.[11]
November	116	From mid- to late November: $3,500	Following the human rights petition to the high court, some detainees released. Cabinet approves increasing payment from $1,500 to $3,500 in mid-November.[12]
December	295	$3,500	Knesset passes new amendment, detaining new asylum seekers for one year.[13]
January–August 2014	Approximately: 3,312[14] Average per month: 414	$3,500	Asylum seekers continue to be detained.[15]

Notes

1. Based on the 128 interviews conducted with returnees to South Sudan.
2. Amnesty International, "Blind to Violations, Deaf to Obligations: Israel's Human Rights Record: Amnesty International Updated Submission to the UN Universal Periodic Review, September 2013," <https://www.

amnesty.org/en/documents/MDE15/015/2013/en/> (last accessed February 27, 2018).

3. Amnesty International, ASSAF, and the Hotline for Migrant Workers, "Israel's Policy towards Refugees and Asylum Seekers: Prolonged Administrative Detention, March 2013,"<http://assaf.org.il/en/sites/default/files/Israeli%20Policy%20of%20Prolonged%20Administrative%20Detention%20March%202013.pdf> (last accessed February 27, 2018).
4. Amnesty International et al. 2013 ibid.
5. Interview with AVR official, Tel Aviv, August 7, 2013.
6. Talia Nesher, "UN Refugee Agency Petitions High Court to Overturn 'Infiltration' Law," *Haaretz*, March 13, 2013, accessed September 1, 2015 <https://www.haaretz.com/.premium-un-agency-to-high-court-over-turn-infiltration-law-1.5233585> (last accessed September 1, 2015).
7. The Association of Civil Rights in Israel, "High Court of Justice Prepares to Hear Petition against Anti-Infiltration Law," <https://www.acri.org.il/en/2013/05/29/anti-infiltration-law-2/> (last accessed February 27, 2018).
8. Amnesty International, June 7, 2013, <http://www.amnesty.org/fr/library/asset/MDE15/005/2013/en/07259891-b209-4058-b370e76c3cdccfe8/mde 150052013en.pdf> (last accessed September 4, 2014).
9. Maya Kovaliyov-Livi and Sigal Rozen, "'From One Prison to Another': Holot Detention Facility,"Hotline for Migrant Workers in Israel, June 2014, <https://www.scribd.com/document/230142608/From-One-Prison-to-Another-Holot-Detention-Facility> (last accessed February 27, 2018).
10. Barak Ravid and Ilan Lior, "Court Invalidates Legislation Allowing Israel to Detain Migrants without Trial," *Haaretz*, September 16, 2013, <http://www.haaretz.com/news/diplomacy-defense/.premium-1.547311> (last accessed February 27, 2018).
11. Ilan Lior, "Israel to Order African Migrants $5,000 to Leave," *Haaretz*, October 30, 2013, <http://www.haaretz.com/news/national/.premium-1.555218> (last accessed February 22, 2017).
12. It was unclear if this was approved in November or December. A civil servant in the Ministry of Interior recalled that the increase was "around November 2013," but some media sources report that the approval took place in the Cabinet in December. Regardless, it was after some detainees were released from detention following the High Court decision. See William Booth and Ruth Eglash, "Israel Says It Won't Forcibly Deport Illegal Migrants, But It Wants Them to Leave."*Washington Post*, January 20, 2013, and interview with AVR official, Tel Aviv, August 7, 2013.
13. Kovaliyov-Livi and Rozen 2014 ibid.
14. Based on total Sudanese and Eritreans who left the country according to Human Rights Watch as of August 2014 (6,400 to Sudan and 367 to Eritrea, for a total of 6,767), minus the total who returned in 2012 and 2013 to Sudan and Eritrea based on labor statistics. For 2012, labor

statistics provided by the Israeli Population, Immigration and Border Agency only give the total number who returned via the Office for the Encouragement of Return (2,600). This includes 1,100 South Sudanese who returned, and the remaining 1,500 are likely from Sudan, as no Eritreans were reported leaving prior to 2013. In 2013, labor statistics report 1,687 Sudanese and 268 Eritreans leaving the country, for a total of 1,955. Therefore, the total number who returned between January and August 2014 was approximately 6,767 − 1,500 − 1,955 = 3,312. See Human Rights Watch, "Make Their Lives Miserable: Israel's Coercion of Eritrean and Sudanese Asylum Seekers to Leave the Country," September 9, 2014, <https://www.hrw.org/report/2014/09/09/make-their-lives-miserable/israels-coercion-eritrean-and-sudanese-asylum-seekers> (last accessed September 14, 2014); Labor statistics <http://www.piba.gov.il/PublicationAndTender/summery/Documents/summary2012.pdf> (last accessed on September 14, 2014); and <http://piba.gov.il/PublicationAndTender/ForeignWorkersStat/Documents/563343n80.pdf> (last accessed on September 14, 2014).

15. Human Rights Watch 2014 ibid.; and Kovaliyov-Livi and Rozen 2014 ibid.

INDEX

EU representative:
Easy Access System Europe
Mustamäe tee 50, 10621 Tallinn, Estonia
Gpsr.requests@easproject.com

www.ingramcontent.com/pod-product-compliance
Lightning Source LLC
Chambersburg PA
CBHW061007280326
41935CB00009B/862